MAKING CARS AT
CREWE

PETER OLLERHEAD

SUTTON PUBLISHING

Sutton Publishing Limited
Phoenix Mill · Thrupp · Stroud
Gloucestershire · GL5 2BU

First published 2006

Title page photograph: Silver Cloud III, *c.* 1964. *(Rolls-Royce Enthusiasts' Club)*

British Library Cataloguing in Publication Data
A catalogue record for this book is available from the British Library.

ISBN 0-7509-4328-9

Typeset in 10.5/13.5 Plantin.
Typesetting and origination by
Sutton Publishing Limited.
Printed and bound in England by
J.H. Haynes & Co. Ltd, Sparkford.

For my father, who, for 30 years, was a setter on the
semi-autos; and for Jack, the great-grandson he never saw.

An early Silver Dawn outside the main offices in Pym's Lane. The curtained windows of the board room can be seen above the entrance. Notice the camouflage shading on the wall of the canteen, in the middle distance. The building beyond the fence is the Ashbank Hotel, built at the same time as the factory. *(B. Fishburne)*

Contents

Preface & Acknowledgements

Even from my childhood Rolls-Royce has been part of my life. As a family we occupied one of the council houses especially built for RR workers at the beginning of the Second World War. We, as children, played in the fields around the factory, even daring to walk on the low wall just outside the main door until chased away by the commissionaire who sat in the alcove at the foot of the stairs. My father, his brothers and the fathers of most of my friends worked there. When the time arrived, I too made my way through the Pym's Lane gates to taste the adult world of work. When I left after sixteen years my relatives kept me up to date with events in the factory. Later, when I opened a second-hand bookshop, so many of the retired employees came to sit and chat that my premises took on the appearance of a geriatric drop-in centre. For their friendship and tales I am ever grateful, as the impetus for this book began with them.

My intention in this work is not to describe the cars manufactured at Pym's Lane, for that has been done many times by more skilled writers; rather, I wish to describe life at the factory and how its development proceeded. Others will decide whether I have succeeded. Regrettably, I was not able to obtain access to the material stored at Pym's Lane when I started to research the origins and development of Royce's in Crewe. However, I should like to record my thanks to John Spragg and Bob Young, who both proved helpful within their remit when I visited the 'visitor experience'.

The unions at the factory were most helpful when I approached them. The senior site representative, Steve Taylor, offered all the assistance available and I am grateful to him and the other union representatives who gave of their time and coffee to further this study of their place of work.

Rolls-Royce Heritage Trust at Derby is doing a good job of looking after the archive material relating to the aero side of RR, and I thank it and especially the Chair of the Trust, Richard Haigh, for granting access to the records relating to Crewe in the 1940s and '50s. I am grateful to Mike Evans of the same Trust who helped me with technical facts relating to the Merlin skew gear. Permission to quote from *Silver Ghosts and Silver Dawn* was granted by the family of the late W.A. Robotham; from *Sigh for a Merlin* by the author, Alex Henshaw; from *Kidnap of the Flying Lady* by the author, Richard Feast and the publishers Motorbooks of the USA; and from the late L.T.C. Rolt's *Landscape with Canals* by Sutton Publishing Ltd. I record my appreciation to authors and publishers for their kindness.

The RR Enthusiasts' Centre at Paulerspury is performing a splendid service for this and future generations in preserving RR (car) material with such care. The welcome there was warm and I thank Philip Hall and the late Peter Baines for the old-world courtesy extended and for the modern-day efficiency that marks the Centre. It is a pity that so much was wantonly destroyed at Pym's Lane in the 1960s before it could find a caring home at Hunt House.

For help with wartime economics, in Chapter 2, I thank Dr Theo Balderstone, though I absolve him from any opinions there expressed, as they are all my own. For clarification of certain facts regarding Spitfires and Merlin engine failures, and in the provision of photographs, Alex Henshaw was extremely helpful and I shall ever be grateful to him. Mike Langley, an esteemed journalist and editor, set me on the road to discovering more about December 1940. I trust I have faithfully followed the trail. As usual, the staff at Crewe Public Reference Library provided never-failing help and assistance, and I am grateful to them. Tim Finch kindly loaned to me his Master's dissertation on industrial relations at Pym's Lane.

I wish also to acknowledge my debt to the members of the Crewe Local History Society, emphasising Joy and Bernard Owen, Harry Jones and his wife Vera, and Pam Minshall, the only chair of the Society. They have sought to keep alive the study of true local history, rather than entering the miasma of nostalgia. My auction colleague, Andrew Turner of Nantwich, placed at my disposal his expertise with computers, and I offer him my thanks.

This leads me to a long list of ex-Rolls-Royce employees who gave of their time to talk of past days, events and people with clarity, cheerfulness and humour, all learned at the factory. I recall their names, in no particular order, with gratitude and appreciation: F.R. Dyson, Alf Jennings, John Epps, Charlie Elson, Reg Spencer, Ronnie Reid, J. and E. Pennington, M. Bourne, F. Ikin, A. Hammersley, J. Platt, W. Lea, Charlie Goodridge, Roy Paine, A. Clayson, M. Reynolds, Brian Stockton, Ted and Marie Penaluna, T. Evans, D. Mason, Neville Sadler, R. Grace, D. Stevenson, G. Roberts, L. Crouchley, M. Roberts, B. Preston, C. Dix, J. Moore, Mr and Mrs J. Fishburne, Mrs J. Elliott, Mrs M. Tomkinson, Mrs D. Dyer, Mrs Healey, Mrs D. Pointon, Mrs E. Cooper, Mrs A. Parke, Roger Bolton, Harry Hulme, B. Platt and Norman Evanson. Some in this list have now passed on and rest in peace, which is more than they ever did at the factory.

I have left the names of two or three to the last, as I am especially grateful to them for all the extra help and many discussions I have had with them. Billy Consterdine was an apprentice in the 1950s, as I was, though he was a true artisan, remaining at RR until he retired. He led me to many ex-employees and I thank him for that and for his friendship over the years. Tony Flood seems to have accurate instant recall of almost anything pertaining to Crewe Rolls-Royce, and I am surprised that other historians of the firm have not made use of his willingness to place his knowledge at their disposal. I am in his debt for access to his unique collection of journals, memos and newspapers published by RR, for acting as an unpaid research assistant, and for reading the script, although any remaining errors are my responsibility.

The late Frank Culley must be mentioned by himself as he was a 'one-off'. The town council honoured him on the day of his funeral by flying the flag at half-mast – an honour they usually reserve for their own. I shall ever be grateful to Frank for the hours he spent in my bookshop. He rarely bought a thing, but his yarns and stories about RR were legion and endlessly fascinating. I salute his memory.

Finally, I must thank my long-suffering wife for her forbearance, patience and encouragement as this work has progressed or faltered since my retirement from the classroom. The most intelligent and far-sighted thing I ever did was to ask her to marry me; the noblest thing she ever did was to accept.

Prologue

One glorious midsummer's day in 1929 thousands of people gathered in a field in the west end of Crewe, a railway town in the north Midlands, to await the arrival of a de Havilland Giant Moth aeroplane named 'Youth of Britain'. The locality had seen little to rival this since 1837, when the first locomotive had steamed through on its way to Birmingham. As an aeroplane touching down was a somewhat novel event, the municipal body had invited the Lord Mayor and Lady Mayoress of the neighbouring city of Stoke-on-Trent, the Mayor of Wrexham, the town clerk of Stone, and other local dignitaries to witness the proceedings. This august party sheltered from the shimmering heat of the sun in a large marquee, specially erected for the visit.

A few minutes after 11 a.m. the biplane, flying from Warrington in Lancashire, slowly circled the town before coming to rest in the fields of Merrill's Farm where, a few days before, the farmer had harvested his hay. Sir Alan Cobham, the hero of record-breaking flights to India and Australia, was the pilot, and, on emerging from the plane, he acknowledged the applause before inviting ten of the waiting civic guests to sample the adventure of flight. Later that day, after a reception in the marquee, the intrepid pilot filled his aeroplane with paying customers, at 10*s* a time, for a short spin over Crewe. Among the interested onlookers, in the early evening, was Frank Culley, a young apprentice in the local LMS railway works.

Before Sir Alan Cobham departed he promised to contact the town council with regard to the makeshift landing ground becoming part of his projected network of civil air stations. During the course of his speech he made the prophetic statement that if an aerodrome were established at Crewe it would also be the site for an aircraft factory. An aerodrome there never was, but within ten years a factory had been built on that very field; a factory which manufactured one of the finest aero-engines of its time; a factory where Frank Culley was to spend the rest of his working life. The following chapters record the story of that factory and its workers.

Chapter One

Merlins Migrate to Merrill's Farm

We have decided on Crewe.

Ernest Hives to Sir Wilfred Freeman, 25 May 1938

One of the consequences of the rise of Hitler and the Nazi movement in Germany was the rearmament of the United Kingdom. If such a policy had not been initiated, Rolls-Royce would not have been asked to increase the production of Merlin aero-engines and would, therefore, never have built a factory at Crewe. So, out of the fear of war, work was provided for the unemployed and migration of labour to this industrial enclave in the rural heartland of south Cheshire was encouraged.

From the very beginning of the railway age Crewe was an important junction, with lines radiating to various parts of the kingdom – although by 1931 its stagnating economy was hardly sufficient to support its population of 46,000. The nearest major conurbation was the Staffordshire city of Stoke-on-Trent, which comprised six separate towns. About 30 miles to the north, Liverpool and Manchester were part of the vast urban sprawl that was south Lancashire. Immediately surrounding Crewe was Cheshire dairy farming country, with the neighbouring typical traditional market towns of Nantwich and Sandbach.

That the municipal borough of Crewe was there at all was owing to the directors of the Grand Junction Railway Company, who had decided to locate a locomotive repair shop in the region in the early years of Queen Victoria's reign. The first locomotive, named *Dr Dalton*, stopped at Crewe on 4 July 1837, when the Grand Junction line between Liverpool and Birmingham was opened. In 1831 the population of Monks Coppenhall, a civil township in the ecclesiastical parish of Coppenhall and the site of the future town of Crewe, was 148. Twenty years later it had risen to 4,571, owing to the economic pulling power of railway wages.

The area had neither natural resources nor a pool of labour, but in 1840 the decision was made to remove the locomotive repair shop from Edgehill, Liverpool, the factors in favour of Monks Coppenhall being that it was a junction for Chester, on the Birmingham–Liverpool Railway, and that land was easily obtainable. When, in 1846, the Grand Junction Railway amalgamated with the Liverpool and Manchester Railway, and the following year with the Birmingham and London Railway, to form the giant London and North Western Railway, Crewe's future was assured. Over the rest of the nineteenth century most of the company's manufacturing facilities were concentrated in the town, making it one of the largest employers of labour in the country. Even as late as 1907 Crewe Railway Works was still in the top ten, nationally.

Crewe being a single industry town, its economy was geared to the railway, yet locomotive manufacture and maintenance were unable to provide employment for all who needed it. Consequently there was always a steady stream of young men migrating to more prosperous areas of the country. As early as 1869 an emigration society had been formed in Crewe to provide would-be migrants with information on the colonies and on other countries where their skills would be welcome. For the entire first third of the twentieth century, the economy of Crewe was declining.

For over seventy years the councillors of the town had endeavoured to persuade other industries to settle in the railway colony, but all to no avail. They were never short of ideas, for out of the fertile musings of the civic leaders came such schemes as boot making, cotton weaving, paper making, hat manufacturing, and a pot factory. In 1877 John Rigg, a railway company official, mooted the prospect of 40 per cent profit by the simple expedient of producing glass. Needless to say, no Victorian, or later capitalist, could be persuaded to invest in such schemes.

When the Labour Party took control of local government in the early 1930s it helped to form the Crewe Industrial Development Council, with the specific aim of increasing employment opportunities. Shortly afterwards John Leach, the owner of a local furniture warehouse, toured an area of Germany to publicise the merits of Crewe as a centre for industrial expansion. What made the town's councillors believe that German investment was available, given the economic conditions of the time, is not known. Predictably, the economy of the borough was affected not at all as a result of Mr Leach's long journey.

The town would have been better served if the council, instead of attempting to persuade firms and companies to settle in Crewe, had set about supplying the borough with an independent source of water. In 1925, because of lack of municipal provision, Michelin, the tyre manufacturer, refused even to consider locating in the town, settling instead in nearby Stoke-on-Trent. From its earliest days, Crewe had relied upon the LNWR Company for both gas and water. At this time (1931), it was still supplied, as it had been since 1864, by the company's boreholes at Whitmore, just across the Staffordshire border.

Eventually the Labour-controlled council did consider the matter, which was more than previous administrations had done, but it was only immediately prior to the Second World War that the details of a scheme for pumping water from Eaton, near to Chester, were placed before the rate-payers in a town-wide referendum. Even then, the correspondence columns of the local paper fizzed with letters condemning the action of the council as unnecessary and extravagant. Fortunately, a majority of the rate-payers was in favour of the scheme, yet it was not until the summer of 1939 that contracts were signed for the work to begin, by which time Rolls-Royce had been in the town for twelve months. Lack of water was as great a threat to the production of Merlin engines, in the early stages of the war, as was enemy action. The supply from Whitmore, supplemented by an emergency main from Eaton, proved equal to the task, until the whole scheme was opened in 1942, but it was a near-run thing.

As has been previously stated, it was the National Government's policy of rearming that was the major factor in Rolls-Royce locating a factory away from its headquarters at Derby. The 'shadow factory' scheme, initiated by the National Government of Ramsay MacDonald, and later Stanley Baldwin, was a device whereby firms such as Rolls-Royce, Austin, Standard and Rover, would produce aero-engines or armaments in addition to their cars. Colonel H. Disney, director of aeronautical production at the Air Ministry, administered the scheme, so it was with him and his officials that two high-ranking RR executives, Ernest Hives and Arthur Sidgreaves, held their negotiations. According to Lloyd's history of the firm, Rolls-Royce considered a shadow factory scheme in 1936, only to reject it, although many months later, in October 1937, the directors of RR finally consented to participate in such a scheme, modified according to their wishes.

The immediate impetus for RR expansion was an increase of 1,900 Merlin engines – on top of a previous order of nearly 3,000 and in addition to a large volume of spares, repairs and Kestrel work. Prior to this last order, Derby had been working to the limit of its capacity, and even with extra plant there, it was clear that a new factory was the only answer. This, it was decided, should be capable of producing complete engines built to drawings supplied from Derby.

Lloyd notes that two schemes had been suggested to meet the rearming crisis. One was to remove (at ministry expense) all car production from Derby to a new factory at Burton-on-Trent, leaving the original plant devoted solely to building aero-engines. The second was similar, but with a new aero-engine factory erected and equipped by the state, yet managed by RR, and with some of the work sub-contracted. Further, the Derby works would have additional land and plant, costing around £250,000. This would raise the Merlin output at Derby from thirty-five Merlins a week to fifty. Talks between the ministry and the board revolved around these schemes and slowly matured during the winter of 1937/8 until, on 16 May 1938, the 'Burton' scheme was formally rejected.

One week later the erection of a shadow factory was approved, but with no location specified. Around this time F.R. Dyson and Wilson Elliott, both young draughtsmen with RR at Derby, were given the task of drawing the outline plans of a factory at three different, unidentified locations. Wilson Elliott, however, by dint of his knowledge of topography, was able to speculate that Shrewsbury was one of the sites. There was now an impasse regarding location; the Ministry of Labour wanted Liverpool, while Hives objected because he did not want a large pool of casual labour. The Ministry of Labour rejected Shrewsbury, leaving Crewe to emerge as the compromise location, partly at the behest of Sir Wilfred Freeman, an influential member of the Air Council.

The main factor in Crewe being on the list of sites at all was the input of C.E. Bates, an Amalgamated Engineering Union (AEU) official at Derby, one-time prospective Parliamentary candidate for Crewe, an alderman and future mayor of Derby. He was a Crewe man who, having served an apprenticeship in the LNWR workshops, had migrated to Derby seeking work. He it was who brought Crewe to the attention of Hives and, although it is not known when it entered the short list, there is, among the papers in the company's Derby archives, an analysis of the town's water supply, dated March 1938. It would be safe, therefore, to conclude that, by about January of that year, the railway town was among the possible sites.

CREWE IS CHOSEN

On 24 May 1938 the decision was made, but kept secret: Crewe was to be the site for an aero-engine factory. The Air Ministry was to pay the capital costs of erecting and equipping the plant, with RR leasing and managing it, at a rent fixed at the prevailing bank rate. The estimated cost to the ministry was around £1,000,000, while RR invested about £750,000 of its own capital. The confirmation of the move was recorded in the minutes of the board for 23 June, when details of a letter from the Air Ministry, regarding Crewe, were discussed. It was item seven on the agenda, and the board formally gave its approval. Meanwhile, Hives had received a letter from Crewe town council with details of three possible sites. They were the disused LMS carriage works and two greenfield plots, and at the end of May two RR officials, Phillips, the architect and Tom Haldenby, who had been apprenticed to Royce Ltd at Cooke Street, Manchester, arrived in the town to meet with a hurriedly formed five-member council sub-committee to view two of the sites.

The first was in the south of Crewe, near the railway station, where Midland Rollmakers eventually settled, on land that was originally part of the Earl of Crewe's estate. It was declared unsuitable, as there were height restrictions on any building on account of its being adjacent to a proposed municipal aerodrome and RR wanted some of its buildings to be three storeys high. The firm did open premises nearby, but not until 1974, when RRM International located its export services branch on the newly opened Weston Road industrial estate.

The second site, an area of about 60 acres, was at Merrill's Farm, in the west of Crewe, adjacent to the Chester railway line. Pym's Lane, a meandering country by-way, was its boundary on the north and west. The farmhouse, formerly occupied by the Pym family, had served in the latter years of the nineteenth century as a smallpox hospital, and stood derelict to the west of the municipal incinerator. This site was accepted as a suitable plot, if a railway siding were constructed to link the site with the nearby railway line; 15,000 gallons of water per hour would be available, and a public footpath would be closed off.

The decision to move to Crewe was reported in the local paper on 4 June, in rather ambiguous language. All the details outlined above were still secret, but the report stated that rumours were circulating, based on good authority, that a large engineering works was to commence activities in the town, subject to Air Ministry agreement. Even the fact that a woman had presided over the council meeting for the first time was presaged with the fact that the mayor was engaged on urgent business, hinting that this was connected with the advent of a new industry. One week later the identity of the firm was revealed.

The Air Ministry agreed to purchase the Merrill's Farm land from Crewe town council at £99 an acre, the average price paid when it had been purchased just after the First World War. This was a bargain, compared with £100 an acre paid by the Grand Junction Railway Company in the early 1840s when it had been looking for land in the Crewe area. In 1846 the LNWR had had to pay £500 an acre for a

How Crewe received the news of a new industry coming to the town, in the summer of 1938.

piece of land in the centre of the town, although the price had fallen to £200 an acre in the 1860s, when the railway company had extended its works westwards.

For its part, the local council promised to provide sufficient housing for the incoming workers and to reconstruct Pym's Lane by widening it and extending its length to reach the A530, the main Nantwich–Middlewich road. The original portion of Pym's Lane that bounded the site on the west was renamed Sunnybank Road. The council also provided the Derby contractors, Gee, Walker & Slater, with temporary accommodation in the corporation garage at the refuse works in Pym's Lane.

BUILDING PYM'S LANE FACTORY

Preparatory work on surveying and pegging out Merrill's fields began on Tuesday 13 June, when everyone present helped the farmer to harvest the hay. Trial borings had established that the sub-clay was suitable for supporting heavy industrial buildings, but unknown at the time was the presence of two underground streams. The western extremity of the site had a potato crop maturing in the ground, and engineer Jack Valentine's intention to use this portion as a recreation ground did not materialise, as it had to accommodate a line of air-raid shelters.

The borough surveyor's department was busy laying water mains at the south and north ends of the site, along with the work of extending Pym's Lane. Planning and installation of the electrical supply was also begun, under the control of A.D. Heagan, the borough's electrical engineer. The local government managers' frenzied reaction to the imperatives of the contractors generated a haze of euphoria that caused certain councillors to imagine they were responsible for RR coming to Crewe, one claiming that the arrival of other firms was imminent. Instead of boasting about its imagined achievements, the council should have been responding more potently to the urgent need for housing.

Before the end of June 1938 temporary office accommodation had been found at Imperial Chambers, Prince Albert Street, and it was there that Rolls-Royce settled in Crewe on 4 July 1938. Responsible for this was an all-Derby, seven-man advance party who arrived at the railway colony in two cars and a lorry. These seven were John Morris, overall manager, W.H. Ward, accountant, J. Valentine, equipment engineer, R. Garner, test engineer, E. Glover, technical assistant, Wilson Elliott and F.R. Dyson. This latter man had a wage rise of 15s on his

On 6 July 1938 John Morris and his team moved into this building, known as Imperial Chambers, in Prince Albert Street to plan the manufacture of Merlin aero-engines in Crewe. *(Author's collection)*

previous rate of £3 for moving to Crewe. They were soon to be joined by S. Doxey, F. Hallows, C.L. Dickin, B. Crutchley, W. Harvey, J.W. Burnett, C. Darby, E. Buchan, H. Hennessey, L.T. Thompson, and Jack Aitcheson, to name but a few of the pre-war migrants from Derby.

One cannot over-estimate the size of the task that confronted this small management team, for theirs was the responsibility to galvanise the builders, as well as to equip the factory with various grades of labour, machine-tools, jigs, gauges and fixtures. Machining, heat treatment, sub-contractors, dispersal centres, air-raid defence measures and welfare facilities were just some of the issues that

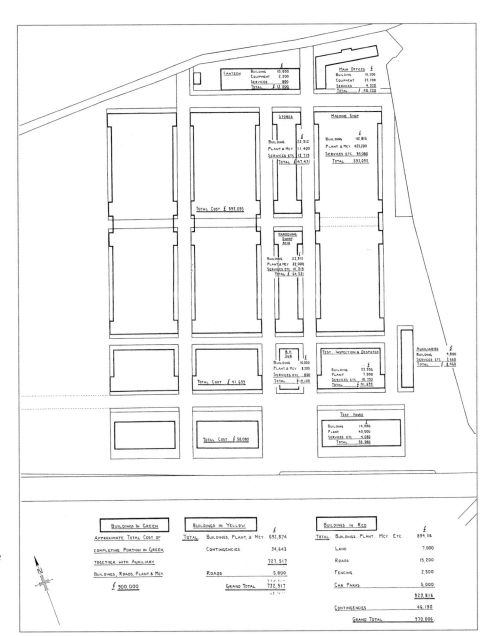

an and estimate costs of the oposed factory Crewe, drawn in June 1938. . Grace)

had to be successfully negotiated. To expedite this, by 12 July Haldenby, Morris and Valentine had produced a scheme outlining the estimated dates by which each stage of the factory would be ready, the growth of personnel at each stage, and the projected numbers of Merlin engines to be built. Despite atrocious weather, the planned dates were adhered to, and by May 1939 the first engine was passed off. By the end of 1939 Crewe RR was two months ahead of its schedule, a telling testimony to the combined efforts of the remarkable Morris and his entire team.

Two odd consequences of the occupation of the rooms at Imperial Chambers were the loss of hot water for the staff at the municipal library on the other side of the road, and the necessity for a group of Christian Brethren to find a new meeting place. The library staff had an informal arrangement to use the water heating facilities at Imperial Chambers. That they had to purchase a heater to replace this supply indicates the lack of facilities in some of the LMS-owned public buildings of pre-war Crewe.

On 6 July, when Jack Valentine officially broke the meadows of Merrill's Farm by removing the first spadeful of soil, building began in earnest under the direction of T. Howard, the Clerk of Works. It was just under six weeks since the decision to settle in Crewe, and such prompt action is indicative of the critical national situation. The rapid reaction from Derby, energised by the ferocious urgings of Ernest Hives, was not matched by the town council when it came to supplying houses, although the fault was not wholly the council's, for it had to wait for loans to be approved by Whitehall. Just before Christmas 1938, when the main machine shop was about half completed and over 4,000 applications for employment had been received, the local authority had not built one extra house. Following a letter of complaint from the firm, and a critical speech to the local rotary club by John

A portion of the Pym's Lane site on 2 August 1938, twenty-seven days after the ground was broken. *(B. Fishburne)*

The site three weeks later, late August 1938. *(B. Fishburne)*

Morris, a special meeting of the housing committee ordered the borough surveyor to proceed, without waiting for ministry sanction.

The administrative team at the Imperial Chambers organised affairs much more efficiently, and job adverts in the situations vacant columns of the local papers soon brought applications by the sackful. John Morris commented later that these replies gave him a dramatic insight into the low standard achieved by the English educational system. A typist, Miss Thomson, was the first local person to be hired, on 4 July. Another early young worker at Imperial Chambers was Frank Dale, who eventually became a section leader in the engine drawing office. Among the hundreds that followed before the end of 1938 was a 26-year-old time study engineer, who recalled the occasion quite vividly.

One evening, after arriving home from work at Joseph Lucas in Birmingham, I noticed, in the newspaper I was reading, an advert for jobs at Rolls-Royce that was being built at Crewe. I decided to apply, though I have to confess that I was not confident that I would be accepted, so prestigious was the name of RR. I thought that it was worth a try as it would probably be more money than I was getting at Lucas. A reply came very quickly calling me for an interview at the temporary offices in Prince Albert Street. The man that interviewed me was 'Big Jim' Burnett, the chief planning engineer. He was well over six feet tall, which is how he earned his nick-name. From the autumn of 1938 I worked in the temporary offices as a rate fixer, visiting the factory for a few hours every day. We usually made the journey from the town to Pym's Lane in Harold Armitage's small Austin saloon. John Morris, a brilliant engineer, was regularly seen around the factory sorting out problems. He was considered by us all to be a father figure who could solve anything. We were all so young in those days that Albert Shepherd, a buyer from Derby, was known as 'grandad' even though he was only forty-five.

The local Co-operative Society's former milk depot in Middlewich Street, rented by Rolls-Royce as its first workshop and training school. *(Author's collection)*

The name of this successful applicant was Neville Sadler, a wartime section leader in rate-fixing, and a product department supervisor when he retired in 1976.

In the animated atmosphere of Imperial Chambers catalogues were combed and contacts tapped by those responsible for purchasing machine-tools and office equipment. The area for miles around was scoured for small engineering firms, to form a sub-contract organisation under the control of J.T. Ward. On 25 July the Crewe Co-operative Society's recently built garage in Middlewich Street was leased for use as a training school.

It was to this building that the first manual workers reported on 8 August. Among them was a 24-year-old fitter named Frank Culley. He had served an apprenticeship in the LMS workshops, only, like all his contemporaries, to be discharged at twenty-one. After leaving Crewe he worked at Fairey Aviation, where about eighty Crewe men were working, before moving on to the Blue Funnel Steamship Line. On learning that RR was setting up in Crewe, he applied for employment and was accepted as an engine fitter. His first task was to strip a Merlin aero-engine, then to rebuild it under the watchful eyes of Bill Harvey and Jack Aitcheson.

The first 200 local workers were employed on this training programme in the Co-op Garage and another 200 were sent on a similar mission to Derby, although Hives soon curtailed the use of Derby for general training. The Middlewich Street garage also served as a tool-room, where Len Harper began the manufacture of jigs and fixtures for use at the new factory.

Meanwhile, back at Pym's Lane, the building work continued apace. Hives had instructed that the factory structure should precede the building of roads, his reason being he did not want the surface of the factory's roads to be damaged by contractors' vehicles. The weather for the summer and autumn of that year was atrocious, with over 11in of rain between July and October, nearly 1in falling on 24 August alone. When Hives slipped off the temporary road of railway sleepers into thigh-deep mud during one of his many visits, he probably wished that permanent roads had been constructed first. One error in planning the building, that manifested itself in future years, was the narrow diameter of the drains. Heavy rain caused water to back up and flood the main shop, to such an extent that production was affected. One such instance was the subject of a severe memo from 'J.M.' to Valentine, the equipment engineer, on 13 September 1943. To try to prevent the flooding, workers soon learned to park a loaded flatbed truck on the nearest manhole cover.

Work on manufacturing the Merlin engines began at the main site, in Pym's Lane, on 18 October 1938, when about 100yd of the north end of the main shop was usable. To quote Jack Valentine, 'The days were hectic. We had to make do with temporary accommodation, even to using a shed in the corporation incinerator yard across the road from the factory.' That yard was also the site of the temporary lavatory facilities for the first workers at Pym's Lane.

Three weeks later Lord Scott, the chairman of RR, came to tour the site. The main shop, which was eventually 1,050ft in length, was built bay by bay, and as each section was completed the contractors would screen off the open end, machines would be moved in, and erection of the next bay would begin. A smaller shop for hardening and heat treatment, that was being erected parallel to it at the same time, was finished around Easter 1939. In May 1939 the main shop was finished, and the engine fitters were transferred from the Middlewich Street garage to Pym's Lane, leaving the vacated space to be filled with machines. From then

Looking south along Second Avenue in June 1939, with the main machine shop to the left. The cycle racks along the avenue were replaced by VW in 2004. *(B. Fishburne)*

until the end of the war, this building was one of the many dispersal sites that RR utilised in south Cheshire and north Staffordshire.

Some contemporary evidence would suggest that engines were being tested by March 1939, but 20 May is the official date when the first Crewe-built Merlin was being run on the test beds adjacent to the Chester railway line, at the southern end of the site, supervised by Dick Garner. The rate of production of Merlin power units accelerated from 5 in May, to 41 in August, 108 in October and 190 in December. The total number of engines produced in 1939 was in the region of 500, at a cost of about £2,200 each.

In August a petition was sent to the council from the residents of the corporation houses in West Street, about 200yd distant, complaining of the noise from Rolls-Royce. A further petition was sent six months later, followed by an official complaint from the town clerk. The Air Ministry wrote to Hives requesting his cooperation in reducing the noise, but he counter-claimed that RR had done everything possible by building 20ft-high baffle walls, as well as fitting large silencers. To alleviate local distress the engines were run at full throttle during daylight hours only, an arrangement that was ignored after the Dunkirk evacuation.

Another complaint, from the west end residents, was of the serious shortage of water, as the supply would often be cut, owing to the tremendous amount being

Looking south down the main machine shop, June 1939. It became far more cluttered as the years passed. (B. Fishburne)

A Merlin engine being tested, showing the water-cooled silencer and exhaust manifold. Notice the large silencers and baffle wall to dampen the noise, for the benefit of the residents of West Street, about 200yd away. (B. Fishburne)

used by the engines on test. The estimated consumption of water, when the factory was planned, was 15,000 gallons per hour; the actual consumption in September 1939, of 40,000 gallons per hour, was expected to rise to 60,000 gallons later that year. The RR water tower, a feature that dominated the west of Crewe, was built at this date to ensure consistent pressure and supply.

THE FIRST STRIKE

On 10 June the first Crewe-built Merlin was despatched amidst small-scale celebrations. There was good cause to celebrate, because it was less than a year since the small group of Derby men had arrived to invest Crewe with its first major industrial plant since the arrival of the Grand Junction Railway works, nearly a century before. Not only had the workshops been erected and equipped in a relatively short time, but a serious labour dispute had also been resolved.

This industrial action was attributable to the use of unskilled labour on jobs that the unionised workforce considered the province of skilled, or rather male, workers. It came to a head early in April 1939, when over 600 men downed tools and walked out of the factory. At a meeting in the Kino Cinema on 16 Sunday April, about one week into the strike, C. Jones, a member of the strike committee, outlined the reasons for the stoppage, claiming that RR had violated agreements by

Small capstan lathes at the north end of the main shop. Operation of the lathes by women led to the first strike, in April 1939. This picture was taken just after the end of the strike. *(B. Fishburne)*

employing girls on lathes, without giving ten days' notice of changes in working practices. One of the Derby union convenors claimed that when the factory was fully operational there would be the prospect of 300 girls doing men's jobs, and that women did not operate capstan lathes at Derby. Financial support of about £100 was received from Derby, as well as a promise of a levy of 2s per man. Such evidence supports the view, as reported by Lloyd, that RR directors believed that the dispute was fostered from Derby. An editorial in the *Crewe Chronicle* stated it was caused by other than Crewe men, although this was, perhaps, wishful thinking as much as informed comment.

Individuals not directly involved in the strike expressed flurries of concern. The town council formed a sub-committee to help resolve matters; however, by the time it had settled its composition, the strike was almost over. A local industrialist, Sir Francis Joseph, was nominated by Alderman Smith, chairman of the LMS works committee, to arbitrate, but Hives would not acquiesce in this. Not that it mattered, because the strike was called off before Sir Francis could have started his consultations. This happened at a mass meeting in St Barnabas church hall on 18 April, when the strikers were informed that the national committee of the AEU refused to make the strike official. A positive outcome of this stoppage was the formation of a liaison committee between the management and the shop stewards, which helped to resolve future disputes before they reached crisis point.

Some historians of the firm have read this industrial dispute as lack of patriotism on the part of the workers. Perhaps there was an element of selfishness, yet so there was in 1941 when Crewe town council was attempting to connect the Eaton water supply to the town; a supply urgently needed to ensure that the LMS workshops, manufacturing tanks, and RR, producing Merlin engines, had sufficient water for their needs. The common peril did not prevent certain landowners and farmers from holding out for twice the going rate as compensation for the pipeline traversing their land. Although most of the farmers settled at around 18*d* per linear yard, a few demanded and received 36*d*. Patriotism, or lack of it, knows no class frontiers when money is involved.

One of the underlying causes of the industrial unrest in 1939 was Hives's determination to increase the use of jigs and fixtures on the production line. The ratio of skilled men to inspectors was low at Derby, when compared with Crewe, where nearly double the percentage of inspectors was employed. The increased use of jigs and fixtures reduced the need for high skills at Crewe, so it was only natural that the unions seized upon a pretext of 'dilution of working practices' in order to prevent further erosion of differentials in rates of pay. What is obvious from a perusal of Frank Culley's notes of shop stewards' meetings is the determination, on the part of the stewards, to 'unionise' the factory. Their desire was for 100 per cent union membership.

The wages paid for the various skills coincided with the locally agreed union rates. These ranged from 29*s* per week for a labourer, to 46*s* for a skilled production machine worker, although for production drillers the rate was 37*s*. Tool-room fitters and tool-makers received 51*s*, electricians and millwrights 46*s*. It must be remembered that the rate was not the actual wage paid, because bonus, based on the rate, made up the amount of cash received. For instance Frank Culley, who had a rate of 51*s*, received around £5 per week without overtime.

The highest paid manual workers were the highly skilled machine-tool setters at 56*s* per week. They were at a premium, and those with management skills were promoted almost as soon as they commenced work. The average wage of a foreman in 1939 was £300 per annum, with an additional £75 bonus. When James Burnett was offered the post of chief production planner in August 1939, his salary was £600 per annum, while Tommy Barlow, who eventually went on to higher things at Shrewsbury, was paid 6 guineas a week as one of Burnett's planners. Barlow is a good example of upward mobility in the engineering industry, for he served his time as a centre lathe turner at Thorneycroft's Marine Works at Reading before moving to Broome and Wade at High Wycombe as a turret-lathe setter operator. From there he travelled to Slough to work as a tool-maker, then as a rate-fixer, before going to Crewe as a production planner. In 1974 he completed the circle, being appointed managing director of Rolls-Royce Motors (car division).

Regarding this pre-war period, L.T.C. Rolt, the respected industrial author, wrote of his experience at Pym's Lane in his autobiography, *Landscape with Canals*:

> I assumed that my new job would prove rewarding, so much did I revere the name of Rolls-Royce. To me it was synonymous with engineering craftsmanship. . . . I now imagined myself fitting up Merlin engines from scratch . . . accompanying them to the test bed to ensure that they performed

satisfactorily. I was to be sadly disillusioned when I left Church Minshull for Crewe on my elderly motor cycle early on the following Monday morning. No daylight ever penetrated the big shop. For twenty four hours a day, mercury vapour lamps blazed over head. I had never encountered this type of lighting before. It made all my new workmates look as if they were suffering from serious heart or liver complaints; their complexions looked ghastly and their lips were blue. They were working a nightshift at Rolls-Royce. Walking from the light and fresh air of an autumn morning into the unnatural glare of this shop, its atmosphere used to hit me like a blow in the face. Warm and stale, it reeked of a nauseating humanity. Instead of assembling engines as I fondly imagined, I found myself tapping the holes for the cylinder-head studs in an endless succession of Merlin cylinder blocks, which appeared before me. . . . It struck me as a job which an ape might have been trained to perform, and I reflected wryly on the care with which my credentials had been scrutinised and on the fact that I had been compelled to join a so-called 'craft union' before being assigned this mindless task . . . I despair of conveying the depths of boredom . . . to which this job reduced me. I even found myself looking forward eagerly to my next visit to the urinal because it relieved the tedium.

The writer goes on to say with what alacrity he left the employ of RR at Crewe, when given the opportunity a few weeks later. Such remarks regarding the monotony of tasks help to place the succession of minor industrial disputes within a sympathetic context. Despite these, however, the majority of the wartime employees at Pym's Lane endured, or enjoyed the years, enabling the plant to produce over 26,000 Merlin engines and 2,000 Griffon engines between 1939 and 1945.

OFFICIAL OPENING

With the trade dispute over and the factory in production, it was an opportune time for the official opening. This took place on 14 July 1939, when Sir Kingsley Wood, Secretary for Air in Chamberlain's National Government, toured the factory along with Harry Bricker, the Mayor of Crewe, before being entertained to lunch by Ernest Hives, where each of the 135 guests received a souvenir brochure to mark the importance of the occasion. Correspondents from various journals accompanied the party on the tour of the works. The report in the *Aeroplane Magazine* contained the observation that it would be an easy target for sabotage by the IRA.

The same journalist also remarked on the youthfulness of the employees. He could, with equal truth, have noted the mixture of dialects, for a small study of the manual workers employed in these early days has revealed a generous mix of origins, representative of every region of the UK, but mainly from the northern and midland counties of the United Kingdom. The rapid influx of workers exacerbated the local housing shortage, a shortage that was a continual grievance of Ernest Hives in his contacts with the town's council. The youthful nature of the employees also meant that anyone who displayed leadership qualities could quickly find himself in a minor management position as there was no need to wait for dead men's shoes. Two examples are Alf Jennings and Bob Banks, who were foremen in their twenties.

Among the mix of workers being attracted to Crewe were some who had exaggerated their skills, as Frank Culley recalled in his own inimitable way: 'We had all sorts here. People who had been butchers, bakers and probably candlestick-makers'. The works committee's verdict was voiced in the words: '. . . the chaos existing in some departments as men are brought from other places without experience'.

In November 1940 a Crewe-built Merlin was stripped, revealing much shoddy workmanship. A special conference of the inspection and engineering departments called for tighter discipline, along with demands to the inspectors not to abuse the practice of extended limits. The inspectors reasoned that the type of men being employed by RR at Crewe were 'a grievous burden' as many were not truly skilled, and they adopted a bullying attitude towards them. The impasse was partially resolved by a management edict that the drawing or blueprint must be adhered to.

Even though the factory had been officially opened in July 1939, it was by no means complete, as a second large workshop was being erected, equal in floor area to the main shop. An underground strong room, which was to house all tracings, designs, patents and accounts, was also being excavated in the summer of that year, although from 1940 it was the Air-Raid Precautions (ARP) control room.

By the end of 1939 the two main workshops, the main office block, the hardening and plating departments, millwrights' workshop, test beds, engine despatch and

General view of the heat treatment department, commonly called the hardening shop, June 1939. Note the electric carburising furnaces and charging machine on the left and gas-fired furnaces to the right. (B. Fishburne)

The laboratory opened in 1939 and was situated in the same range of buildings as the hardening shop until VW commissioned a new one in 2000. *(B. Fishburne)*

boiler house were all complete. The water tower, which could be seen on the skyline of the west of Crewe until RR was separated from Bentley at the beginning of the twenty-first century, was also in place, except for the initials 'RR', which did not appear until after hostilities ended, presumably to keep its location secret.

HOUSING THE WORKERS

By the time of the declaration of war in September 1939 the problem of housing the influx of workers had still not been solved, by either private or public bodies. Most blame must be laid at the door of the town council, for it was the councillors who had promised to deliver sufficient houses for the company's needs. These had been assessed in July as 2,000 houses, but there was no way that the corporation could have erected such a number. The borough surveyor, Leonard Reeves, one of the most competent to hold the job during the twentieth century, would never have agreed to build as many as 1,000 houses before the end of 1938, as is stated in some accounts of Rolls-Royce in Crewe. In a report to the council in August 1938 he stated that plans had been passed for over 400 dwellings to be built by the local authority, with nearly 300 planned by private builders. It could be claimed, in defence of the council, that its hands were tied to some extent, as they had not the power to build without sanction from Whitehall. The facts are that, on 4 June 1938, the full council pledged to erect 102 dwellings north of Timbrell Avenue, yet the building contract was not signed until three days before Christmas of that year. Even then the contract had to be reassigned to another firm in the early days of 1939 because the previous contractors, Fletcher and Sons of Crewe, had been declared insolvent.

Once the newly appointed builders, Eadie & Company of Wolverhampton, had received their contract, they began immediately to construct the street of around eighty dwellings that became known as Smith Grove, along with another twenty houses in the same area. Four months later the first of these houses, each costing the council on average £320, was ready for occupation, the whole of the estate being completed by September 1939. The same builders were then given the contract for the 250-house Selworthy Drive estate, about a mile from the factory, although this decision was criticised by Whitehall as the council had not waited for official approval. As a tribute to the builders, one of the streets on this estate was named Eadie Grove. The houses on both of these estates were available for rent only.

During these months Hives was demanding the date when sufficient housing would be available, because lack of it was hampering the recruitment of staff. Lloyd claims that by March 1939 a decision had been taken not to extend the Crewe factory, owing to insufficient housing. It should be pointed out that the original seven who had come from Derby in July 1938 also had to find themselves accommodation – unlike those who came from Clan Foundry in 1950, when Rolls-Royce moved heaven and earth to provide housing in the south Cheshire region. John Morris bought a large house on the main Nantwich road at Wistaston, which he shared with the Stafford family when Fred Stafford started working at Pym's Lane early in the war. Ronnie Dyson moved into lodgings in the south of Crewe and Wilson Elliott lived in rented property in Newfield Drive.

Private speculators responded with a little more urgency, although they never shouldered the massive schemes that were really necessary. In September 1938

A group of wartime employees – all but one residents of Smith Grove, built in 1939 especially for RR workers. Front row, left to right: Martin Connellor, George Watson, Ted Ollerhead, John Rawcliffe, Stan Watkins, ? Mills, Harry Jones, Fred Jones. Back row: Frank McCuaig, George Sleigh, Bill Briggs, Eric Booth, Derek Booth, Stan Frost, Sam Henshaw, Jim Breakey, Peter Abraham. *(Author's collection)*

Houses in Mossford Avenue and Selworthy Drive, built by the town council in 1939–40 to house Rolls-Royce workers migrating to Crewe. *(Author's collection)*

Sparkes and Stephens started to build around 100 semi-detached dwellings in Holland Street, at a cost of £415 each. An estate of 1,200 houses, adjacent to Valley Road and bounded by the Queen's Park, was planned by the Wistaston Green Company. Unfortunately this was not built until the postwar era, and even then it was a local authority project.

Between 1938 and 1940 small groups of houses were built by private speculators on existing thoroughfares such as Mablin's Lane and Remer Street, as well as a larger estate of about 175 dwellings north of Crewe Road, near to the railway station. A Manchester firm came to grief in its attempts to cash in on the need for houses, leaving its estate near to Valley Road partly completed. For around twenty years the Wistaston Green end of Danebank Avenue was Marsden Road, the name given by the original builders. The 22-year-old Bob Banks, Alf Jennings and Bob Hill were three early workers at Pym's Lane who occupied property on this estate. The first of these cycled about 35 miles from Manchester for an interview at RR, obtained accommodation for his wife in Woodside Avenue, and returned home to Manchester the same day on his bike. Within three years he was a foreman.

The result of these private building ventures was the erection of approximately 1,000 dwellings between 1938 and 1942. This has to be compared with the need, for Rolls-Royce was taking men on at the rate of 100 a week even before the war started, reaching a total of 8,752 by December 1942. Some people interviewed remember having to share their bedrooms with lodgers, so rigorous were the emergency regulations empowering the authorities to billet homeless workers. Accommodation was desperately needed, for some homes were grossly overcrowded.

The ease with which the population acquiesced to these wartime regulations has almost been forgotten with the passage of time. Incursions into personal freedoms were many, but, owing to the serious struggle against fascism, such measures were submitted to with equanimity. Unfortunately, interpretation of the emergency regulations left scope for self-important bureaucrats to impinge needlessly upon personal freedoms. When the war was almost over, some residents of Crewe were admonished for demolishing their Andersen shelters without first gaining official permission. This was in the spring of 1945, when there had not been an air-raid for over two years.

Six days after the declaration of war a conference was held between representatives from the council, the Ministry of Health, the Air Ministry and the Public Works Loan Board to discuss the urgent need for housing, leading to a decision to build 500 dwellings on 65 acres at Totty's Hall Farm in the west of Crewe, about 1,000yd from the factory. The plan was for a first phase of 150 houses at a cost of £65,000, then a further 390 dwellings costing £189,000. Rolls-Royce, on being offered the chance of contributing towards the cost of this estate, politely refused. A few weeks into the contract the council realised that it would not be able to complete the building of the second phase, so in June 1940 the Ministry of Aircraft Production (MAP) took over the project, substituting maisonettes for houses. They proved to be notorious in postwar Crewe, for they were damp, with unattractive flat roofs, and very unpopular with some tenants. The solution to the perennial problem of these flats was their demolition, some twenty-five years after they were built.

Even during the war the maisonettes were not easy to let, as is demonstrated by a letter from the MAP to the town council, in June 1942, insisting that no council houses were to be rented to incoming RR employees so long as any maisonettes remained unoccupied. Difficulties were also encountered with the collection of rents on the Totty's Hall estate, the Ministry's suggested solution of docking the rent from the workers' wages being rejected by the company.

Besides the maisonettes, the Ministry also erected a hostel for the single women drafted into the town to work at the Pym's Lane factory. Mainly from the Glasgow area, a few of these ladies soon gained a reputation for fighting and entertaining men. (The hostel became an annexe to the College of Further Education in postwar Crewe.) As late as 1944 the company was complaining to the town council that houses originally built for RR employees had been re-let to other workers. Wartime regulations were so stringent that workers, directed to a factory, were not allowed to leave without official sanction, despite having no satisfactory dwelling place.

The wartime hostel built for conscripted female labour on an estate planned for RR workers. Between 1940 and 1960 it was surrounded by maisonettes that were never very easy to let. After the war the building became an annexe to Crewe College of Further Education. *(Author's collection)*

All of the extra homes, along with the wartime needs of the railway works, as well as the demands of Rolls-Royce, led to a shortage of town gas, meaning that the LMS Railway Company had to construct three new carbonising arches at its local gas works in Stewart Street. Gas production had increased from 256 million cu ft a year in 1938 to more than 500 million cu ft

Looking north across the Company's Pym's Lane car park in 1943, with Minshull New Road to the right. The ground slopes down to Leighton Brook and Totty's Hall Farm can be seen in the distance. The barrage balloon is flying above the Totty's Hall housing estate. RR sports ground is at the top of the hill opposite the farm. *(Martin Bourne)*

six years later, with around 100 million cu ft being consumed by the Pym's Lane plant.

Demands on the bus fleets of the Crosville Motor Company and similar firms, to provide transport for RR workers from outlying communities, were too great, when combined with the needs of the LMS. Each day the Potteries Motor Traction Company brought in over 700 persons from the Staffordshire pottery towns. The resulting chaos of buses (Crosville alone sent forty-five vehicles) seeking parking space around the factory can easily be imagined. Many times, ARP wardens protested about torches being shone at the destination boards of the buses – such practices were an infringement of blackout regulations.

The chaos meant that at the height of the war a bus station had to be constructed, preliminary discussions beginning in the autumn of 1941. Yet such was the bureaucracy, and the multiplicity of interested bodies, that it took nearly a hundred letters, over a period of twelve months, before the plans were approved. The bus station, opened in February 1943, is now the company's car park in Pym's Lane.

For most Crewe-based employees, a popular way of travelling to work was by bicycle, meaning that West Street and Badger Avenue were flooded with cycles when the factory disgorged its workforce. Cycling within the factory precincts, however, was an offence that could be penalised by three days' suspension. The practical effect of the ban was that most cyclists dismounted to walk through the gates, then, after walking another few yards, would remount and ride to their cycle shelter.

Chapter Two

The Merlin Years, 1939 to 1945

Work again. No time for pleasure.
Frank Culley's diary, 11 November 1940

By August 1939 it was obvious that war with Germany was near. The confirmation of this was the signing of the Nazi-Soviet Pact on 23 August, freeing Hitler's hands in the east and allowing him to gain *Lebensraum* at the expense of Poland. Locally the effects were many. The longest item on the agenda at the monthly meetings of the Crewe town council was the report of the ARP sub-committee. All over the town preparations were in hand to protect the people from air-raids, to regulate food rationing and to search for emergency mortuary accommodation, to mention but three responses to the crisis.

At Pym's Lane, declaration of war meant that working hours were increased by the addition of overtime. This was not as onerous then as it was later, for Frank Culley still managed to visit the cinema twice a week, which was more than he could do after May 1940. Each employee had to wear an identity disc, to be shown to the security staff on entering the factory. The walls of the main buildings were camouflaged, as were the immediate surroundings. Roof lights were blacked out and air-raid shelters were constructed inside the factory perimeter, on the unused acreage adjoining Sunnybank Road. Jack Valentine requested the town's ARP committee to have the electricity sub-station that fed the factory protected by sandbags. This man, known to successive generations of RR employees as 'JV', worked tirelessly to introduce all known air-raid protective measures into the plant. Strangely, air-raid precautions had not been included in the original plans for Crewe Rolls-Royce. They were pencilled in on the Morris/Valentine scheme of July 1938, as was a revised estimate of costs that included £14,000 for thicker walls, splinter-proof sub-stations and wired windows.

Other actions were taken by government departments to protect the factory from air-raids. There was a line of smoke-screen chimneys along Pym's Lane and Sunnybank Road, which were regularly serviced by 821 Smoke Company of the Pioneer Corps. These smoke-screens had a cylindrical base filled with cotton waste soaked in diesel oil, and on receiving a warning the service men on duty ignited the cotton waste. This did not burn fiercely, but smouldered, giving off dense clouds of evil-smelling smoke through a 4ft chimney. The theory was that it would drift over the factory, masking the buildings. The smoke affected the long-suffering residents of the houses surrounding the factory, more than the bomb-aimers of the

Luftwaffe. Barrage balloons and anti-aircraft (AA) gun sites ringed the plant to protect it from low-flying bombers, and there was even a gun on the roof of the main office block until November 1941, when it was removed because the regular movement of its crew was damaging the roof. These guns were under the control of the 135th Light Anti-Aircraft Battery. Thirty-two barrage balloons, controlled by 949 Barrage Balloon Squadron, protected Crewe, the nearest to the factory being just to the west, in Sunnybank Road. Emergency water tanks were placed at strategic points for dealing with incendiary bombs. The lake in the nearby Queen's Park was drained, owing to its being a marker for enemy aircraft, only to be filled again, in January 1941, on the instructions of the Chief Fire Officer, because he needed the water as an emergency supply. Later in the war a census of nineteenth-century wells was taken, in case the civic water supply failed. Fortunately they were never needed. The western approach to Rolls-Royce, through the dairy fields of south Cheshire, was along the newly constructed extension to Pym's Lane which, in the early stages of the war, had stone blocks laid across it to prevent hostile aircraft or gliders using it for a landing ground.

The outbreak of war brought dispersal of the staff in the main office block fronting Pym's Lane. The plant and equipment department moved into the Baptist

Aerial view, looking north, of the factory with its wartime camouflage. Pym's Lane runs from east to west at the top of the picture. The last building on the north side, going west, is the dilapidated remains of the Pym family's farm. A balloon can be seen in the top left corner, protecting the factory from low flying hostile aeroplanes; a protection that was not in place on 29 December 1940 when the factory was bombed. Notice the 'spiked' field in the foreground to deter gliders and enemy aircraft from landing. The triangular portion of ground between the Chester railway line and West Street is now filled with housing. *(Author's collection)*

German reconnaissance photograph showing the Rolls-Royce factory and the LMS railway workshops. Queen's Park is the oval-shaped area in the left centre and RR is the rectangular area of buildings near the top left corner. *(Author's collection)*

Schoolroom in Waterloo Road, Haslington; others went to Stoke Hall, near Barbridge, leaving the vacated office space for an army unit and an ARP contingent. When new premises were built at Glasgow some of its managers came to share these offices for training in RR methods, as did some from Ford Motors.

Once enemy action began, dispersal was repeated, this time to a greater number of sites, for the duration of the war. It also meant a further increase in working hours under the Essential Works Order, with double shifts being introduced in virtually every department. Day shift 'normal' hours were 7.40 a.m. to 7 p.m., while the night shift clocked on at 8 p.m. and ended at 7.30 a.m. Further overtime was added as and when it was deemed necessary. Later in the war a barber was provided 'in house' to allow workers to have their hair cut, because of the unsocial hours they were working.

Yet more disruption to normal working patterns was occasioned by air-raids. When the warning siren was heard everyone at Pym's Lane was supposed to assemble in the shelters. Once there, they were not let out until the wail of the 'all clear'. In Crewe the worst year for raids was 1941, when in total 112 warnings were received, of which 58 occurred between March and May. These impinged upon working hours in a very real way, since if the siren sounded just before a shift ended, another hour or two could be added by having to remain in the shelter. An example of this was on 7 April 1941, when a warning sounded at 9.40 p.m., yet clearance was not given to leave the bunkers until 3.55 a.m. It must be said that workers were not encouraged to obey the 'alert' warning, especially when Merlin parts were urgently needed. This was in response to Beaverbrook's appeal to all workers in the aircraft industry to remain at their machines or benches until enemy bombers were virtually overhead, before they sought shelter.

A glance at Frank Culley's diary reveals that the events of May 1940, culminating in the Dunkirk retreat, created a distinct imperative at Crewe:

20–5–40   Intense speed up at work as Germans advance near coast.
25–5–40   8.00 a.m. to 9.00 p.m. On again at 10.17 p.m. Home at 8.00 a.m.

There is no doubt that the shock of the crushing defeat of the French Army and the British Expeditionary Force by the Wehrmacht energised the workforce at Pym's Lane and elsewhere. An interesting corollary to the Dunkirk retreat was that four French engineers who were flying home after visiting the USA were diverted to the UK, along with five multi-spindle drilling machines that they had purchased. They eventually arrived at Crewe, along with their machines, where they spent the rest of the war working in the jig and tool drawing office at Pym's Lane.

Perhaps Frank Culley's feelings are best summed up with a comment recorded on 27 May 1940: 'Really done to the wide. Everybody is just thoroughly fed up with this hum-drum, day in day out, existence. Weather is perfect. Worked to 8.00 p.m. Attended union meeting.' This, and many other entries, all help to show that when Beaverbrook became Minister of Aircraft Production, with a brief to increase aeroplane production, his ministrations were not needed at Crewe RR.

In August 1940 the town of Crewe received its second official visit by a reigning monarch, when the Pym's Lane factory featured in the King's itinerary, and being taken to watch that visit is one of the author's earliest memories. King George VI and Queen Elizabeth made a ninety-minute tour of the main shop, in the company of John Morris, before moving on to Crewe's football ground, where various local dignitaries awaited them. The abiding impression of many workers who saw the

King at close quarters on that occasion was that he was wearing make-up. As the royal couple left Pym's Lane, the factory's Home Guard paraded as a mark of honour and respect.

BOMBING AND ITS CONSEQUENCES

One safety measure that was proposed by the AEU district committee, but not carried through immediately, was a suggestion, in September 1940, for a 'spotter' to be always on duty at RR to give warning of enemy aircraft in the vicinity. Perhaps it was an air-raid on 3 October, when a number of bombs were dropped about 300yd from the factory, that consolidated the 'spotter' system, for by November it was complete, being linked with the Observer Corps at Shrewsbury and Manchester, as well as with local observers at Radway Green Royal Ordnance factory and the LMS works. On 14 November Rolls-Royce received its second near miss, when twelve bombs landed in a field adjacent to Pym's Lane. No damage was done, yet 'Lord Haw-Haw', in his news bulletin from Germany, declared that the factory had been destroyed. It seemed as if the management's promise, that 'all necessary precautions would be taken to safeguard the employees', was being fulfilled.

Despite these near misses, and all the measures outlined above, none of balloons that ringed Crewe was flying and no warning was given when, just after 3 p.m. on Sunday 29 December 1940, a Junkers 88 bomber approached Crewe from the south-west. It was on a mission that brought devastation to Pym's Lane, and the worst catastrophe in the history of Crewe Rolls-Royce. According to observers, the bomber flew across the town, making a dive over the west end, where it released two bombs at a height of around 200ft, immediately afterwards climbing to safety in the cloud cover. These bombs exploded on the north-west corner of the factory at 3.09 p.m. and Frank Merrill, a young schoolboy at the time, gave this account of the incident many years later:

During the second world war I lived in Darlington Avenue in the West End of Crewe. On the Sunday afternoon, I now know to have been 29 December 1940, I was ten years of age and suffering from mumps. I mention that because as a result I was confined to the settee in front of the living room window and not supposed to go out. I heard the noise of an aircraft. There was a lot of low broken cloud and as I looked out of the window the aircraft appeared briefly, quite low. It was twin engined and I thought at first it was British. When it appeared again, I couldn't see any roundels. It appeared dark all over without the usual camouflage. I turned to the other members of my family in the room and said that I thought the plane was German. Within minutes there was the sound of aircraft engines again, much louder and as I looked up it was coming very low down, head on at right angles to Darlington Avenue heading west. The mumps forgotten I ran to the back door. The plane shot overhead, its German markings unmistakable at that height. I was amazed to see that the bomb doors were open and as it passed over Minshull New Road two bombs tumbled out. My father grabbed me, slammed the back door shut and shoved me under the stairs. There was a tremendous bang and the back door was blown open and slammed against the sink. The next thing I remember is everyone crowding outside, and staring at a huge column of black smoke rising from the direction of Rolls-Royce. We could hear people shouting and yelling from the direction of Minshull New Road as hundreds of people who lived in the adjoining streets converged on Rolls-Royce to find out what had happened to their family members working there. Mr Hough, who lived across the road, appeared carrying a piece of metal about the size of a sewing machine. He said it had landed on their Anderson air raid shelter in the garden. It was said later that it was a piece of RR machinery. I suddenly thought 'bomb shrapnel'. Like all boys of my age, I was obsessed with collecting war souvenirs and started to look around our garden, not very hopefully. To my amazement, there was, sticking out of the ground, a piece of bomb shrapnel about the size of my hand, still warm.

One of the bombs landed just inside the west wall of 16 shop, causing fifteen outright deaths, with another man dying a few hours later. The second struck the adjacent electrical sub-station, killing an electrician who was making a weekly inspection of the equipment. These seventeen deaths helped to bring the total killed across the UK in air-raids in December 1940 to 3,793.

The average age of the dead was 28 years, which, when compared with 43½ years average age in the Derby RR bombing of July 1942, provides further evidence of the youthful composition of the workforce at Pym's Lane. Of the Crewe deaths, four were females and thirteen were males. Around sixty were injured, including one man with a large stake of wood through his thigh, and John Morris with shrapnel wounds to his legs. Fred Stafford, who was present at the

Entrances to wartime underground air-raid shelters immediately adjacent to the bombed 16 shop, looking south. If a warning had been given on 29 December 1940 the workers could have assembled in these shelters in a few minutes. (A. Flood)

Bomb damage to the corner of 16 shop inflicted on Sunday 29 December 1940. Seventeen people were killed in the incident and many injured. As no warning was given the workers had no time to congregate in the shelters. At the top of the picture an interesting vehicle, known as a Beaver-Eel, can be seen. It was a Leyland lorry with an armoured body, hurriedly built for the Ministry of Aircraft Production to defend factories manufacturing for the RAF. It was armed with a single gun. *(Author's collection)*

time, managed to escape injury by taking evasive action. He was from the Coventry area, and therefore had stark experience of raids, enabling him to recognise the sounds of a bomber and falling bombs. Although this raid was not the first to bring fatalities to Crewe, it was a greater cause of loss of life than any other local wartime incident. Some of the injuries must have had long-term implications, as a dance was held two years after the tragedy to raise money for the victims.

Elsewhere in the factory, the first that the workforce knew of the incident were a tremendous explosion and instant darkness as the lights went out, due to the damage to the sub-station. In the ensuing chaos there were many minor accidents as workers tried to vacate the premises, until order was established and rescue work began. The injured were taken to the local hospital, while the bodies of the dead were removed to a makeshift mortuary in the canteen, to await preliminary identification. Alf Jennings, foreman of 121 department, which had borne the brunt of the damage, identified most of the dead. Only 23 years old, he found it a terrible ordeal, as the following account makes clear:

I was standing by one of the semi-autos discussing the progress of a particular job with one of the operators when there was tremendous noise and a sudden blackness. It was a few seconds before I realised what had happened, in fact it was only when I saw the side wall had gone that I realised it was a bomb exploding. I had fallen to the floor by instinct I suppose and was uninjured. The man I had been talking to was underneath the machine that had been blown on top of him. He was dead when we got him out. All the lights had gone out but as the side of the bay was blown out and part of the roof you could see the awful mess and damage. When the bomb exploded the machines all stopped working and you could hear shouts and cries, especially from the injured. One of the worst casualties I helped with was a man with a large spar of wood sticking right through his thigh. It must have been part of a duck board or pallet. The bodies of the dead were taken to the canteen where I had to help to identify them as many of them worked for me. Another man that could have helped with the identification could not face it so I had to do it alone. I was twenty three. It was an awful day. So many killed and injured and no warning.

Alf gave this account sixty years after it had happened. It had obviously deeply affected him, yet it was work as normal next day. No stress counselling was offered, or expected, in those war-torn days.

In the gathering gloom of a winter's evening it proved impossible to examine the site closely, meaning that one of the bodies was not discovered until the following day, when an inspection of the roof was made. Needless to say, there were many nameless individuals who laboured long hours to relieve suffering and to release trapped colleagues. While this rescue work was in process at Crewe, a massive raid was taking place on London, when over 10,000 incendiary bombs, along with hundreds of tons of high explosives and land mines, set fire to the city, killing many civilians, destroying hundreds of houses, eight Wren churches and the medieval Guildhall. This was the occasion of one of the most famous photographs of the war on the home front, when the dome of St Paul's could be seen undamaged amidst the smoke and flames.

Later in the week justified anger occasioned vigorous complaints from the workers at Pym's Lane. Hives sent a furious letter, along with the following 3,000-name petition from the local employees, to Max Beaverbrook, the Minister of Aircraft Production:

Sir,
We, the undersigned, workers in the Crewe Division of the Rolls-Royce Engines, (Aero), wish to lodge a most vigorous and solemn protest against the inefficiency of those responsible for our protection from air attack. Most particularly we would deplore the lack of individual initiative evident in the control of ARP and Military personnel.

On the 29th ult. 16 deaths [the 17th victim died after the letter was sent] and many casualties can be attributed directly to this factor. Only the inaccuracy of the German airmen prevented a very heavy casualty list, yet, had proper precautions been taken, the probability is that no lives would have been lost, as no shelter was damaged. Again had the defences been on the alert, the German airmen should have paid dearly for their audacity. During the night attacks on Manchester and Liverpool, alarms were sounded at Crewe, presumably on instructions from some outside source, and many hours were needlessly spent in shelters whilst on the occasion of a direct attack on this Factory in broad day-light, we had no balloon barrage, no warning of any description, and no AA fire.

As this matter is most urgent, we respectfully request an early reply.

We are, Sir, your obedient Servants,

3,000 Signatories.

Had Hives known that radar and the Observer Corps had tracked the bomber from the moment it crossed the English Channel, he would have been even more incensed, as would have been the workers in 16 shop. Sir Donald Somervell, the MP for Crewe, also registered a strong protest regarding the lack of a warning and the absence of balloons.

The official enquiry established that the Barrage Control Officer at Crewe had been informed that a lone bomber was 35 miles away and was heading for the town. This yellow warning was given eight minutes before the raid, insufficient time for raising the balloon barrage, but not for evacuation of the workers to the shelters. The sad and inexcusable fact is that no one need have died if this warning had been given to the workers at Pym's Lane.

At 3.08 p.m., when the LMS 'spotter' saw the lone bomber approaching RR, he gave the full danger signal. A minute later the bombs exploded, giving no time for workers at either factory to congregate in the shelters. There were complaints from the unions that the workers at the LMS railway works, less than a mile away, were in the shelters when the bombs were dropped. Pearce, the personnel manager, who stated that both RR and the locomotive works had received only a yellow warning at 3.01 p.m., vehemently denied this.

Another complaint raised by the unions was that a group of 'first-aiders' from the LMS works who came to offer assistance had been refused admittance by the commissionaires. Again, the management defended this action because no intimation of their arrival had been given, an excuse that had no validity considering the urgent nature of the incident. As a result of the letter from Hives and the local MP's interest, a Court of Inquiry was ordered by the Director of Home Operations and was held by Lt-Gen F. Pile of Anti-Aircraft Command. The results were kept secret until 1971, when all relevant documents were released under the thirty-year rule. From these papers it can be gleaned that no warning was given because it was not a mass raid, for apparently the rule was that sirens were not sounded for an incursion by a lone enemy plane. The balloons were at close haul on account of the perceived threat of stormy weather. In the absence of warnings, AA guns were forbidden to fire unless the aircraft was clearly identified as hostile, a rule made because of the sizeable loss of friendly aircraft. In any case, the bomber was too low to form a suitable target for heavy AA guns. There were four light guns available, but their line of fire was impeded by the sandbag perimeter of their emplacements.

The latest research would suggest that the lone Junkers, with its four-man crew, escaped to the safety of its base in northern France despite the efforts of the RAF to intercept it. Fighters had been sent up during its inward flight to the extent of one section from No. 10 group and five sections from No. 9 group; two further sections from No. 10 group were unavailingly scrambled on the Junkers' outward flight. It would also appear that the same aeroplane, with the same four men aboard, attempted to bomb Crewe again next day, but returned to base after bombing a secondary target nearer to the coast, because the weather was too clear. This bomber crew was transferred to the Baltic region in the spring of 1941, only to be reported missing a few months later in the fierce fighting following the invasion of Soviet Russia. There is no truth in the local myth that the pilot of the Junkers was once a premium apprentice in Crewe railway works. This same type of fable was peddled around Derby following the bombing of the Rolls-Royce works there.

Lessons were learned from the bombing of the factory at Pym's Lane. It is ironic that within a week 3,000 tin hats had been received for workers at the factory. Although these had been requested months before, none was ever made available, despite all of the workers at Derby having them. Hives made the point, in his angry letter to Beaverbrook, that, as most of the deaths were due to head injuries, steel helmets should be provided forthwith. Fourteen-inch thick blast walls were erected in the machine shops; first-aid facilities were increased and a van was fitted out with stretcher racks. Len Huntley, superintendent of the labourers, was placed in charge of rescue work in any future emergency and fire fighting was put under the control of Crutchley and Woolridge of the millwrights. The shop stewards' request for the gun on the roof to be manned continuously was refused, as nearly 300 men would be lost from production if it were allowed. These innovations hint at the chaos that was effected by the air-raid.

A further major innovation that outlasted the immediate consequences of the bomb was the increased medical facilities at the factory. The staff at the ambulance room was enlarged to seven nurses at £2 15s a week, four non-staff nurses and three assistants. In May 1941 Dr Lloyd was appointed on a salary of £1,000 per annum – twice as much as Fred Stafford, the future works manager, was receiving. Lloyd was responsible for all first-aid facilities and for the general health of the employees, visiting most of the dispersal centres every week, in addition to having nurses permanently stationed at them. Plating shop operatives, and other workers on dangerous processes, were examined regularly for signs of industrial disease. The principal ambulance room was at the centre of the east side of the main shop, so Lloyd established a smaller one in 16 shop for the duration of the war. In six months the two ambulance rooms dealt with nearly 71,000 incidents. Over 3,000 of them were eye injuries, for wearing of goggles was not accepted as necessary by most engineering workers. There was also a high incidence of cuts that turned septic, attributable mainly to the oil and coolant used in the machining processes. Errors and omissions revealed by the bombing tragedy at Crewe RR also had to be rectified by the local ARP committee. Perhaps the most poignant was the need for a suitable mortuary, as the premises selected in 1939 were the old, abandoned public baths in Mill

Street. Complaints were received regarding the inhospitable and unsympathetic nature of the building, where the bodies were all laid out in an extremely cold, dirty and dilapidated room.

For Rolls-Royce the bombing did not impair production, as nearly 700 Merlin engines were dispatched in January and February 1941, eighty-eight more than in the last two months of 1940. Undamaged machines from the affected premises were moved into 17 shop and were operating again within two days, although such details did not prevent the firm from applying successfully to the local authority for a reduction in rates on the basis of damage by enemy action. The report of this tragic incident in the local paper ran to only around 250 words, without even identifying the dead. This, surely, is indicative of the rigorous wartime censorship, as is the fact that the obituary notices stated that the casualties had died from injuries received at work, without specifying the location of the factory.

In the postwar years a few of the personnel involved in this incident sought to persuade the management to erect a plaque to commemorate the deaths of the young workers. BBC Radio Stoke produced a special programme to mark the fiftieth anniversary of the incident, but nothing in the way of a permanent memorial was erected. Usually, on the anniversary of the bombing, Frank Culley or Alf Jennings would write to Pym's Lane regarding the possibility of some tangible marker to the seventeen dead, only to be met with chronic indifference. Ironically, it was Volkswagen, the new owners of the factory, who answered the request, in the year 2000, by mounting an imitation Spitfire propeller in 16 shop, on the same wall that had been demolished by the German bomb sixty years before. Sadly, Frank Culley was not there to witness the unveiling, having died a few weeks earlier.

OTHER WARTIME MEASURES

The dispersal of more of the non-manual personnel also dates from the bombing incident, although the machining centres in north Staffordshire were set up because of lack of housing in Crewe. Eventually there were about twenty of these satellite sites, which included the LMS workshops at Stoke and Longton, and small factories or garage premises at Newcastle-under-Lyme, Holmes Chapel, Haslington, Wistaston, Winsford, Sandbach and Nantwich. Later in the war, Newcastle was separated from Merlin production so as to allow machining for the nascent jet engine project to be established there.

Hives always intended that Crewe should utilise as much sub-contract labour as possible. J.T. Ward gave priority to the search for such facilities long before the factory was finished because Crewe, unlike Glasgow, would not have its own foundry or forge. Winston Churchill's inauguration as Prime Minister increased the pace of requisitioning floor space to accelerate Merlin production, until well over 100 firms were sub-contractors for Crewe Rolls-Royce. These were as scattered as Preston, Birmingham, Coventry, Burnley, Blackpool, Enfield and Grimsby. Even Linotype of Altrincham and Terry's Chocolate of York were pressed into service, as was Sheffield University. Locally, the LMS works also manufactured aero-engine parts via the sub-contract department at Pym's Lane.

During this middle period of the war, Crewe had its first direct contact with the RR unit at Clan Foundry in Derbyshire, a wartime site for engineering personnel dispersed from Derby. It was under the supervision of W.A. Robotham, technical assistant to Ernest Hives, who had started working for Rolls-Royce in 1919. Robotham and his team of erstwhile car designers were endeavouring to increase the power of a Crusader tank by replacing the existing Liberty engine with an un-supercharged Merlin that could run on 'pool' petrol. Within a comparatively short time the immense design problems had been successfully faced, and the new engine, known as the Meteor, was brought to Pym's Lane for testing. In his autobiography, *Silver Ghosts and Silver Dawn*, Robotham describes the visit to south Cheshire: 'When the first engine was assembled we took it over to the Crewe factory since Derby had no spare test-bench capacity. To our immense relief the drawing office had made few mistakes; the parts went together and the engine developed the predicted 600bhp on pool petrol.' Besides providing the test facility, Crewe also machined some of the parts for the Meteor engine. Robotham and the design team did not know then that Crewe would be the locus of all their car designs after the ending of hostilities.

The plant at Pym's Lane had, by now, almost attained the limit of its development, as the 1943 building programme inspired by the Griffon engine was the last of the wartime expansion schemes. The main shop, along with 16, 17 and 18 shops, was where seemingly endless lines of capstan and turret lathes, bar autos and semi-autos, universal grinders, vertical and horizontal millers and gear cutters, along with specialist machines, were stationed. The home army of men, women and boys set or worked these machines unceasingly, night and day, manufacturing the many finely machined parts needed to build Merlin engines. Every known manner of machining metal could be viewed at Pym's Lane, along with the accompanying smell of suds or coolant and sounds of a busy workshop. Heat treatment, hardening, plating and metal polishing took place in the smaller building that filled the space between the main shop and the other large machine shop. At the south end of this narrower building were the millwrights and the boiler house.

Perusal of the mass of wartime correspondence and memoranda pertaining to Crewe, located in the company's archive at Derby, stimulates admiration for the managers, indeed for the whole staff. Shortages and problems on production were monitored regularly and eased with febrile haste. Liaison with the many dispersal sites and sub-contractors was a constant task. Forecasts of production had to be made well in advance to qualify for the delivery of rationed resources, for there was very little metal of any kind, and every allocation had to be accounted for.

Each week production figures were sent to Hives, and these returns were brief and to the point. This amazing man seems to have been everywhere, even finding time to visit Crewe and Glasgow almost every week. His energy was boundless and, according to Llewellyn-Smith, he was responsible for 'the light of intelligent and humane management filtering into many parts of RR'.

The southern ends of the main shop and the second large shop were utilised by the engine build department. From there, engines were taken to the test beds, under the control of Dick Garner, and thence to strip inspection, situated at the

Strip inspection after endurance engine testing in June 1939. All the parts from each dismantled engine were laid out in fifteen specially designed trays, occupying one length of conveyor. *(B. Fishburne)*

south end of 18 shop. If all was to the satisfaction of final inspection, the completed engines had their controls checked and set by Frank Culley before travelling the few score yards to the despatch department, a large building near to the factory's Merrill's Bridge gate. Here they were painted and loaded onto heavy lorries, to be transported to wherever they were needed. When the factory had been planned, it had been hoped that the LMS rail system could be utilised, whereas for many reasons, road transport was substituted for rail. At the peak of production over 500 Merlin engines a month were leaving Crewe to power Spitfires, Lancasters and Mosquito aeroplanes, to name but three.

The strike of 1939 did not settle industrial relations, for the early years of the war witnessed a spate of stoppages, and until Nazi Germany invaded the Soviet Union a few militant stewards seemed anxious to foster stoppages. The politically left of centre yet sensible Frank Culley, who had been elected secretary of the works committee, recorded in his diary on 23 April 1940: 'Had a meeting from 6 until 9 p.m. after a lightning strike.' Again on the following day a similar comment: 'Was at another stewards' meeting tonight, until 10.30 p.m. then was up late doing the typing.' He, along with Charlie Elson, the convenor, and the other saner members of the works committee, sought to filter the genuine grievances from the sinister political protest. Further evidence of communist influence and agitation at this stage of the war is suggested by the action of a few workmen who jeered at soldiers from the Pioneer Corps working in the vicinity of the factory, and made seditious remarks involving comparisons in pay. Management found a pretext to discharge the leading agitator and troublemaker when he called an unofficial union meeting during working hours. The union district committee acquiesced in his dismissal, on the grounds of some injudicious remarks he had made about them.

Matters between management and manual workers degenerated to such a pitch that, in June 1940, a member of the works committee sent an unauthorised telegram to Ernest Bevin, the newly appointed Minister of Labour in Churchill's first coalition government, warning him about the possibility of a strike. Bevin's response to this unofficial action was typically brusque, threatening the militants with being 'conscripted into the military'.

This did not end the petty industrial strife, for on 23 July 1940, five weeks after the fall of France, there was an unofficial strike in one of the machine bays. A series of short wildcat strikes in the bar auto lathe section during September occasioned an enquiry by the local representatives of the Ministry of Labour. This time the cause was dirty conditions, attributable to the use of reconstituted oil. John Morris must have had a direct, if secret, source to union discussions, because he was aware that non-RR persons were at a union meeting on 4 October 1940, agitating and urging industrial action. The result was not a strike, simply a letter to the management complaining about poor working conditions. This letter was an item on the agenda of a joint meeting where Morris revealed that he knew it was nurtured by other than RR stewards.

It was suggested that a more permanent cure for industrial relations would be to send a few of the strikers to London to view the bomb damage. At Derby, Hives actually did arrange for four members of the works committee to visit the capital to see the devastation, though that action was to motivate production, rather than to improve industrial relations. The deaths and bomb damage inflicted on the Crewe factory later in the year did much to curtail the incidence of stoppages; another cause of the decline was the invasion of Soviet Russia in June 1941, which meant that the mother country of communism was now allied with the British. This generated another cause for local agitation, led by RR workers, with a sprinkling from the LMS works. Up to 1944 rallies were regularly held demanding that a second front be opened to relieve the pressure on the Red Army. The main leaders of this campaign were Charlie Elson and his wife Eileen, who also worked at the factory, and the Glaswegian Communist Peter 'Jock' Abraham, a machinist from the main shop. It must be said, however, that niggling labour disputes in certain departments continued at fairly regular intervals up to the end of Merlin production, when the workforce was drastically reduced.

GEARED FOR PRODUCTION

Among the vast majority of the workers at Pym's Lane there was complete support for the war, despite the long hours of work. When the Lord Lieutenant of Cheshire organised an aircraft victory fund the employees responded well, with Crewe raising enough to pay for two Spitfires. The sad fact that one of them failed to return from operations on 17 July 1941, fourteen days after having being received by 234 squadron, was kept secret at the time. Regular factory-wide collections were organised, and two typical examples, from 1943, were the Reginald Mitchell memorial fund and the Stalingrad week. This latter did not seem to cause any objection from management, which was not always the case in other engineering factories. In addition to these ad hoc collections, the workers at Pym's Lane adopted a minesweeper, which they supported through most of the war years. In July 1945 six employees were invited on board for a demonstration, as a token of gratitude. This was, perhaps, more acceptable than the treat suggested by Stafford Cripps on his visit in January 1943, when he proposed that the best workers and timekeepers should be rewarded with a flight in a bomber.

War weapons week, a seven-day thrift campaign in 1941 saw the employees at Pym's Lane subscribe over £20,000 to the savings scheme – about 10 per cent of the town's target. Moreover, it must be remembered that, at the same time, along with the rest of the UK they were paying for 55 per cent of the war through taxation. Income tax was 10s in the pound and purchase tax was introduced in October 1940, while postwar credits, a tax under another name, took yet another bite from the weekly pay packet. As their name implies, these credits were supposed to be repaid by the Government at the end of the conflict, though in the event it was many years after. Savings were higher than they had been pre-war, partly for patriotic reasons, partly because more people were in work, but mainly because there was nothing to spend money on. It was reported in January 1941 that the people of Crewe had saved over £1 million the previous year, compared to £30,000 in peacetime.

By 1942 the austerity measures championed by Sir Stafford Cripps meant that the small petrol allowance for pleasure motoring was cancelled, the clothes ration was reduced, and a limit of 5s was placed on meals in restaurants. Fresh citrus fruit was so scarce that a lemon was auctioned in Crewe for £2 10s in 1943, about half of a standard week's wages. A banana, in a town-wide raffle in the winter of 1944, was a much-desired prize. No doubt things were far worse in the bomb-ravaged cities of Germany and Russia.

In his book on the period A.J.P. Taylor calculated that, compared with 1938, 20 per cent less was spent on food, 38 per cent less on clothes and 43 per cent less on household goods. Committees of civil servants planned all production, even down to the manufacture of such items as umbrellas – decreeing that, from 1943, all umbrellas should be produced with fewer spokes. Three grades of cotton would be released for umbrella covers, and decoration would be confined to the borders. Such was the planning in Churchill's wartime administration.

During these years the number employed at RR rose steadily, reaching almost 10,000 by 1944, about 30 per cent of them being women. At the Holmes Chapel dispersal centre the ratio of women to men was even greater, with almost half of the 900 employees being women. Between April 1941, when there were 800 females employed at Pym's Lane, and April 1942, over 1,700 women were added to the pay-roll. As the company did not provide crèche facilities it was not easy, especially in the early years of the war, for working mothers to juggle their time around school hours – which accounted, perhaps, for the 9 per cent rate of absenteeism among this group. In 1942 the town council helped to alleviate the problem by opening two nurseries, partly in response to a letter from Ernest Bevin.

Such were the wartime conditions that many single women came unwillingly, having been directed to Crewe under the regulations introduced by Churchill's Emergency Powers (Defence) Act. Although direction of labour was necessary in so great a crisis as Britain faced in 1940, it was a mixed blessing. Much of the scrap, poor time-keeping and indifference emanated from those who were at Pym's Lane reluctantly. The minutes of a wartime production meeting record that Elson, the convenor, blamed them for shortages, because they were, apparently, spending a lot of time doing very little.

It is worth noting that, despite the unusual confusion and breakdown of the traditional social order, in the first three years of the war only eleven illegitimate births were recorded among the directed girls, billeted mainly at the hostel on the Totty's Hall estate. This is not, perhaps, the true figure, for the town's percentage of illegitimate births rose from 1.7 per cent in 1941 to 5 per cent four years later. So great was the social opprobrium for the unmarried mother that most of the local girls who achieved that status went to another town to give birth. By 1943 the Ministry of Health was instructing all local authorities to give urgent attention to the problem of illegitimate babies.

In 1941, a typical year, about 150 conscripted women left the employ of RR. Of these, twenty-eight enrolled in one of the women's services, twenty-six refused to work, thirty-three went absent without leave and thirty-two were declared psychologically unsuitable, whatever that might mean. Despite these vagaries, the contribution of the women operatives during the wartime years was crucial. John Morris made the final judgement in 1956, on his return to Pym's Lane for Hives's retirement celebrations, when he said that without the women they could not have achieved what they had.

By 1944 the floor area stood at 1,236,000sq ft, a figure that is indicative of the mobilisation of the British economy. It is often presumed that it was solely Germany's preparation for war, coupled with the Allies' lack of readiness, that brought the initial German victories. This, however, begs the question of tactics, weapons and strategy. Undoubtedly, Germany armed earlier, and with greater determination, than the UK. It is equally obvious that the superior strategy of *Blitzkrieg*, or lightning war, yielded the overwhelming victories that Germany experienced between 1939 and 1941. Thereafter, the economic superiority of the Allies began to tell, as the flow of armaments increased.

Mark Harrison, in *The Economics of World War II*, indicates that in 1939 about 15 per cent of the UK's national income was devoted to war, while Germany's figure was 23 per cent. Four years later this had risen to 70 per cent for Germany and 55 per cent for the UK. Of course, these statistics do not tell the whole story, for Britain had the benefit of lend-lease that was bringing armaments across the Atlantic in ever-increasing quantities. At the same time, Germany's exploitation of the wealth and manpower of the occupied countries added to the plus column of its balance sheet. Further facts can be deduced when these figures are examined more closely. Germany's military budget was divided into roughly equal portions between pay and munitions. For the UK, in 1941, the ratio was 3.4 to 1 in favour of military equipment and weaponry. This weaponry was being created for a second front, for North Africa, for bombing purposes and to a lesser degree to supply Russia, where the Red Army and the civilian population were making great sacrifices that ultimately prepared the way for the victory of 1945.

When the mobilisation of the German and the UK workforces is compared, a similar picture emerges. In the first year of the war nearly 16 per cent of British industrial workers were employed on war work, with a further 2.8 per cent in the armed forces. For Germany it was around 14 per cent, with 4.2 per cent in uniform. By 1943 the percentage of the British workforce in the armaments industry had increased to 23 per cent, with almost the same percentage in the services, while the German figures were 14.2 per cent and 23.4 per cent respectively. It could, therefore, be argued that, in contrast to Britain, the German economy, for much of the war, had areas of untapped reserves.

The appointment of Churchill as Prime Minister coincided with the fall of France, and the release of energy that this brought about has been commented on before. It is worth emphasising that, in the days following Churchill's assumption of office, the British economy followed the pattern set by Chamberlain, to become ever more centrally controlled within a taut bureaucratic system administered by the steady hands of Sir John Anderson. This all-powerful centralised system was able to prioritise resources according to immediate needs and medium-term plans, effecting an immense transfer of labour, capital and materials to the war effort.

In Berlin, it would seem that divided authority, exercised by powerful individuals jealously guarding their own personal provinces, was the rule. For instance, Goering controlled both the aircraft industry and the destiny of scarce imported materials, while Speer held sway in the ministry of armaments. This state of fiefdom proved adequate while there was slack in the economy, and as long as occupation reaped a harvest of resources and enforced labour. By 1942, however, Speer was convinced that such a harvest was finished. He tried to persuade the Führer that full centralisation of control over resources was urgently necessary but, fortunately for the Allies, was not wholly successful as Sauckel, Martin Bormann's placeman, retained a clenched grip on German labour. Other factors and persons also militated against Speer, such as his inability to tap the rich vein of Himmler's SS empire, though it is generally accepted that there was a sea-change in German war economic management, when Speer took the helm. Economic historians are still not agreed as to the cause of the large increase in German war production from 1942, some claiming that civilian consumption had been left undisturbed in the assumption of a quick victory. Others claim that the utilisation of resources became far more efficient than under the previous ramshackle party management of Goering.

At the height of the struggle the enlarged plant at Pym's Lane was producing about seven different marques of Merlin engines at any one time, and for a short period in 1942 the number was eight. Between 1939 and 1945 eighteen separate marques were produced at Crewe, with demand for the Merlin X, at 4,589, exceeding all others. Other high production figures were XX (3,391), III (2,012), and the Merlin 21, with just over 2,000 being built. One of the later marques, the 66, also rated highly, with production figures of 2,588. The last of the Merlins to be manufactured at Pym's Lane was the 76, of which 1,200 were built between January 1944 and May of the following year. Lloyd and Pugh, in their account of Hives and the Merlin engine, point out that the production flexibility at Crewe and Derby enabled RR to cope with manufacturing different marques, but with reduced output. This is one reason why the total number of Ford manufactured Merlins is higher than the Crewe or Derby numbers. However, in wartime numbers were not the only criterion.

Judged by any standard, the Merlin was a remarkable engine. It had twelve cylinders, arranged in two banks of six at an angle of 60 degrees to each other, and saw wartime action in nineteen differing types of aeroplanes. Intensive development increased its power from around 1,000bhp to 2,000bhp. For instance the Merlin III gave just over 1,100bhp at an altitude of 16,000ft in 1940, whereas two years later the Merlin 61 could produce the same power at 30,000ft. By the end of hostilities around fifty versions of the engine existed. In addition to Crewe, they were manufactured at Derby, Glasgow, the Ford Motor Company at Urmston, Manchester, and the Packard Motor Company, Detroit. Somewhere in the region of 25 per cent of all the Merlins built in wartime Britain came from Pym's Lane.

The Griffon engine also went into production at Crewe, four months after the Normandy invasion, and around 2,200 were made locally, with the last one going to the plane makers in December 1945. Eight different marques were covered, the Griffon 61 being the most in demand and the 69 the least in demand. As a result of the successful prosecution of the war, the engine build programme was drastically curtailed in a letter from the Ministry of Aircraft Production, dated 27 November 1944, meaning that redundancy became a certainty for many of the workforce at Pym's Lane.

CREWE ENGINES FAIL

Of the 26,000 Merlins dispatched from Pym's Lane to the many aircraft factories and depots around the country, a large proportion went to Castle Bromwich, a suburb of Birmingham, where a large shadow factory had been constructed under the auspices of Morris Motors. Building started the same week as it began at Pym's Lane, with the first Spitfire being delivered on 21 January 1940. On a site of over 1,400 acres, it was estimated that about sixty aircraft a week could be built, most of them Spitfires, each powered by a single Merlin engine.

For much of the war Alex Henshaw was the chief test pilot there. As he records in his book, *Sigh for a Merlin*, it was a very exciting, as well as exacting, time. Here he gives an account of failures that occurred as he was testing Mk VB Spitfires powered by Merlin Mk 46 engines. At its most basic, the problem of these engine failures concerned the bronze skew gear, positioned on the upper vertical drive shaft, responsible for driving the magnetos. On the top end of the drive was a bevel that drove two other bevel gears, and fitting these was critical, on account of having to ascertain the required setting of backlash. This whole assembly, along with other essential drives, was contained in the wheel-case bolted to the rear of the engine.

R.W. Harvey-Bailey, a senior engineer at Derby, had identified this as a potential cause of trouble, even as far back as the Kestrel engine, for when these gear assemblies were routinely serviced some of them displayed signs of malfunction. Alec Harvey-Bailey, the son of RW, has written that, despite many attempts to rectify the fault, the odd failure still occurred. What was so critical about those that provoked Henshaw's anxiety, in June 1942, was that they were not occasional, but dramatically frequent.

The first incident occurred around the middle of June in Spitfire EP 499, when Henshaw was forced to land in an arable field. A few days later, on 17 June, it happened again, although this time he was able to glide down to complete a landing at Desford. After two colleagues encountered further similar engine failures, Henshaw, considering enough was enough, demanded immediate investigative action from Rolls-Royce before any fatalities occurred. He described the problem quite succinctly in his book: 'These skew gear failures were more disturbing because there was no warning of any kind and they often occurred after a machine had climbed, dived at full throttle, and probably had several landings and adjustments.' On 18 July he was almost killed in a horrendous crash-landing in the gardens of a Black Country suburb, and it was only thanks to his consummate

Damage to a house in the West Midlands, caused by the crash of a Spitfire that was being tested from Castle Bromwich. It had crash-landed owing to skew gear failure and the Merlin engine had become detached from the airframe. This series of engine failures, in 1942, caused Hives to initiate an intense investigation that ended up at Crewe. *(Alex Henshaw)*

skill, and a fair slice of luck, that he walked away from the wreckage of Spitfire EP 615 without serious injury. Tremendous efforts then went into tracing the cause of the skew gear failure, as Alec Harvey-Bailey outlined in *The Merlin in Perspective*.

Eventually, all of the malfunctioning engines were traced to one source, as Henshaw records:

> One of the top technicians rang me up from Rolls-Royce and said he was sure I would be pleased to hear that they had traced the cause of the skew gear failures. The story he told me was almost unbelievable. Apparently they had traced all the defective engines to one source and here for some reason they were assembling the engines in the opposite way to those normally turned out. The conclusion reached was that all bearings and gears were subject to the same clearances and inspections but for some reason it was thought this change in the assembly position reduced slightly the clearance that should have been given to the main skew gear assembly.

As Alex Henshaw states, the story was almost unbelievable, yet the given explanation begs a number of questions. Why should the failures suddenly occur with such frequency? Why only one source? Why was only one marque of Merlin involved? There is an alternative explanation that answers the problem more neatly, known to a few at the time, but kept secret from all not directly involved.

The single source of all of these engine failures was, in the opinion of this writer, the Pym's Lane factory. Over fifty years later Frank Culley, who was working in the department involved, could recall the episode with remarkable clarity:

> I didn't know then anything about engines failing but I couldn't fail to notice all the top brass suddenly appearing about the place. Dick Garner, Cecil Darby, Bill Harvey and all the AID [Aero Inspection Directorate] men were crawling all over the engines. All hell had broken loose. If my memory serves me it was one of the inspectors on engine test that found a Merlin 46 with the nut loose on the upper vertical drive shaft. It had been on test and he'd removed the complete wheelcase for checking. It didn't take them long to find out who'd signed for it.

It was an inspector named Howe who, on stripping an engine that had just been tested, discovered that one of the nuts in the wheel-case assembly was not as tight as it should have been. This led to another eighty-one engines being dismantled and examined, which revealed nineteen Merlin Mk 46 engines, with the same sub-assembly, having incorrectly tightened nuts, all signed for by the leading hand of the section. Before May 1942 many of the wheel-cases fitted at Crewe were manufactured and assembled by a sub-contractor. From May, Merlin Mk 46 engines, including the wheel-cases, started to be made and assembled at Pym's Lane.

The main cause of these skew gear failures in the Crewe-built Mk 46 engines, stemmed from the difficulty, on the part of the fitters, in correctly assembling and tightening the nuts on the upper vertical drive shaft, as well as ensuring the relevant backlash. To put things simply, this meant that the skew gear was locked in position after fitting a distance piece, adjusted to suit the alignment of the centre bevel gear. In making these adjustments, a procedure was adopted to check the squareness of the distance piece, after which, the backlash of the gears was checked. If that was incorrect, the whole procedure was commenced again, until the specified backlash was obtained, with the nuts correctly tightened. As the job had a time allowance, it was difficult to obtain any bonus.

To assist in the new task of coping with the assembly of Mk 46 wheel-cases, four extra fitters were drafted into the wheel-case section in May 1942. Although the men had had no experience of this work, the leading hand was told he had to maintain his production target of eight engines every twenty-four hours. To achieve this he completed the most difficult part of the job himself, including fitting the skew gear and obtaining the specified clearances. Unfortunately, it seems that he did this by tightening the nuts until the gears were solid, and then slackening them to obtain the necessary backlash, meaning that in effect the nuts were loose.

Consequently, when running at the operational speed of 3,000rpm, with incorrectly tightened nuts, too great a load was transmitted into the wheel-case bearing support system. The result was that the steel worm wheel, which should have meshed with the bronze gear that drove the magneto, acted more like a cutting tool and the skew gear stopped working, causing the engine to cut out. There can be hardly any doubt that Harvey-Bailey, who was the chief technical production engineer for the whole of RR, and outstanding at his job, was not cognisant of the facts. It is highly probable that he confided the real cause only to Hives and a few of the inner circle, when he issued the appropriate formal assembly instructions, namely Technical Instruction Sheet BY 70, to ensure that correct procedures were adhered to in the future.

Thus the alternative explanation for the skew gear failures is that it was mainly a matter of incompetence, exacerbated by production schedules and a bonus system dependant upon performing a task in a specified time, that was at the root of the problem. Add to this the fact that the leading hand was working an 86-hour week, then a scenario begins to appear that, even if it does not excuse the working practices, partially explains how such things could happen.

After a police inquiry the leading hand, who had been employed at RR since August 1939, was arrested and charged with industrial sabotage. Following a hearing at the local magistrates' court, he was committed for trial at Chester Assizes, and among those who gave evidence for the prosecution were Bill Harvey, superintendent of the fitters, and Cecil Darby, of the inspection department. On being found guilty of an offence under the Defence Regulations (1939), he received a sentence of three years' imprisonment. At his trial the judge went into great detail about the serious nature of such an offence when the country was at war, yet, one would feel, there has to be a degree of deliberation to warrant a charge of sabotage. It must be emphasised that it was not politics, or a malicious spirit that motivated him; it also has to be said that it was inexcusable and extremely foolish.

From such an incident it could be construed that inspection procedures at Pym's Lane were somewhat lax, and there is evidence that the Derby hierarchy was concerned about standards at Crewe. A memo from Hives to John Morris, dated

8 April 1942, accused him of producing engines that were of a lower standard than those from other RR factories, an accusation that Morris vigorously refuted. Despite this, he did acquiesce in the replacement of his chief inspector and agreed to an inquiry into Crewe's inspection procedures by Miller, from RR Glasgow. To avoid trouble with the unions, Miller's mission was represented as a drive to improve the inspection techniques at Hillington. Incidentally, Miller remained at Glasgow after the war, rising to become chief executive and helping to ensure that RR retained a presence in Scotland.

A perusal of Frank Culley's notebooks for the wartime years presents another picture, which helps to crush the illusion that all Crewe inspectors were duds. The entry for 18 January 1943, regarding magnetos on test, records: 'rejected for excessive backlash which increased on test from 0.0055 to 0.009 . . . fibre gear teeth worn along roots. . . . Ball-race in distributor sleeve loose in housing also two retaining screws loose.' Two further entries from the same day state: 'RX-M 15188 rejected for loose screws, wear along roots of fibre gear teeth, backlash from 0.0045 to 0.006 gone to 0.006/0.010. Skew gear scrapped for plucking,' and 'RX-M18585 failed condenser'. These entries, it must be stressed, are but a representative sample of many.

KEEPING ORDER

With such a large and recently formed workforce gathered from many parts of the country, various forms of ill-discipline were bound to be manifest at times, as not every workman at Pym's Lane was there in a voluntary capacity, as has been noted. This could, and did, lead to confrontations that were dealt with by the local magistrates, and many incidents are recorded, in the minutes of the works committee, of complaints of laziness, absenteeism, lateness and insolence, from directed workers. In February 1942 a tool-maker wanted desperately to leave, but was refused permission by both RR and the Ministry of Labour. He was fined £10 for moving to a similar job in Sheffield, although, because of requests by his new employer, he was allowed to stay there. Another example is that of a fitter, fined £20 by Crewe magistrates in 1943 for persistent lateness.

Other employees were prosecuted for thieving, either from the firm or from their fellow workers. Two inspectors were caught, in July 1941, taking unofficial paid leave by the simple, but illegal, expedient of clocking each other in, for which they were prosecuted and fined £20, with the option of three months' imprisonment. Usually, however, the offences were of a petty kind, not requiring recourse to the courts. The works committee met at regular intervals to discuss complaints and minor misdemeanours, until June 1942, when a separate disciplinary committee was formed to standardise penalties. Curtailment of bonus payments was the usual punishment for scrap or faulty work, with a few days' suspension being reserved for more serious infringements of industrial practices. Another perennial complaint of the management was that employees ceased work at lunch-times before the official stopping time. The power curve of the factory began to drop from its maximum at 12.40 p.m., not returning to full output until 2.10 p.m. Lunch-time, which lasted for sixty minutes, was at 12.55 p.m. Other matters causing concern during 1942 were poor bonus payments, cycling within the works, unfunny comedians and awful singers at workers' concerts, gambling or card playing during working hours, absence without leave, abusive language, sleeping on night shift and poor service from the canteen.

The first plans of the factory show that the original intention was to site the canteen where the main offices now are, and to have the offices where the canteen was built, at the eastern edge of the site fronting Pym's Lane. Until it was completed, all meals were prepared at the borough refuse disposal works, across from the factory. Eventually, the canteen occupied the whole of the ground floor area, incorporating a stage and public address system. The upper storey was the venue, and April 1940 the date, for an opening ceremony at which Jack Payne and his band were the main attraction. Regarding this, Frank Culley noted: 'Finished at noon. RR dance at night, rained very heavily. 1400 attended Jack Payne's Band. Good time, home at 12.30 a.m.' John Morris also provides a comment about this event in the handwritten fragmentary recollections of his time at Pym's Lane. Apparently, when Hives, on arrival at Crewe, started to dress for the occasion, he found he had forgotten the trousers to his dinner suit. Not to be frustrated he wore his own jacket and borrowed Haldenby's navy blue trousers, leaving the top button unfastened to accommodate his ample girth. Incidentally, the source document for this story was deposited by Morris's sole remaining daughter into the custody of Crewe and Nantwich Borough Council for safekeeping. Within two years it had gone missing.

Shortly after the opening ceremony the upper portion of the canteen was partitioned off into three sections, with the eastern portion remaining as a concert hall for dances and similar social functions. Planning engineers, along with a jig and tool drawing office, filled one section, with the remaining portion becoming a canteen, mainly for weekly salaried staff.

During the war the concert hall, or Welfare Hall as it became known, was the venue for weekly concerts or film shows. In the autumn of 1943 some of the films shown were *Desert Victory*, *Worker's Weekend* and *Men from the Sea*. Gracie Fields made a visit, as did the Hallé Orchestra and the BBC Northern Orchestra. The Crewe RR brass band entertained regularly, along with the RR male voice choir. This latter group broadcast more than once on the BBC Home Service, as the Merlin Singers. Lectures by military or air force personnel took place about once every eight weeks, often accompanied by displays of artefacts or photographs. It would be true to say that, all through the war, there was something arranged at least twice a week.

Not every employee patronised the canteen, as many used the one-hour lunch break to travel home for their midday meal. The proximity of the council housing estates enabled many of the men to cycle or walk home, to eat and return within the permitted time. Even those living on the outskirts of the town were never more than 2 miles away, and the Crosville Motor Company sent sufficient buses to transport them home for a hurried meal, and then back for the afternoon shift.

A form of canteen apartheid quickly appeared, with about five different sections of eating facilities being provided. Manual workers occupied most of the space, but women, salaried staff, superintendents or monthly paid staff, and lastly senior managers, all dined off different crockery, in allocated sections.

The canteen facilities were managed by RR for the first couple of years, not altogether successfully. Even before the factory was working at full capacity, complaints were raised regarding the inordinate amount of time involved in serving cups of tea from the canteen trolleys wheeled around the departments. The main excuse, according to the canteen manager, A. Jones, was the high level of crockery abuse. In a report submitted in December 1940 he claimed that in fifteen months over 22,000 cups had gone missing, 2,200 in the preceding ten days. This loss was, perhaps, the cause of another complaint, that the price charged for the meals was too high when compared to neighbouring engineering factories. Jack Valentine and Pearce, the personnel manager, went on a fact-finding mission to Fairey Aviation, Leyland Motors and Foden to ascertain the cost, quality and portions of the meals. On their return they agreed there was a case to answer, although, if the manager had to recover the cost of his missing crockery, the difference in price was fully justified. At other times, there were cases of petty thieving, when a few members of the canteen staff were prosecuted for stealing cigarettes, chocolate and foodstuffs. In the dark days of shortages, rationing and queues, the temptation to service the black-market must have been very great.

In addition to providing meals, the canteen received an allocation of cigarettes and chocolate for sale among the workforce. Again, there were grumbles from the shop floor that workers were being deprived of their fair share, by the items being offered only to the staff in the main office block. The canteen manager was instructed to distribute all available supplies in an equitable manner, meaning, in theory, one cigarette per person per week.

Yet another complaint was concerned with the small portions of food that made up a meal. The manager counter-claimed by citing the amount of waste food that was binned after each sitting. The solution, proffered by the works committee, was two different sizes of meals. The position of the canteen manager at Pym's Lane, in the wartime years, was no sinecure.

With the high level of complaints continuing to stream in, the management, in November 1941, contracted the canteen service to Barkers of Reading. They were already running the canteen service at the RR plant at Hillington, but at Crewe they were only slightly more successful than the local management had been. A joint committee, formed in October 1942 to rectify matters, also failed to provide a satisfactory service.

Service deteriorated so much that over 4,000 manual workers, led by Charlie Elson, began a boycott of the canteen lasting for over three months. One of the first mentions of Harry Grylls, in the works committee minutes, was when he was cited as saying that the contract of Barker and Company, canteen caterers, would not necessarily be renewed. This comparatively innocuous dispute turned into a confrontation, with the ridiculous scenario of stewards distributing meat pies and sandwiches to every department at meal times. John Morris, along with the senior management team, was determined not to back down, considering it more than a dispute about food. Eventually Sir Stafford Cripps, the Minister for Aircraft

Production, became involved, along with officials from the Ministry of Labour. The long-term solution to the dissatisfaction only came with the reduction in the number of employees at the end of the war, enabling a more acceptable level of service to be offered.

Such a prolonged dispute was symptomatic of the state of labour relations during the latter years of the war. Undoubtedly, the urgent need for workers during the frenzied build-up of Merlin production brought some to Pym's Lane who were less than skilled, to put it kindly. A few motivated by undemocratic politics, and proficient at fomenting grievances, also managed to slip through the security screening, along with war dodgers, although the overwhelming majority of employees were ordinary members of the British working class. They had no political axe to grind, unless it was the wish for the war to end and for conditions to return to normal.

There are letters and memos in the company files at Derby that detail the feelings of large sections of the workforce, channelled to official notice via Charlie Elson, the works convenor, who, from about 1941, was employed full time on labour relations. That there were not more stoppages of a severe nature was attributable, in no small part, to Elson's negotiating skill and common sense. He led the shop stewards responsibly, walking a tightrope between justified grievances and political pretexts. The period between 1940 and 1945 witnessed the labour force approaching 10,000. Many workers were forced to travel every day, others lived in crowded lodgings, and all worked long hours. There was a greater potential for labour unrest than at any other period of RR's sixty years in Crewe. Like most of the workers, Elson was comparatively young, being just under thirty when he moved from a tool-room milling machine to the convenor's office. There is no gainsaying that he earned his wages. He was also the first RR employee elected to the town's council, although not the first to serve, for Pearce, the personnel manager, was co-opted during the middle period of the war.

The last tangible reminder of these wartime years was the unveiling of the Battle of Britain Memorial Window at Nightingale Road, Derby. Designed by Hugh Easton, it was unveiled on 11 January 1949 before a congregation of distinguished guests. Among these were Sir Stafford Cripps, Lord Tedder, Viscount Trenchard and Lord Dowding. Also present were over seventy Battle of Britain pilots, as well as Jeffery Quill, the Supermarine test pilot. Crewe's fifteen representatives at the proceedings included Jack Aitcheson, C. Beavers, Dick Garner, Harry Grylls, Bill Harvey, Harry Moore, Jack Valentine and Arthur Smaller, a tool-maker, and one of the few Crewe manual workers invited.

Chapter Three

A New Dawn

. . . the formidable task of turning the Crewe factory over from Merlin to car production.

W.A. Robotham

As the combined forces of the allied armies gradually halted the momentum of the Axis powers, by the summer of 1943 it became apparent that, although it might be a long haul, the war would be won. In June of that year working hours were cut from 236 a month to 229, not much, but indicative of a trend. Consequently, the directors of Rolls-Royce also entertained thoughts of a postwar economy that included the manufacture of motor cars.

When, in February 1944, the Board of Trade gave permission for the design and development of cars to be commenced, the directors established a sub-committee, chaired by Llewellyn-Smith (LS), deputy works manager at the Hillington factory and, until late in 1942, senior manager at Crewe, to consider all options. Among its other members were Robotham, Bleaney, S. Gill and Denning Pearson, and it reported back with a resolution that car production should be at Crewe. To quote LS's words: 'Our committee proposed that the firm should pick up the threads of our pre-war ideas and rationalise our range by adopting standard bodies. . . . The obvious answer was to phase out aero-engine production at Crewe pretty quickly and build new cars there.' The suggestion, in *The First Cars from Crewe*, that the Cheshire town was chosen for car manufacture because the company owned the plant is not true, for Pym's Lane was leased from the government until 1973. According to Alec Harvey-Bailey, Glasgow was considered by Hives as a possible car site, especially as the factory there had its own foundry, only to be rejected owing to its proclivity for militancy and industrial action. Shortly afterwards Hives recommended Llewellyn-Smith as general manager for car production, with Robotham taking the lesser position of chief engineer. Thus it was that Crewe became the sole manufacturing centre for the best car in the world.

It is no secret that Robotham was very disappointed at being passed over for the top position, especially as he had spent many years in the employ of Rolls-Royce designing and developing cars. It was the second time that he had been rejected, for Hives had appointed Harvey-Bailey in preference to Robotham as chief engineer of the chassis division in 1937. It must also be said in LS's favour that he had already had management experience at Crewe, as well as at Hillington. In 1933, after finishing his studies at Manchester University and Balliol College, Oxford, he had started to work for Rolls-Royce in the experimental department, on a salary of £3 15s a week. From all the evidence it would seem that there was never a chance that Robotham would ever move to Crewe to serve under Llewellyn-Smith.

erial view of the factory in 1954. The fence separating RR from Kelvinator, erected in 1946, can be clearly
en going south along the northern end of Fourth Avenue. Pym's Lane is in the foreground. *(Martin Bourne)*

Meanwhile, the main concern of the works committee was the inevitable redundancies that would come with the war's end. Having first hand experience of the parlous state of the town's economy before 1938, the local union leaders were anxious to retain as much employment as possible. To deal with the obnoxious task of making men and women redundant, a special committee was set up, with officials from the Ministry of Labour, Rolls-Royce and six of the principal unions. An analysis of the ages of the redundant workers confirms once more the youthfulness of the wartime employees at Pym's Lane, where the largest group (36 per cent) was between 25 and 30 years old. Those in their fifties comprised the smallest group (9 per cent).

Once the Derby board had made Crewe the location for car production, Hives lost no time in approaching the Ministry with an offer to purchase about 63 per cent of the available floor space. Although the Air Ministry refused to sell, it offered RR a 10-year lease at a rental of £20,000 a year. Some time later County Clothes, an American-owned manufacturer of fine garments which already ran two small factories in the town, agreed to share the vacated space with British Celanese, an arrangement that carried the promise of employment for about 1,400 women and 400 men. June 1946 came and went, but all the released space was still in use, for storage of surplus government-owned machine-tools.

Despite public meetings and continuing pressure from the local councillors and union officials the spare floor space was not released, mainly because the Board of Trade considered that Crewe, being in an agricultural area, was non-priority. This delay caused British Celanese to withdraw and set up a factory in east Denbighshire. As it had been expected to use about two-thirds of the spare capacity, this left a yawning gap in the postwar employment plan of the town. Fortunately, the refrigerator manufacturer Kelvinator Ltd, a firm that had been bombed out of its London premises, stepped into the breach. Production of refrigerators began in July 1947, soon reaching 100 units a week, mainly for export. Despite a promise that it would be in by the spring of 1946, County Clothes did not receive its accommodation until April 1947. The American owners must have been irritated by the sluggish nature of decision-making within the English Civil Service.

MORE HOMES FOR WORKERS

Many factors curtailed postwar production and sales of highly priced luxury cars – not least the austere times prevailing over much of western Europe. The high level of purchase tax and scarcity of steel inhibited manufacture, as did the fact that only Australia, Switzerland, South Africa and the USA would import RR cars before 1949. Another aspect of concern was the critical lack of fuel and power, a shortage exacerbated by the severe winter of 1946/7. So extreme did matters become, that the workforce had its employment terminated on 14 February 1947, when electricity was virtually unobtainable for any length of time. All were re-engaged early in March, when the power supply to the factory was restored. During the interim a small amount of power was produced by harnessing generators to the engines on test – sufficient, it was said, to keep about 300 men in employment.

Present levels of affluence make it easy to forget the austerity that gripped postwar England as the UK emerged victorious from six years of fighting, but with its economy crippled. Receipts from exports had declined by around 60 per cent of the pre-war level. The merchant marine capacity was nearly a third less than it had been in 1939, a dreadful loss for a maritime nation. The Americans abruptly ended lend-lease, throwing still greater strain onto the straitened economy, and ensuring that the incoming Labour Government, elected by a war-weary population with great expectations, faced massive economic problems.

Rationing was continued at virtually the same level as in wartime. Few families could afford to run a car, even when it was possible to find one that was worth buying. The Crewe of the 1940s still retained vestiges of the nineteenth century. Unmarried mothers were not officially allowed the facilities of the borough maternity home. A single coal fire provided heat and hot water in most homes, meaning that all rooms, excepting the main living room, were extremely cold in winter, so much so that many children went to bed wearing gloves, socks and even balaclava helmets. Over 57 per cent of the houses in the borough had no bathroom. A visit to the lavatory meant a trip outdoors in many dwellings, and for a few these were privy pails. Some dwellings still had gas lamps, while in some of the outlying areas candles and oil lamps were the only means of lighting. The majority of homes had no telephone. Milk was delivered in open containers, and many tradesmen used a horse and cart for street sales.

Another factor – more local than the austerity – that depressed postwar employment at Pym's Lane was lack of workers' housing. Despite the drastic fall in numbers on the pay-roll, there was still an extreme shortage of suitable dwellings for incoming staff. The number of unemployed men in Crewe in January 1946 was only 246. Twelve months later it was 133. Thus it will be appreciated that specialised labour had to be attracted to the town. In December 1946 the personnel manager, Bill Edge, and Reg Currall, chief of car assembly, interviewed the council's housing officials, requesting over fifty houses to accommodate the families of the staff of the trim and paint shops that were then being formed at Pym's Lane.

The obvious answer, to build as many new dwellings as possible, and as quickly as possible, was negated by the postwar building regulations. Nationally, in excess of 210,000 homes had been destroyed by bombing, and 250,000 more had been made uninhabitable, some authorities reckoning that one-third of the nation's housing had been affected by the war. The first call on exceedingly scarce raw materials was from the dollar-earning export market, so priorities were settled by government decree. No building or decorating work of any kind that cost more than £10 could be initiated without a licence provided by a government department.

Crewe's permanent population, instead of declining as it had during the 1930s, showed an 8 per cent increase by 1947. The councillors were very aware of the housing problem and sought to alleviate it, even before the end of the war. Two estates of prefabricated bungalows were planned early in 1945, at a total cost of around £14,000. In April loan sanction was received from Whitehall for fifty permanent dwellings on the Totty's Hall estate, followed by another ninety in 1946, meaning that by midsummer eight dwellings a week were being let by the council.

The end of the war also saw the resurrection of the pre-war plans for a housing estate east of Middlewich Street, that had the potential for over 900 houses. Unfortunately, the council was only allowed to build 200 houses in 1946, with another 250 the following year. Around this time the infamous Totty's Hall flats were purchased from the Ministry of Aircraft Production and renovated. Even with rents as low as 14s a week, compared with 22s a week on the Middlewich Street estate, these Rolls Avenue flats were never popular. Despite all the measures taken by the council, housing remained an acute problem for Rolls-Royce.

Other local industrialists were also clamouring for their needs to be recognised immediately. County Clothes wanted 20 dwellings for key workers, British Rollmakers 23, Calmic Ltd 3, and Kelvinator 7. In addition, the council had 2,400 applicants on the waiting list, 1,600 being priority cases. Shortage of suitable housing was, according to LS, the reason why the Clan Foundry personnel stayed at Derby when the experimental machine shop was established at Crewe in 1948. The *Crewe Chronicle* also blamed the housing crisis for the inability of the Crewe Alexandra football club to attract new players. Apparently nobody wanted to play for the Alex if it meant living in lodgings. Needless to say, Llewellyn-Smith did not have to enter his name on the list for a Totty's Hall flat, as in June 1945 he moved into The Limes, a recently purchased company house in the nearby market town of Nantwich.

The Limes, Park Road, Nantwich, purchased by the company for Llewellyn-Smith in 1945. It is now a residential hotel. *(Author's collection)*

Early in May 1949 LS wrote to the town council stating, 'the Company is experiencing difficulty in increasing its labour force. If further expansion of skilled engineering industry is to take place in Crewe, it will only be effected by the vigorous pursuit of an adequate housing policy to provide further accommodation.' As already stated, the council's hands were tied, for the number of dwellings it could build was dictated by a higher authority. This pressure for rented accommodation remained a perennial problem for RR, and as late as 1974 the factory's personnel department asked for forty houses although, even then, the council's housing committee could only make twenty available, owing to demolition of Victorian dwellings in Crewe town centre.

A FACTORY FOR CARS

Once firmly ensconced at Crewe, LS began to plan for car production, and by the summer of 1945 the equipment department at Pym's Lane, under the direction of Valentine, was feverishly laying out the plant for the manufacture of motor cars. To quote Wilson Elliott: 'When peace was restored we began the change over of Crewe factory to motor car production, bringing in entirely new jobs for car body work, painting, woodworking, trim-shop etc. New engine test facilities were needed and we had to design and manufacture new test rigs for various auxiliaries such as shock damper test rigs and so on.' Larger boilers were installed to provide the new paint-shop with steam. Ted Glover had the responsibility of supervising the transfer of any necessary machinery from Derby. Once aero-engine production had ceased, the number of machine-tools needed at Crewe was around 700, a steep drop from the 2,500 being run at the height of the war.

By the winter of 1944 Grylls and Evernden were more often at Crewe than Derby, working at Wistaston Hall, one of the Crewe dispersal centres utilised by LS as a design office. Here, engineers, in concert with their colleagues at Clan Foundry on the southern outskirts of Belper, could grapple with the problem of turning Crewe into a car factory. Robotham was rarely seen at Crewe, so Grylls's presence would suggest that LS wanted a leading member of the design office to be part of the changeover at Pym's Lane. Frank Dodd, chief of road test, was another of the Derby car team implanted at Crewe before the manufacture of Merlin and Griffon engines ceased.

The difficulties of running down aero-engine production while initiating car manufacture were enormous, especially when it is remembered that the necessary skills for manufacturing complete motor cars were unknown at either Pym's Lane or Derby. Robotham freely admitted that he knew nothing about the mysteries of trimming cars, paint-work or panel beating, matters that required him to take advice and to learn new tricks.

The problems faced by Morris, Smith and the other senior managers were immense, with no skilled body workers, no trimmers, their steel requisition cut to 30 per cent and a shortage of speedometers, road springs, lamps and other bought-out parts being only a few elements of their quandary. Bonus disputes as the car operations were re-timed, combined with the high expectations from a lethargic and war-weary workforce, produced a most contentious mix. That the first car rolled off the assembly area in February 1946, less than three months after the last Griffon engine left Crewe, is a massive tribute to all involved.

The presence of a prototype for the early postwar cars has been outlined by many authors, including Ken Lea in his work *The First Cars From Crewe*, published by the Heritage Trust. Consequently, many of the detail drawings pertaining to the chassis and engines already existed, which meant that H. Varley, Tom Barlow and the rest of the planners could commission the jig and tool drawing office, under Freddie Green, to design all the necessary jigs and fixtures. Lesley, chief of the purchase department, was responsible, under the direction of the production planners, for buying parts not manufactured at the factory. Among these were all the castings and forgings, such as crankcases, crankshafts, valves and connecting rods – for Crewe had no forging or casting facilities. Obviously the machining of these bought-out parts to Rolls-Royce tolerances was done in-house.

When alterations were made to existing cars, or as new models were planned in later years, the various design teams, originally at Clan and later at Pym's Lane, would raise design schemes that would be drawn into individual parts by detail draughtsmen. Each of these parts had a unique number, and designers would endeavour to use as many existing parts as possible, to avoid repetition and cut down on costs. Production planners would take over at that stage, producing a layout that itemised, in sequence, all machining or heat treatment that was necessary to produce the part. This was a highly skilled job, needing a minute knowledge of machining and workshop technology. All of this planning took place in one half of the large room above the canteen. Besides jig and tool draughtsmen and planners, this area also contained the rate-fixers, headed by Harold Armitage and later Norman Wiggett. This latter job was a thankless task, because the rate-fixers timed each element of the production process, enabling the worker on the shop floor to make his 'time', or not, as the case might be. As this determined the amount in the weekly wage packet, a rate-fixer was not a popular man.

From the planning department, information was passed to the various offices, such as material control and progress, ensuring that the correct steels or other metals and materials were available when needed. Most jigs, tools and fixtures were made on site in the tool-room, under the control of Len Harper and Jimmy Rozell. Harper, the superintendent, had been recruited by John Morris from Sunbeam of Wolverhampton in August 1938, and soon achieved a position of responsibility, even, for a while, being in charge of the jig and tool drawing office. Production machining took place in the northern and central areas of the main shop. Once the parts had been accepted by inspection they were passed to the finished parts stores.

The southern end of the main shop, which had formerly seen the erection of Merlin engines, was adapted into an assembly line for cars, engine build and small unit assembly. Nothing as crude as a moving belt was seen at Crewe for fitting together the many parts onto the chassis, but there was a continuous line of frames, in various states of build, as teams of fitters added their particular contribution to the final assembly under the supervision of Bill Harvey and the gentle Frank Hallows. Jack Aitcheson controlled the engine assembly area, which was positioned between the chassis line and the machine-tools.

Engine assembly line, *c.* 1951. Ernie Scott is investigating the stretch of a connecting rod, watched by (left to right) Jack Aitcheson, foreman of engine build, Harry Worth, an inspector, known in the factory by his stage name 'Marco', traceable to his spare-time occupation as a magician. The man in the jacket is Reg Tapley, an inspector. *(Rolls-Royce Enthusiasts' Club)*

Fitting a straight six engine into the chassis, *c.* 1953. The fitter controlling the hoist is the author's uncle, Albert Ollerhead. The man guiding the gearbox is an apprentice named Lindop. One of the jobs performed by apprentices when they started on the fitting bay was 'pop' riveting the instructions onto the oil filler cap that can be seen on the top of the engine. The bulge in the back pocket of the fitter is probably the horse racing pages of the daily paper. *(Rolls-Royce Enthusiasts' Club)*

Before the engines were fitted into the cars they had to undergo eight hours of controlled running on the test beds at the southern extremity of the factory, supervised by Arthur Willacy. Following this, one engine in twenty was dismantled and meticulously inspected. It was not only engines, however, that were tested, for most units and new parts were evaluated on specially designed equipment in the rig test department or in the electrical laboratory.

What was novel and unknown at Pym's Lane, indeed at Rolls-Royce generally, was the art of coach fitting and trimming. It ought to be emphasised that the south Cheshire region had no large-scale experience of the manufacturing techniques needed to finish cars. Foden and ERF at nearby Sandbach, respected manufacturers of heavy lorries for most of the twentieth century, did not need trimming skills, consequently there was not a ready pool of labour that could be tapped or easily trained. Crewe railway workshops had not manufactured passenger rolling stock since about 1870, as carriage building for the LMS was centred at Wolverton, in Buckinghamshire. Carriage repair work had been executed at Crewe until 1932, when that too was transferred to Wolverton, meaning that most of the skills necessary for car body building and finishing had to be attracted into Crewe.

As there was no tradition of coach-building at Derby, Robotham had to find someone to establish and lead an appropriate department whose finished product would be equal to the standard of pre-war coach-builders. In his autobiography he tells of the experience when a man named Green, who came as highly recommended and experienced in producing quality bodies in quantities, was employed: 'Green, in his turn, introduced me to his homonymous friend Greene, who had been trained to make drawings of body panels suitable for Pressed Steel tools. We were progressing. In May 1944 John Blatchley . . . walked into the office and said he wanted to return to body design. . . . A month later I took on Currall, recommended by Green as a body production expert, and shortly afterwards Seely, a specialist in the manufacture of seats and interior trim.' The Currall mentioned here was Reg Currall, 'poached' from Singer Motors late in 1944. Eighteen months later he and Bill Edge, the personnel manager, travelled to Coventry in an unsuccessful attempt to persuade skilled coach-builders to migrate to Crewe. When one compared hourly rates in the car manufacturing heartland of the UK with those paid at Pym's Lane, failure was a foregone conclusion. By such methods were departments established in those days.

Edgar Lowe, the senior body foreman from 1945, had, prior to 1940, owned a small car body repair business in Browning Street, Crewe. Others, such as Jack Hewitson, the body inspection supervisor, adapted their skills to new procedures. Quiet and unassuming, Hewitson had been travelling mechanic for Sammy Davis, one of the Bentley boys, and he joined RR as a member of Robotham's body team in 1946. He was also ever-present at Minshull New Road sports ground during the summer months, when the RR cricket eleven played at home. Perhaps this was a factor in his appointment as welfare manager in the 1960s.

Although the community of Crewe did not have a pool of workers skilled in body trimming techniques, it did have persons experienced and highly skilled in sewing and tailoring. This was attributable to County Clothes and other local clothing factories, which had been present in the town for sixty or seventy years. Some of these skilled workers were hired and trained, thus forming the nucleus of the trim department.

The body trim department was located at the southern extremity of the main shop. Vic Seely, who had learned his trade in the Black Country, was in charge of the trim shop, with Edgar Holt as foreman. The first of the trim processes was to cut the hides into the required shapes for the seats. These would then be sewn into place by one of the machine operators (usually female). Carpets would be treated in a similar way, for, at over £4 a yard in 1950, there was no room for careless work. In charge of this latter operation was Oscar Harrison, formerly of Thrupp and Mabberley, who bore a middle name of Hamil in honour of the famous pioneer aviator. Incidentally, Oscar Hamil had been the first man to land an aircraft in the Crewe area, in 1913. Although most of the interior trimming had to be done at the outset by workers who had been attracted from other employers, by the early 1950s apprentices trained on the job were emerging to provide a constant stream of skilled labour.

Very early in 1946 an application to build a paint mixing shop was submitted to the town council's planning committee, and Basil Wilman was brought in as chief of the paint laboratory, two developments indicative of the seriousness with which the problems thrown up by unfamiliar processes were being met. The laboratory, built towards the north-western end of the site, contained many devices that aimed to replicate the varied meteorological motoring conditions. A 'weatherometer', a large-diameter stainless steel drum, contained painted panels that were subjected to infra-red and ultra-violet rays, conforming in strength to the power of a tropical sun, and rotated at three revolutions an hour. Jets of water would also be played onto the paint samples as they passed around the drum, producing, in two months, the equivalent weathering they would receive in two years of use. Different atmospheres were also created, to correlate with urban, rural and seaside conditions.

The main laboratory was still under the control of the wartime chief metallurgist, B.A. Beckley, and was to remain so until his retirement in 1962. He had formerly worked at Sunbeam, as part of the team that produced the artificial fog used in the

iew of part of the trim-shop, c. 1951, showing
rk on sewing the hides for covering seats.
nming cars was a completely unknown activity
Rolls-Royce when it started to manufacture cars
in in 1945. *(Rolls-Royce Enthusiasts' Club)*

The 'weatherometer' in the paint laboratory, c. 1951. Various paint samples were subjected to ultra-violet rays and water to test for fading. The drum revolved at a pre-set speed to provide a determined amount of ultra-violet, water or both. It was organised by Basil Wilman, the chief paint technologist. The identity of the man here is not known. *(Rolls-Royce Enthusiasts' Club)*

Looking south down Third Avenue, immediately outside 174 department or car test, *c.* 1957. A Lister truck driven by Ted Williams is towing a Silver Dawn. Traces of wartime camouflage can be seen on the covered way. *(Rolls-Royce Enthusiasts' Club)*

Zeebrugge raid of 1918. Many of the early workers came from Sunbeam, obviously sought out by John Morris, who had worked there before starting at Rolls-Royce.

Finished cars were road tested by a team of around a dozen experienced testers, trained for such a purpose by Frank Dodd, once Sir Henry's personal chauffeur, and a highly skilled driver-mechanic. He was transferred from Derby to head road test and car repair at Crewe, yet chose to live at Knutsford, almost as far away as the town from where he had come. To set up both the road test department and a service station was not an easy task because, before Crewe became the car plant, many cars were serviced at the London service station. Consequently Dodd had to find testers and mechanics for both road test and the Crewe service station – or car repair, as it became known locally.

This department was situated in the former Merlin engine despatch stores, adjacent to Merrill's Bridge at the south-eastern corner of the site, and many older models were renovated and serviced under the watchful eyes of Dodd and his deputy, Joe Williamson. Len Fisher, one of the earliest foremen in the service station, had been employed in Paris between the wars, and it has been recalled that he had a successful, if unorthodox, way of timing the twenty-four sparking plugs of the Phantom III. Using a device designed by him, and made in the tool-room, Fisher taught his favourite fitters how to set the timing accurately in the minimum of time. When Fisher retired, Billy Bull was promoted to senior foreman, remaining in post until he, too, retired in 1968, with over forty years of service to his credit.

When the car repair department was fully operational in the late 1940s it had around 200 workers under its auspices, if not under its roof. This was when Doug

Fox was brought from Derby to head road test under Frank Dodd, eventually taking over in 1958 as chief tester, when Dodd was promoted to quality engineer. Fox, himself, was promoted in 1967 to factory public relations officer.

Some of the problems of testing cars on the roads of Cheshire had been anticipated, some had not, for, in 1947, the company was warned by the district coroner not to test cars at high speeds on public roads. The context of this was a death, caused by a road traffic accident on the A530, about a mile from the factory. A car out on test had collided with a cyclist; at the subsequent inquest it was established that the car had been travelling at just under 40mph, so perhaps 'high speed' was relative.

FROM CLAN TO CREWE

By the late 1940s the only departments missing from Crewe were the design and development teams, and the detail drawing office. Although still at Belper, owing mainly to the shortage of housing in the Crewe area, their input was immense, as an article in *The Autocar* for 16 July 1948 makes patently clear. Experimental machining, transferred late in 1947, was under the supervision of Ike Whitehouse, formerly at the Stoke-on-Trent wartime dispersal centre. Another man who came from the Stoke factory in 1945 was Jack Penaluna, appointed chief cashier in 1953 on the death of Halliwell. Seven years later, John Vernon took over this position, when Penaluna died at the early age of 45. Vernon remained in place as paymaster and cashier for the next thirty years.

The real controlling figure of experimental machining was the enigmatic Stan Smith, whose career included experience of the PV 12 engine (forerunner of the Merlin) while a member of the 1931 RR Schneider Trophy team. He was transferred back to car work late in 1946, having been employed at Rotol, and later the Ministry of Aircraft Production, with R.H. Coverley. The experimental garage was housed against the southern wall of 16 shop, the border between Rolls-Royce and Kelvinator. This garage, organised at Crewe by the recently transferred Vaughan Lewis, had the same problem that had faced Frank Dodd four or five years earlier. Where could highly skilled test drivers be found? Some, such as Percy Rose, Lol Ward and Stan Dean, were ex-Derby. Others were added from the ranks of Crewe fitters, so that by 1955 Bob Webb, Bob Guyton, Doug McNeil, John Gaskill, Alec Bayliss, Alan Wells, Walter Lea, Jack Edwards and Roland Bridges were just some of the men who earned their livings by testing experimental cars.

One of the major design figures who did not transfer from Clan Foundry in 1951, as he had moved two years earlier, was the technical production engineer Harry Grylls. There was no love lost between him and Robotham, his erstwhile boss, nor was there between Llewellyn-Smith and Robotham, so it was amenable for LS to have Grylls at Crewe as the virtual chief of the design team, even if Robotham was the titular head at Derby. Fortunately, a prospective altercation was avoided in 1951, when Robotham decided against moving to Crewe. According to Robotham, Hives gave him a choice between developing motor cars at Crewe and directing his energies towards the diesel engine. He chose the latter, thus opening the door for Grylls to be crowned as chief engineer of cars.

In the spring of 1951 the decision to locate car development and design and detail draughtsmen at Pym's Lane was made, and the company allocated capital to purchase houses in Manor Way and Stanhope Avenue. Until these were ready, some of the relocated employees managed to obtain rooms or lodgings in the area. Reg Spencer, then a young design engineer, recalls living in a pub at Burleydam, about 10 miles from the factory, while others commuted each day from Derby.

For the first year the designers and detail draughtsmen worked out of the recently erected, bungalow-type building that bestrode the strong room at the rear of the main office block, while they awaited new accommodation fronting Pym's Lane. These offices, opened in the early months of 1953, provided room, in the upper storey, for the various design sections led by Charles Jenner, and later Jack Phillips (engines), Frank Tarleton (transmission), Reg Davis (electrical) and George King (chassis). This design office was connected by an elevated, covered walkway to the suite of offices in the main block occupied by Bert Jeal and the body office, Blatchley's small styling department, Ivan Evernden, Ray Dorey and eventually, a little further along the corridor, next to the board room, Llewellyn-Smith, guarded by his personal assistant, Eric Moore and the gracious Edna Norris.

On the ground floor Harold Peak, a scratch golfer, was chief draughtsman supervising the detail drawing office; assisting him were Ted Holland (chassis) and George Cooper (engine), each having about a dozen detailers to interpret the design schemes and break them down into individual parts that could either be contracted out or made in the factory. The specification office was also on the ground floor, with Ernie Nibbs as the section leader, while another of the leading technical engineers with accommodation in this building was Tony Martindale. Joining RR in 1934, he spent his wartime years in the RAF at Farnborough, where he is reputed to have piloted a Spitfire at 0.91 mach. After being awarded an Air Force Cross and bar, he returned to RR, where his main involvement was in the design and development of brakes and suspension, together with duties as technical production engineer. Unfortunately, he died in 1959, three years after being appointed chief development engineer.

Another change in the management in these early postwar years occurred when John Morris, the works manager, left in 1949 to take over as technical director of the Engineering Group of Metal Industries Ltd. He had been a good servant to the firm, and as one of the original seven had performed a Herculean task in rapidly establishing RR as a productive unit in Crewe. Morris had responsibility for the whole of manufacturing, hiring, and on occasions 'firing' employees as, during his years, the labour force approached 10,000 spread over seventeen sites.

His job was taken over by Fred Stafford, his deputy, who had worked for Birmingham Small Arms before moving to Crewe as a technical assistant on £500 per annum in 1941. Although he was Morris's nephew this was not a case of nepotism, for he performed well enough to be appointed a car division director in 1960, another member of a Rolls-Royce board never to have graduated from university. A further change at this time was the promotion of Alan Brogden to assistant works manager.

CARS AND COSTS

In early September 1945 LS reported to the board, giving the estimated costs of adapting the Pym's Lane plant for car production as £300,000 for tools and £65,000 for the paint-shop, most of the machine-tools being purchased from the government at approximately 20 per cent of their 1939 installation price. Two months later he suggested that the expenses, before revenue began to flow, would be £392,000 for the current year, with another £1,595,000 for 1946. Within two years, according to his projected figures, the plant would be manufacturing thirty-five cars a week, without the need for a night shift. His tentative estimates suggested that fitting a standard body would necessitate a 76 per cent increase over pre-war prices.

Early in 1946 LS was promoted to general manager over the whole of the car side of the business, which included, in addition to Crewe, the London sales and repair departments and the Lillie Hall branch. From this lofty perch, so desired by Robotham, he supplied the directors, in the middle months of that year, with details of the junior car project, code-named 'Myth' by Hives in 1939. Llewellyn-Smith suggested that the price of a 2-litre car with a standard steel body would be about £1,000 before tax. October 1947 was fixed as its launch date, with a flow of 100 cars a week. The expected sales of the Bentley Mk VI, in 1946, were 300 cars. At another meeting in July he reported that the deposits received against new vehicles were £86,705 (303 Wraiths) and £234,288 (1,008 Bentleys), with another £71,396 brought in through servicing and spare parts.

At this same meeting the Silver Phantom project was cancelled, but work was continued on the Silver Dawn, the 8-litre Bentley and the Junior car, this latter project only to be revoked, in rather brutal language, at the July meeting of the directors, after five experimental models had been made. Descriptions and details of cars in the rationalised range may be found in works such as Ian Rimmer's *Rolls-Royce and Bentley Experimental Cars*.

Consideration of the RR board minutes can lead to the opinion that LS was never enamoured of the enterprise of a small car, and that there was a dichotomy in the camp, for the policy of LS and the views of his chief engineer often seemed to diverge. After completing a tour of some American car factories Robotham compiled a report detailing his observations on future strategy; observations that seem to have been summarily dismissed by the board, with very little consideration. By the late 1940s Robotham was disenchanted by his long-term prospects within the car division, leaving on record that its policy was a source of continual criticism. Part of the cause was the pique he felt over the promotion of LS. Another factor was that he was convinced that a larger volume of vehicles ought to be produced to keep the car division solvent, an argument that carried much weight and can be traced back to the years of Harvey-Bailey. All of these reasons led to his enthusiastic embrace of the diesel or oil engine project, as he called it, a fortuitous decision because there were, in effect, two chief engineers of the car division, one at Clan and one at Crewe.

The crucial importance of the rationalisation of parts to reduce overall costs, initiated by Harvey-Bailey and Robotham in the years immediately prior to 1939, cannot be over-emphasised, especially in the trading conditions of the postwar world. The first of the peacetime Bentleys was based on the pre-war Mk V, powered by a six-cylinder, 4.5-litre engine, with an aluminium head, side exhaust and overhead inlet valves. Unique in the history of RR, a car was to be produced that had an all-steel body, fitted and trimmed at the home factory. In so doing, the company was venturing into the unknown and there is, perhaps, more than a germ of truth in the cynical hypothesis of Frostick in his book, *Bentley Cricklewood to Crewe*, where he writes that there was no way the RR design team, steeped in the traditions of Derby, would allow a car bearing the famous radiator to be part of an experiment that might go wrong. Thus the marrying of a RR chassis to an all-steel body had to wait until it was a proven success.

The second of the postwar Crewe models was a Rolls-Royce, known as the Silver Wraith, which was offered for sale as a chassis only, with the body fitted and trimmed at a specialist coach-builder's chosen by the customer. It was a Silver Wraith, with coachwork by H.J. Mulliner, which occupied pride of place in the Transport Pavilion at the Festival of Britain, on the south bank of the Thames in 1951. Half-way through the Festival it was changed for a Crewe-built Bentley.

When the numbers of Mk VI Bentleys produced each year up to 1950 are analysed, on average seventeen cars a week were built, although in 1946, when production began, less than one a week rolled off the assembly line. Obviously the number of finished cars grew as the experience and skill of the workers increased. Devaluation of the pound by the Labour government in 1949 helped to boost sales, especially to Switzerland and the USA. By 1951 the workforce at Pym's Lane was building about thirty cars a week, including Bentleys, Silver Dawns and Wraiths, meaning that between 1946 and 1952 just over 5,200 Mk VI Bentleys were manufactured. Nearly 1,000 did not roll along the Crewe assembly line, going rather to be trimmed at such firms as H.J. Mulliner, Park Ward or James Young. At the same time, two or three Silver Wraiths a week were being sent on to these or similar coach-builders. Surprisingly, considering the emphasis on exports, only fifty of the whole Bentley production run were left-hand drive, as, until 1949, RR did not countenance such practice. Perhaps this helps to explain the failure of the US sales campaign in 1947.

To gain an estimate of the effort that Llewellyn-Smith and John Morris, along with the workforce generally, had accomplished, it is worth glancing at the financial figures for the car division for 1949, when a total of 1,163 cars, with a value of £3,262,347, had been sold. In addition, 119 B range engines brought in £59,340 and spare parts another £138,369. It is to the B range engines that we now turn.

THE B RANGE ENGINES

During the war the Clan design team continued to work on the development of four-, six- and eight-cylinder petrol engines, especially after the return of Robotham from the Ministry of Supply in 1943. The original design of these engines dated back to pre-war days, with the decision to produce a rationalised range with 97 per cent of the parts interchangeable. Always alert to increasing the revenue of the firm, Robotham saw the value of utilising this common range of engines for military and civil purposes, and like others of his projects, it proved a very successful and far-sighted venture.

These engines were of conventional design, with in-line cylinders, overhead inlet and side exhaust valves. Charles Jenner led the team at Clan Foundry responsible for the successful design of these engines, and not least among its members was Jack Phillips, who became responsible for all engine design after he moved to Crewe. It was, however, another young Derby designer, Reg Spencer, who worked on the B range project, from its beginning at Clan, almost to its end at Crewe, in the late 1980s.

The B80 developed around 165bhp at 3,750rpm, while the B40 and B60 grossed 80bhp and 160bhp respectively. From Pat Ware's excellent volume on the B series engines, it can be calculated that, in total, over 27,000 were produced. This book also gives the cost of a B40 engine, in 1952, as £200, making the B range project a successful revenue raiser, which was all the more gratifying, considering that 'the B range engines had been embarked upon as a precaution against the collapse of the motor car business'. From 1948 the B range became the standard power unit for all of the British Army's wheeled combat vehicles, and particularly close links were forged with the Fighting Vehicle Research and Development Establishment at Chobham. The Austin Champ, Alvis Stalwart and Saracen, along with the Daimler Ferret scout car, are but four of the military vehicles in which these engines were installed, and by 1960 twenty-seven overseas armies were using them. One example of foreign use was the West German contract, worth £8.5 million, negotiated in 1957, ten years after the commencement of production.

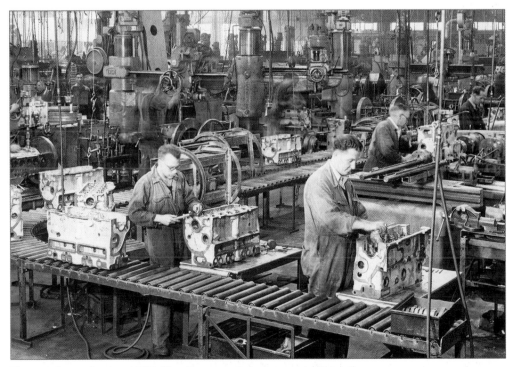

The crankcase line, c. 1957. The B range engines were built on the conveyors, as can be seen in this picture where two fitters are working on B60 engines. This was half-way along the main machine shop. (Rolls-Royce Enthusiasts' Club)

In addition to their military uses, these engines also powered commercial vehicles, and Walter Sexton can be named as one representative of the development engineers who mastered the problems of fitting B range power units into fire appliances, airfield mobile equipment, luxury passenger coaches, snow ploughs and even a Vickers Heavy Hovercraft. Further details of these engines, along with their many installations, can be found in Ware's definitive work *In National Service*.

To cope with the flow of orders for the B range engines another 1,000 employees were needed, taking the pay-roll up to around 4,000. Unfortunately this £60,000 expansion programme coincided with the housing and skills shortages at Crewe. There was a great need for capstan operators, millers and grinders, only they were not easy to find and, despite a recruitment drive, the first four months of 1949 saw a net increase of only four. Unemployment in the Crewe area was down to 33 per cent of the national average, with five times as many vacancies as registered unemployed. At that time just over 800 people travelled daily to work at Rolls-Royce, some from as far as Liverpool and Manchester. About 5 miles away, the Royal Ordnance Factory at Radway Green was also trying to locate skilled machine workers, especially after the start of the Korean War in 1950.

APPRENTICESHIPS

One long-term measure taken by the company to reduce the skill shortage was to refine the apprenticeship scheme. Teenage lads had been employed before the war started, and one of the causes of the 1939 strike was women performing machining tasks that the unions expected lads to do. Many of the youngsters stayed longer on one job than they would have done under different circumstances, and the works committee wartime minutes reveal more than the occasional complaint that apprentices were not receiving sufficient skill instruction, even though a training scheme of sorts was in place, under the supervision of a Mr Rothery. An article by Lawrence Allen in the *Rolls-Royce Enthusiasts' Club Bulletin*, No. 267, also notes the ad hoc training during this era, even to the point where the teenage Allen himself had to request a move to another department.

In 1948 Bob Moulton was the first Crewe lad to be indentured, when the scheme was introduced into Pym's Lane, with the appointment of F.R. 'Ronnie' Dyson as apprentices' supervisor following a year or so later. This man, one of the seven Derby men who opened up the RR enterprise in the town, organised and controlled the scheme that trained more than a few who later moved into managerial positions. Ron Ashley, production director, and Bernard Preston, UK operations director, are two examples of those who could be named.

Many of the young males who joined RR often had relatives working at the factory, although too much can be made of the 'son following father' syndrome when youth employment is considered. It happened at Pym's Lane, as it had been happening at Crewe locomotive works for over a century. The author's father, and three uncles, were pre-war employees, though the six Dobson brothers easily beat this, spending all their working lives at the factory. There were few other career opportunities locally for the secondary modern school pupil, so the horizons of most of Crewe's school leavers were limited to an apprenticeship at the LMS works or 'Royces'.

The lowest rung of the four divisions of training, in the 1950s, was apprentice machinist, where the candidate was selected to spend his working hours on the production line, operating capstan lathes, milling or grinding machines. One step above this was the trade, or craft, apprentice, who was given a more general training, moving around the various departments according to aptitude and ambition. The final destination was chosen at around age 18, and could be as varied as tool-making, maintenance electrician, coach trimming or fitting. In the early 1950s the yearly intake of trade apprentices numbered around forty.

A sense of the shock to the raw youths on entering an engineering workshop in the early 1950s can best be gained from the following account given by Billy Consterdine, a highly skilled tool-maker, about eight years after he had retired.

Two weeks after leaving Bedford Street Boys' Secondary Modern School in April 1951 aged fifteen I started to work at Rolls-Royce. This was not my choice for I wanted to work on locomotives in the British Rail Workshops in Crewe but my father, who worked for the railway, wanted me to serve an apprenticeship at RR. On arrival at the Employment Office I was taken by a boy, who had been in my class at school, to my allocated place of work. On the way he took me into the main shop where my first impression was of the colossal, deafening noise. I didn't know then that much of it was coming from the bar autos. Another thing was the size of the main shop, it seemed enormous, with machines stretching right into the distance. There was also a peculiar smell that I soon learned was always present. It was the smell of suds or coolant. I was then taken along a gangway to my place of work in 119 department, the Polishing Shop. Unfortunately Mr Dykes, the foreman, said he wasn't expecting any new starters and anyway apprentices were never put with him so I was taken back to the Employment Office where it was found that someone had misread the information. I should have been taken to 219 department not 119. I began yet another tour of the factory to the department where I was to spend the next forty years. My guide delivered me to a well built man at a table in the corner of the shop. When he spoke to me I was surprised that his voice was so highly pitched for such a big man. 'Are you the new lad?' he said. I had started work at Rolls-Royce.

He goes on to talk about the many machines that he was trained on, and the variety of work in 219 department, manufacturing parts for machine-tools and the millwrights, as well as the tool-room.

Some of the more academic trade apprentices were selected for one of the drawing offices, or similar technical departments. To initiate prospective draughtsmen into the company's methods and procedures, a drawing training school was organised in the late 1940s in the 'cock-loft', above the boardroom. Its first instructor was Bernard Slawson, who had joined RR in 1940 from Sunbeam, as assistant superintendent in the main shop. Outstanding apprentices could be nominated for prizes or awards, given every year by Hives and W.O. Bentley.

A higher rank of apprentice training was for those from a grammar school, or one of the minor public foundations. These were engineering and commercial apprenticeships, sometimes called student apprenticeships, when training fitted the candidates for management roles or more prestigious positions as they 'came out of their time'. Three typical products of this training were Dave Buckle, eventually customer manager, John Smith, company secretary, and Peter Hill, a chassis development engineer.

Late in 1956 the company opened the apprentices' hostel in Minshull New Road, on a portion of the sports ground. It was not for every apprentice, only those who needed accommodation, for the locality could not provide sufficient lodging space to satisfy the needs of the engineering apprentices. The hostel had two storeys and could house twenty-four youths, in addition to Henry Carmichael and his wife, who acted as warden and matron. Trade apprentices were expected to live at home.

An important feature introduced into the schedule of a trade apprentice in the early 1950s was structured elementary skill training. A few square yards of the car test department were partitioned off for use as an apprentice training school. Part of this was used as a schoolroom, where Ronnie Dyson gave lessons in mathematics and technical drawing. (One of Dyson's stated ambitions was to live until the twenty-first century, an ambition that he achieved by a margin of eleven months.) The rest of the schoolroom was filled with machine-tools, and the quiet, inoffensive Ernie Ward, a highly skilled tool-maker, was appointed in 1952 as instructor. About thirty apprentices a year received basic training in grinding, milling, drilling, centre lathe turning and setting capstan lathes. Needless to say, many of them also received unofficial training in practical jokes.

Opening of Leighton House, the apprentices' hostel in Minshull New Road, November 1956. Left to right: F. Tomkinson (architect), Jack Valentine, G. Hodkinson (Mayor of Crewe), D. Tomkinson (architect), F. Llewellyn-Smith. The hostel was closed in 1983 and is now a nursing home. *(Author's collection)*

The first apprentices' training school, cobbled together from a section of the car test department. The machines were scrounged from production and had seen better days. Arthur Hammersley, the second instructor appointed, is in the centre of the picture. A youthful John Harrop, who became a development engineer, is working the capstan lathe on the left. Ronnie Dyson's office and schoolroom are through the door on the left. *(A. Hammersley)*

Arthur Hammersley became the second instructor in the mid-1950s, partly to stiffen the discipline, but also to extend the training. Once the apprentice had done his stint in the school, he would be sent to other departments to complete his apprenticeship. Day release to study at the local technical college for an Ordinary National Certificate or a City and Guilds qualification was all part of the scheme.

Holidays, at resorts such as Llandudno, were organised by Dyson and E. Hunstone, the welfare manager, for any apprentices wishing to participate. Rewards for consistent good work were also part of the regime. A month at an Outward Bound school was gained by Bill Bailey and David Chambers in 1955; the former was an apprentice from the tool-room, and the first to be recognised in this way. Others were sent on special residential courses, such as one at Brereton Hall, near Sandbach, entitled 'Adjustment to Industry', also in 1955.

Although girls were not apprenticed at this time, it is perhaps opportune to include them this section, as many of Crewe's female school leavers found employment with Rolls-Royce, usually as shorthand typists or clerks. Their initial service would be in the mail office or the typing bureau. The mail office, under the jurisdiction of Len Horrocks, contained half a dozen teenage girls, some of whom had to walk up to 5 miles a day, taking the internal mail around the various departments. In the 1970s and '80s, when the supervisor was Mary Long, the duties remained essentially the same as in the 1950s, three rounds of mail delivery a day, as well as sorting the incoming letters and memos. Marie Penaluna (nee Hill) lived locally and recalled her time at Pym's Lane with some degree of affection:

I started work at Rolls-Royce in 1953 in the Mailing Office, where we were all young girls with an older supervisor. The job was to send out letters and parcels all over the world and receive all incoming mail for delivery around the company. There were different rounds within the factory, which we took in turn, so walking everywhere we saw the manufacture of the cars from start to finish, which was fascinating. The job I really loved was taking the correspondence (after work finished at five-o-clock) to Crewe station for the company's offices in Derby and London. Not only did we get overtime pay, but we were driven to the station in one of the firm's cars by a chauffeur in full uniform. We carried the mail in big leather cases, which we handed to the guard. The London bound train was the Red Rose, Liverpool to London. After meeting the London train we went down, on a ramshackle lift, to a tunnel under the lines, coming up at the bay where the Derby train was standing. We were told that this tunnel was infested by rats! I think this was just to frighten us, but we dashed through pretty quickly. After handing the Derby mail over and negotiating the Terrible Tunnel we were driven home.

In overall control of female training, such as it was, was Nellie Lofkin, who also played for the ladies' cricket team in the 1940s and '50s.

THE SILVER DAWN AND OTHER DEVELOPMENTS

The third postwar model from Pym's Lane, the Silver Dawn, was a Rolls-Royce with an all-steel body, revealed to the world at the Toronto International World Fair of 1949. It was basically the same vehicle as the Bentley Mk VI, having a similar wheelbase, chassis and body, and as around 1,500 steel-bodied Bentleys had been built, all of the production snags had been ironed out. As the Bentley had not answered the government's prayer for foreign exchange (only about 18 per cent went abroad) the Silver Dawn was for export only, especially the North American market, to earn those much-needed dollars. To assist market penetration it was supplied with a left-hand drive, as were the Mark VI Bentley and the Silver Wraith when so required. Part of the problem of increasing sales to the USA, according to Llewellyn-Smith, was a marked tendency on the part of customers to prefer a more transatlantic design, a phenomenon that began to exercise the minds of Ivan Evernden, Blatchley and other designers and stylists, whether at Crewe or Clan.

It was around this time that Robotham was invited onto the board of Rolls-Royce, a belated recognition of his acumen and consistent contribution to the growth of the firm. Policy decisions regarding the current models were also made, at the June 1949 meeting of the directors, when the board accepted the crucial necessity of developing the existing car, a decision that led to the two major modifications to the Silver Dawn and Bentley VI.

The first, in 1951, was to the engine, where the cylinder bore was slightly enlarged, increasing the capacity to 4,566cc. The second was forced upon the company, by the spring of 1952, when orders declined – attributable, so the board was informed, to the obsolescent shape of the body. In order to rectify this John Blatchley, now promoted to chief stylist, altered the profile of the cars by increasing the size of the boot, as well as the overall length of the car.

Another feature for export-only cars, introduced around this time, was the automatic gearbox, based upon the General Motors 'Hydramatic', but

Preparing Silver Dawn bodies before spraying, after being brought by road from Cowley, *c. 1951. (Rolls-Royce Enthusiasts' Club)*

manufactured under licence at Pym's Lane. The outbreak of war had prevented Robotham from pursuing his 1939 intention to develop such a box after he had obtained drawings from GM. When car production was recommenced he instructed Evernden, who was considered to be the UK's expert on automatic transmissions, to scheme it into the Silver Phantom. It was then brought to the attention of the board in Robotham's report of December 1949, in which he claimed that, even if work on it was begun immediately, it would be at least two years before it became a standardised feature. As it was 1952 by the time the automatic gearbox was available for export-only models, Robotham's forecast was reasonably accurate.

In his book, *A Living Tradition*, J.R. Buckley recalls that the performance of the first RR-manufactured automatic gearboxes was less than satisfactory, until it was discovered that there was too fine a surface finish on some of the components. What Buckley does not say was that this discovery was made by Ivan Evernden and Fred Stafford on a prolonged investigative visit to Detroit. One of the best descriptions of the stages involved in the manufacture of the automatic gearbox is given in *A Living Tradition*.

Initially the new gearbox was produced in the main shop, near to engine build, until the board sanctioned investment of £75,000 for a purpose-built machine and fitting shop for its production. Eventually, Ike Whitehouse was transferred from the experimental department to act as superintendent of the transmission department, as the gearbox shop was called, remaining there until his death in 1966.

The Bentley R type Continental, unveiled in the spring of 1952, was, and still is, very highly rated by respected judges of motor cars, and as so few were built (208) they remain eagerly sought after to this day. Again, there is no wish in these pages to repeat tributes to its lines and features, except to state that this car was the last collaborative creation of Robotham and Evernden before the former took over as chief of the oil engine division at Shrewsbury. For many motoring enthusiasts this car, which could reach 50mph in first gear, is a worthy tribute to their collective engineering genius. Two Bentley Continentals were on view at Earls Court, London in October 1954 – a four-seat sports saloon and a convertible coupé, with coachwork by Park Ward.

The winter of 1952/3 witnessed a small-scale spate of redundancies, mainly from the paint-shop, which was often subject to cyclical staff adjustments during the 1950s. Production machining was also the subject of a comb-out of workers over retirement age and these, who had been kept working on account of postwar skill shortages, received notice to leave. Part of the reason for this was the flow of apprentices who had completed their training and their two years of national service.

While the sales team, led at Crewe by Walter Holmes and at Conduit Street by Jack Scott, successfully introduced the R type Bentley in 1952, the design and development engineers worked on the next project, code-named 'Siam'. It was the first car to be fully styled by the Crewe styling department, headed by John Blatchley. Park Ward, the company's London-based coach-builder, built the prototype body that was transported to Crewe in September 1952 to be endurance tested in the spring of the following year. Another Siam, built in the winter of 1952/3, had its first outing in March 1953, with further rigorous testing in the following months, despite a serious factory fire.

FIRE INTERVENES

The conflagration in July 1953, which inflicted the worst damage to the fabric of the plant since the bombing of 1940, started at lunch-time in the experimental department's wood shop, adjoining Kelvinator. The works fire brigade, under the control of O.G. Valentine, was first on the scene, but fire appliances from Crewe and five neighbouring stations were eventually needed to deal with the flames, as road test, with its many finished cars, was only about 40yd away. As the works was due to close down for the annual holiday, the indefatigable Jack Valentine cancelled his break and, with the help of paid volunteers, organised the clean-up, and although complete restoration took some time, there were no fire-induced impediments to production in any of the departments.

In autumn 1953 the third experimental car in the Siam project went to France, in the care of Stan Dean and Doug McNeill, for extended trials – cut short by its being involved in an accident. Besides this continental testing, some of the models were tried out at MIRA (the motor industry research establishment), near to Nuneaton. Testing of the fourth Siam was under the control of Geoff Bastow for most of 1954. This was also the year that Bastow played the part of court chamberlain in the annual pantomime at the RR Christmas party, a fact that presents another view of this august and gifted development engineer.

Despite the cancellation of the Myth project in 1947 the idea of a small car comparable in size to the Vauxhall Velox had not evaporated, for a further feasibility study was made in 1954 under the code-name of 'Tibet'. Grylls considered that a four-cylinder engine would be ideal if 'we could stomach it, both engineering-wise and politically'. The cold light of reality dictated that, at RR specifications, it would cost considerably more than the Velox or any other comparable vehicle, and the project was stifled by prolonged consideration. Around the same time a request was received from Armstrong Siddeley to be supplied with automatic gearboxes, a request that brought only a short-term revenue relief.

Another design project initiated in the early 1950s was the V8 engine that was to power the firm's cars for the rest of the century. The six-cylinder engine that had powered many of the previous cars had reached its limit, as, according to Harry Grylls, it had been continuously developed since 1923 without altering its stroke or the length of the crankshaft. During those thirty-six years the power output had been increased four-fold. Need for increased power was the major factor in moving to an eight-cylinder engine, yet despite having a straight eight available, the senior design team chose to produce a V8. Grylls and Jenner determined the original specification, with Jack Phillips, who became chief engine designer when Jenner died in 1955, bearing the responsibility and the credit for actually delivering it. Phillips allocated design of the crankcase to Les Robinson, the crankshaft and con-rods to Fritz Feller, the induction system to Harry Bamford, and the cylinder head and valve gear to Reg Spencer. All the detailing was completed by George Cooper's engine section of Harold Peak's drawing office.

V8 engines being tested. The test beds were at the southern end of the factory, adjacent to the Chester railway line. *(Rolls-Royce Enthusiasts' Club)*

Fred Lewis examining a dismantled V8 engine after it had been tested. Unlike fitters in the days of Merlin strip inspection (see page 35), Fred could be seated to perform his inspection duties. *(Rolls-Royce Enthusiasts' Club)*

After a couple of years the project had advanced sufficiently to enable an engine to be run on test, allowing another four years of development. In its initial stages there were many problems that had to be faced, and Grylls predicated two of them in an issue of the *Rolls-Royce News*. One was the different ratio of expansion between the aluminium cylinder block and head and the surrounding metals, giving problems in maintaining clearances between the contacting metals. Coolant was circulated around the block at an equivalent rate of around 40 gallons a minute. The designers countered the expansion problem by ensuring that the coolant around the cylinder block was at high pressure and low flow, while around the head it was at high pressure and high flow.

Another quandary was how to cool the engine. Because the use of aluminium precluded water as a coolant, glycol was used instead. Unfortunately, that also brought problems, especially as the V8 had 'wet' liners. As glycol had a habit of searching out weak seals, it was vitally important that there were no weak spots at the top and bottom of the liners, where they fitted into the block. Other, more minor, problems were smoothed away by the ministrations of Ron West, the leading engineer on the engine development section. More information regarding the design and development of this engine can be found in Jack Phillips's own account in the *Rolls-Royce Enthusiasts' Club Bulletin*, Nos. 182 and 183.

As the first postwar decade ended the senior management could be congratulated on what it had achieved. The Pym's Lane plant had been recast from manufacturing aero-engines to producing luxury cars; the wartime pay-roll had been drastically reduced; the premises had been adapted, and staff had been trained for the novel processes (novel to RR) of building complete cars. In the difficult trading conditions of a world just emerging from a catastrophic war over 10,000 cars had been sold, an even more admirable fact, considering the punitive rate of purchase tax. Export markets had been re-established, providing the UK with much-needed foreign exchange. In addition, with the B range engines, another highly profitable string had been added to the RR bow. A more powerful engine was in its early stages of development, and lastly, another range of cars had been designed and developed, to the point where it was almost ready for unveiling.

Chapter Four

Silver Clouds with Blue Streaks

*Boys in Crewe grow up dreaming of going to work for
Rolls-Royce Motors.*

RRM Journal, vol. 2, no. 4

At the end of April 1955 the Silver Cloud and the Bentley S type were offered
for sale, or rather displayed to the world's press, at the Hind's Head Hotel in
Bray. Regarding these new cars Llewellyn-Smith said: 'The announcement of
a new car is a very big event for us. It represents many years of development, design
and preparation work for production. In terms of cash something not far short of
£2 million. That might be small money for some motor car manufacturers but not
for us.' These were the first cars that were wholly designed and developed at Crewe.
Perhaps it would be more truthful to use the singular, for they were not two separate,
completely different models, but rather the same car with different radiators.
According to an article in the *Rolls-Royce Bulletin* of January 1956, the merging of the
models was a deliberate aim of the design team and senior management, even if the
article boasted that 'the Bentley is now a Rolls-Royce and the Rolls-Royce a Bentley'.

Improvements had been made to the braking system, steering and suspension,
and automatic transmission now came as standard. On sale at £4,796 for the
Cloud, and £4,669 for the Bentley, they were not excessively more expensive than
the Bentley R type when it had been offered for sale at £4,392 in 1952, and
considering it had cost about £2 million to develop, a rise in price of around 6 per
cent was not enormous. The Mk IX Jaguar was selling for just under £2,000, the
Humber Super Snipe for £1,493, and the Ford Consul cost only £818. They, of
course, were not aimed at the rich and powerful, or the great and the good.

The world into which the Silver Cloud was launched was a different one from
that of 1946, when the Bentley Mk VI went on sale. A queen, not a king, was head
of state; Anthony Eden was head of the government, having just replaced Churchill
as leader of the Conservative Party. Motorways were being scheduled for
construction and ration books were obsolete, leading to the closure of Crewe's
Food Office in Hightown. Mainly through the American-sponsored Marshall Plan,
the economies of the defeated nations began to recover, powered by massive
investment in plant and infrastructure.

Beneath the surface, however, there were worrying signs, as the attack on
exports and home markets from the Japanese and German car makers was

beginning to bite. By 1955 Germany had replaced the UK as Europe's largest manufacturer of cars. Workers in the UK car industry demanded wage increases that outstripped inflation, causing Fred Stafford, in a talk to the local rotary club, to claim that workers were pricing themselves out of the market. A multiplicity of craft unions, each with its own demarcation procedures, bedevilled labour relations nationally, yet, despite the number of unions being into double figures, no major labour disputes hit Pym's Lane during these years, other than token one-day stoppages called by the national officials of the Amalgamated Engineering Union. Not all of the inefficiency in the industry was the fault of labour, however, and British managers and investors must shoulder a large share of the blame, for investment levels between the UK and its erstwhile enemies were hopelessly out of balance. Both Germany and Japan were beginning to re-equip with the latest machine-tools, which left Britain even further behind.

In 1951, when the board sanctioned £79,000 of expenditure at Pym's Lane, only 39 per cent was for machine-tools. Three years later £86,500 or 27 per cent of total capital investment was dedicated to machines. Much of the plant and machinery at Pym's Lane was very dated, compared with that in the USA. Another typical example of a UK car maker whose machine-tools were well past their sell-by date was Singer Motors. William Rootes began his career there on a lathe in 1910, and when he took over Singers in 1955 he was amazed to see the same machine still in operation.

The majority of the machine-tools at Pym's Lane dated from the late 1930s and had been worked hard, day and night, for the whole of the war, before being purchased from the Ministry in 1945. That they continued to work reasonably efficiently was largely due to the skill of the machine-tool maintenance department, led by Ted Glover and the courteous Sydney Slaney. Machine-tool fitters were stationed at strategic points throughout the main machine shop, ready to deal with any emergency. One of the main functions of 219 department, the former 17 shop tool-room, was the manufacture of spare parts for broken down machines.

THE NEED FOR *LEBENSRAUM*

While the designers and development staff could feel complacent with the launch of the Silver Cloud and its Bentley equivalent, the production and equipment engineers faced a dilemma that had been confronting them, with increasing urgency, for a number of years. Whereas they needed, approximately, an additional 80,000sq ft of factory floor, all available acreage was in use. Expansion was barred by the Chester railway line to the south and Pym's Lane to the north. When the factory was partitioned off at the end of the war, the spare ground at the west end of the site became part of the Kelvinator lease, meaning that it was not available to RR.

In November 1950 the company negotiated with the town council to purchase about 7 acres of Mingay's Farm, west of Sunnybank Road, for £1,500, and further portions for £11,000 in 1956. No reason was given why the land was needed, although the supposition remains that it was for expansion purposes. The main impediment to expansion was that Kelvinator and County Clothes intervened between RR and its newly purchased site.

View of the car assembly line in the early 1950s. *(Rolls-Royce Enthusiasts' Club)*

By mid-1955, with no other ground available, the management was glancing with acquisitive eyes at the 10 acres of land on the other side of the eastern boundary, which were supposed to be a buffer zone between the factory and the houses in Minshull New Road. A planning application for factory expansion led to a five-day inquiry in September 1955, when strenuous objections were raised by the locals, only for the town council to side with the company. Hopes were extinguished when the inspector's report, published six months later, found in favour of the locals.

The decision proved a body-blow to the plans of the directors, for they wanted desperately to increase the productive capacity of the plant. As a cyclical trade depression at the refrigerator manufacturer's coincided with this planning rejection, LS quietly approached his neighbours, enquiring as to their long-term intentions. The bouts of redundancy at Kelvinator occurred at regular intervals, occasioning the dismissal of up to 25 per cent of the workforce. Llewellyn-Smith's overtures were rebuffed by a definite refusal to allocate Kelvinator's lease to Rolls-Royce, so an offer was then made to County Clothes for its portion, at a cost to RR of £475,000. This was turned down as the clothing firm was expanding, having opened two more manufacturing units, one at Audlem, about 10 miles from Crewe, and another at Wrexham, just across the Welsh border. Matters seemed to have reached a deadlock. Fortunately for RR another factor, which gave the car firm the answer it had been looking for, now entered the equation.

This was early in September 1956, when a disastrous fire occurred at Kelvinator, involving over ninety firemen from seven brigades. It was the worst in Crewe's

Tyre and wheel test, *c.* 1957. The technicians are Albert Davies and Michael Mason. *(Rolls-Royce Enthusiasts' Club)*

history, and at £1.4 million was, according to the *Manchester Guardian*, the most costly fire in peacetime Britain. Starting in the paint-shop at midday, it raged for over four hours, destroying 120,000sq ft of factory space. Within a fortnight LS received a secret message that Kelvinator was prepared, for a price of £250,000, to relinquish the lease. In order to expedite the matter LS and W. Gill, the finance director, privately agreed to settle for around that amount, despite the company valuer's estimate of £150,000. In the event, the compensation was whittled down to £175,000, a reasonable figure for a lease with another twenty years to run.

Five months after the fire production commenced at a new Kelvinator plant at Bromborough, on the Wirral, capable of manufacturing 250 refrigerators a day as compared with 200 at Crewe, yet it was still claimed publicly that both plants were necessary to meet production targets. A few months later, in November 1957, Kelvinator publicly announced that the Pym's Lane plant was closing and that, henceforth, all its products would be made at Bromborough, leaving the way open for Rolls-Royce to move back into the rebuilt section. County Clothes disclosed in January 1961 that it, too, was moving to a new site, meaning that RR could reoccupy the whole of its wartime premises.

When the details of this latter relocation are examined, its genesis was in the fertile mind of LS. Although this is not recorded in the press, RR agreed to compensate County Clothes to the tune of £175,000 for releasing its portion of the factory, at the same time making a similar sum available as a loan for a new factory, secured by mortgage at 5 per cent interest, to be repaid over twenty years. The whole move was completed by the spring of 1962.

Secure in the knowledge that Kelvinator was vacating its portion of the site, the main board resolved, at its last meeting of 1957, to transfer various service, spares and sales functions from Hythe Road and Conduit Street to Crewe. In preparation for this, W.S. Bull was appointed general service manager, with a seat on the car division board, although the full transfer of all the relevant sections was not completed until the autumn of 1959. This service department, including clerks, technicians, technical authors and artists, was located, as a temporary measure, in the rebuilt 18 shop. Day-to-day matters were administered by Stuart Quigley, Reg Shore, Jack Wrighton, Ken Hargreaves, W. Wills, Bill Trimming and C.A. Nutt, all transferees from the metropolis. The small drawing office, dealing mainly with spares, special tools and customer requests, was administered by Bob Hill, a wartime compatriot of Dick Garner. Lying in the filing cabinet of this drawing office was a part number book from the 1920s, containing many examples of Henry Royce's signature. Eventually, George Telford, who had transferred from production machining to a technical artist's board in 1960, became manager of the renamed marketing services department. The opportunity was also taken, early in 1958, to construct an access gate from Sunnybank Road into the south-west corner of the factory.

Training of apprentices also received a boost by gaining space when Kelvinator departed to Bromborough. It had been obvious, for a long time, that the screened-off portion of car test did not provide sufficient space for modern industrial

All of these would be familiar faces to apprentices from the 1950s and '60s as they were instructors in the apprentices' school. Left to right: Bob Wildgoose, Arthur Hammersley, F.R. 'Ronnie' Dyson, Doug Irlam, Ernie Ward, Tommy Mason and Ted Thorley. The occasion was the retirement of Ernie Ward, the first instructor, appointed in 1953. (A. Hammersley)

training. This was especially noticeable when compared to the grand lay-out of the British Rail Training School, opened about a mile away in 1955, and overlooking rose gardens and ornamental lakes. It had five lecture rooms, a common room, a library and a 19,000sq ft workshop housing seventy machines, fifty-two of which were lathes, seventy-four benches, a smith's hearth, a moulding furnace, a core oven and welding equipment. Trades taught in the school were turning, copper-smithing, fitting, pattern-making, sheet-metal working, brick-laying and electrical work. Even if some of these trades were not in use at Pym's Lane, the scratched together facilities in the small, even minuscule, workshop partitioned off from road test paled into insignificance when compared to the lavish provision at Crewe Railway Works.

Five years after the opening of this rival school the directors voted £19,000 for a training school on the south-western extremity of the premises. The larger space enabled extra machines to be brought in (most of which were in need of attention, having been worn out on production) and the number of instructors was increased to four, still under the control of Arthur Hammersley. Bob Wildgoose's training school for draughtsmen, as well as Ronnie Dyson's office, were integrated into this space at the same time.

DIVERSIFICATION

It was crucial that RR had managed to acquire the extra space, because several new projects were on the stocks. In an attempt to enhance the revenue of the car division, Ivan Evernden had been instructed to examine anything that would increase the output and profitability of the factory. From this survey negotiations with the Twin Disc Company, of North America, were completed in July 1955, when an agreement was signed allowing Crewe RR to manufacture torque converters under licence.

A torque converter is basically a change-speed transmission without gears, and at its simplest is a centrifugal pump driven at constant speed. The fluid from the pump drives a turbine at such speeds as it can attain dependant upon the load connected to it. In many ways Crewe RR was ideally suited for this type of work, as it was already engaged in the production of gearboxes and car transmission systems. A further factor in its favour was that the oil engine division, at Shrewsbury, was manufacturing rail cars, meaning that Crewe-built torque converters could be utilised as the transmission units for them. In order to test the torque converters a special rig, 40ft long, was built on the test beds at the southern fringe of the site, where any rail route could be simulated by means of three big flywheels and a dynamic brake. These would produce the resistance set up by the weight of an engine, gradients and rail car brakes.

At its meeting in January 1958 the board was informed that the first Crewe-built torque converter had passed all its tests. Later that year, Crewe was supplying units to British Rail, South Australian Railways and Malaysian Railways, as well as for use in earth-moving equipment and dumper trucks. For the short time that it was in Crewe, responsibility for design work and amendments was under the control of the amiable Frank Holt, who had commenced at RR in 1918 as an apprentice draughtsman. Most of his design career was spent on transmission projects, which is why he took much of the responsibility for the torque converter installations. Unfortunately for the car division, the enterprise was transferred to Shrewsbury in the early 1960s.

Another venture that touched the fabric of the Crewe factory in the 1950s and '60s was the Blue Streak rocket project. Hives had expressed keen interest in rocket propulsion from the late 1940s, seeking to ensure that RR would be part of any UK venture. The Conservative government of Winston Churchill had taken office in 1951 with a strong defence element in its manifesto. It must be remembered that this was the era of the cold war, when the UK, mainly because of its empire, was erroneously considered to be a superpower. Another factor in this illusion was its victorious emergence from the world war, having fought the longest of all the allied nations, unfortunately losing much of its wealth in the process. As the war had been fought to restore freedom to enslaved states, it was difficult for the UK to resist the onward march of democracy in the countries of its empire. Thus, the dilemma arose in which the government endeavoured to display the vestments of a world power, without having the means to pay the wardrobe bill. For many years it tried to finance defence commitments that it could ill afford, even to the point that when the Labour government left office in 1951 about 14 per cent of the gross national product was spent on defence. This decline in national fortune had a drastic effect upon the Blue Streak project, as we shall see.

In the early 1950s the UK's nuclear weapons delivery system centred upon the aptly named 'V' bombers, known as the Vulcan, Valiant and Victor. One of the government's strategic aims was the replacement of aeroplane delivery of atomic bombs by medium range ballistic missiles.

As the USA was supreme in the technical development of rocket propulsion, it made commercial sense to form a liaison with relevant companies, so agreement was reached, in July 1955, between an association of British companies that included RR, Marconi, de Havilland and Saunders Roe, with Rolls-Royce agreeing to build rocket motors to the designs of Rocketdyne, a division of the North American Aviation Corporation. For the privilege, RR agreed to pay Rocketdyne a sum of $500,000, along with annual instalments of $100,000. These motors already powered the Thor missile, then in service with the RAF. From the summer of 1955, the RR rocket division was based at Duffield Bank House, Derby, with the work contracted out around the RR divisions at Barnoldswick, Hucknall, Glasgow and Crewe, in addition to the main works at Derby.

The Crewe contribution was entrusted to the experimental department, under the eye of Stan Smith, with day-to-day control and occasional liaison with the test site at Spadeadam mainly in the hands of Ernie Pointon. As these engines, known as RZ 2, were considered secret, most of the local work was completed away from casual eyes, in the area of the factory known colloquially as the cathedral. By the end of the 1950s, the RZ 2 engines were being tested at Spadeadam, a RR-managed site in the bleak moorland of Northumberland. Prudently, the Conservative government of Harold Macmillan cancelled the whole enterprise in the spring of 1960, owing to expense and its growing obsolescence.

It needs to be said that the technical input of RR was not in any way a contributing factor to the obsolescence; rather was it the rapid development of other delivery and defence systems by the Americans and Soviet Russia. By 1960 its fixed launch sites, and the use of liquid oxygen as fuel, meant that Blue Streak could not adequately act as a deterrent.

Cancellation of Blue Streak, as a ballistic missile, did not signal the winding up of the whole project, for the government sought to incorporate the enterprise into the nascent European Launcher Development Organisation. When, eventually, this attempt at continental cooperation crawled into life, the Blue Streak development was used as the first stage in the launch of a communications satellite, and it was this new project that filled the cathedral at Pym's Lane, rather than the ballistic missile programme. History shows that this attempt at pooling national resources in a commercial push towards the stars was a failure as far as the UK was concerned. By the early 1970s Britain had withdrawn, although not before thirteen firings of Blue Streak had been achieved at Woomera in Australia with a 100 per cent success rate, a statistic indicative of the engineering expertise of the RR group.

Precision casting was another process introduced at Crewe in the middle 1950s, following ratification by the main board in December 1956. Another term used to describe this was investment casting (where 'investment' is used in the sense of enrobing), a process based on the age-old lost wax process, a manufacturing procedure that is credited to the Chinese before the Christian era. At Pym's Lane a pattern die, made from steel or aluminium, had molten wax injected into it, thus forming a solid wax pattern of the part that was to be produced. On cooling, the wax pattern was removed from the die and coated with several layers of clay slurry and sand to produce a ceramic shell. This was the investing process. To complete the die, the wax had to be removed, hence the 'lost' in the nomenclature 'lost wax'. The ceramic shell was heated with steam until the molten wax ran out, leaving a pattern which, after further processing, could be filled with hot metal. On breaking open the shell, a perfect replica of the pattern emerged. This is a simplistic description of the process that was introduced into the car division in 1957.

The first home of the investment casting department was near to the test beds, moving a few months later to a permanent location at the southern end of the premises recently vacated by Kelvinator. This was bordered by Fourth Street and Third and Fourth Avenues, and soon became known as the aero shop, where Ted Crouch (manager), G.A. Whittaker (metallurgist) and Henry Clayson exercised the main day-to-day supervision. The latter had been a senior foreman in 16 shop machining during the war. His son, Tony, eventually became foreman in the wood shop. Jeanne, his daughter, was severely injured at the factory in a terrible accident in December 1947, when she fell down the lift shaft near to the canteen.

Needless to say the lost wax process was employed at Derby about fifteen years before it appeared at Crewe, the immediate stimulus being when the company, in association with Power Jets, took over gas turbine work from Rover Cars. Hives obtained a licence to employ the process after visiting the Austenal Company in the United States. From 1942, it was under the control of the foundry manager at

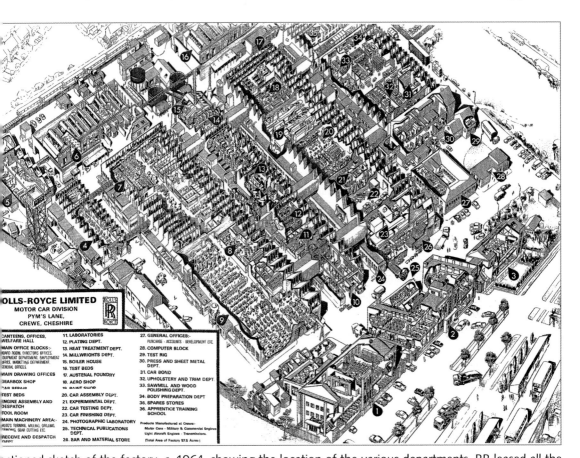

...ctioned sketch of the factory, *c.* 1964, showing the location of the various departments. RR leased all the ...uildings from the government and most of them were built during the war. *(A. Flood)*

Hillington, before being transferred to Derby in 1946. By the early 1960s the precision foundry venture at Crewe had its own machining section, an X-ray department and a standards room.

Until 1971, when it began to expand its operations, the Crewe foundry only manufactured castings for its own use, or under sub-contract for Derby RR. After a couple of years, following Plastow's reorganisation, the Investment Foundry Division (IFD) became an officially organised 'centre for profit' within the ambit of RRM. Despite this division of corporate interests, there was not a corresponding geographical split, for the IFD remained firmly ensconced at the south end of the Pym's Lane site, having its own board, with Ian Nelson as chairman, Ron Hampshire, managing director and Alan Whittaker, technical director. A planning-cum-drawing office, with a complement of twelve or so planners and draughtsmen, was established, along with a sales department with sufficient virility to win its first export order from the USA by 1973. By the end of the decade such items as chain links for woodworking machinery, bushes for beer barrels and hip replacement joints were being made by the IFD, along with the staple products such as mascots and nozzle guide vanes for jet engines.

This expansion called for increased investment and by November 1973 six new machines had been purchased, allowing casting to very fine tolerances. It was claimed that some of the items cast required holes with diameters of one hundredth of an inch, limited to an error of one thousandth of an inch. Some of the castings required little in the way of finishing; others needed to be machined on angled faces or apertures that could not be cast, meaning there was heavy investment in such services as turning, grinding and milling. By the autumn of 1974, Rennie Steele, the future product director who was rapidly moving up the hierarchy, reported a 10 per cent increase in manpower on the machining resources of the IFD, and a similar increase in its foundry labour force. There was at this time a slight altercation between the workers and the management regarding poor ventilation, especially when new and expensive creep grinders were being operated. The alternative to these was a workshop full of milling machines and, as £2.5 million had been invested, there was little sense of a return to machines that were, in any case, rapidly becoming obsolete.

In the 1970s the new generation of aircraft on the drawing boards of the plane makers called for engines that would operate at much higher temperatures, so modifications in the manufacture and casting of materials were also necessary. It was known that vacuum-cast steels would not oxidise when subjected to these higher working temperatures, hence further capital investment in the IFD at Pym's Lane in the form of a Balzer vacuum melting furnace. Other features of the late 1970s investment plan were air melting and automated shell making equipment, a numerically controlled drilling machine and the installation of a vacuum casting facility, purchased from West Germany at a cost of £320,000.

The usual complaint of restricted space bedevilled the plans of the IFD, and so a resolution for increased production space was sent to the main board. In the absence of a positive response, additional capacity was leased on a small industrial estate in Underwood Lane, about 1,000yd from the main factory, where around thirty people were employed under Jack Taylor, superintendent of the foundry. This expansion in floor space and production potential was typical of the 1970s, when optimistic sales forecasts were made most years. For example, there was a healthy 66 per cent increase in turnover in 1979, and the first month of the next year saw Hampshire clinch a deal with Fiat that was trumpeted as a harbinger of work for many years. This increase in business resulted in the purchase a new and complex grinding machine, costing a third of a million pounds. As it was too large for the available space in the aero department, it was located in the main shop, where its installation was a cause of curious interest for, as the doorways were too small, it had to be lowered through the roof by means of a large crane.

Another venture that LS and the board considered in 1958 was the manufacture of a small aero-engine to power light aircraft, under licence from the Continental Motors Corporation of America. This firm was probably the leading American producer of such engines and by the autumn of 1959 negotiations between RR and Continental Motors had produced a draft agreement, with three planned stages, to introduce light aircraft engines into the factory. The first was to import engines direct from the manufacturer at Mobile, Alabama; the second was to purchase engines in kit form to be assembled at Crewe, while the third stage was to manufacture complete engines in-house.

The results of a six months' investigation into the costs of the project revealed that a turnover of £1 million would be necessary before it became profitable, a target accepted as achievable by the directors. They certainly had to cement their intentions with more than fair words, because the cost of exercising the option to build light aircraft engines was around £1.5 million. One factor in the decision to proceed must have been the merger between Pressed Steel and Auster and Miles to form the Beagle Aircraft Company, in 1960. Beagle Aircraft needed engines, and the Crewe car maker had done business with Pressed Steel over many years. The agreement between Continental and RR, besides allowing Crewe the selling rights in Europe, Australia, Africa and parts of Asia, also included provision of spare parts, overhaul and part exchange transactions.

This latter clause was a good money-spinner for Crewe Rolls-Royce, as the recommended period between overhauls was 1,500 flying hours. When engines had reached this limit the operators had the choice of an overhaul or, if their schedules were tight, a factory replacement supplied on a part-exchange basis. The cost of a new 0-240 engine in the late 1970s was around £2,600 for a four-cylinder engine with oil-cooled pistons and valve rotators, capable of producing 130bhp at 2,800rpm. Many of its parts were interchangeable with those of other RR Continental engines.

By the spring of 1962 tooling for the Continental engines had reached an advanced stage, and it was hoped that Crewe-built engines would be ready before the year's end, a hope not realised before the spring of 1963, when the first RR-badged engine left the factory. It was envisaged that the first year's production run would total 1,000 units, with further revenue being earned by repairs to engines already in service, although, in fact, the repair work preceded the manufacture and build by many months. The repair line for these engines was established in the vacated car repair paint-shop, near to the Chester railway line. Eventually six different models were made at Crewe, ranging from 225bhp down to 95bhp. By 1971, RR had delivered more than 6,000 units, with over 80 per cent of the total being exported. As usual, there was no one at Crewe whom the board felt to be capable of overseeing the project, so J.E.P. Herriot was sent from Derby, and among those who helped him to get the project off the ground were Graham Williams, R. Salisbury-Jones, R. Taverner and L. Marshall.

Again, it must be emphasised that establishing this enterprise was neither easy nor cheap. Production space, along with machine-tools and all the appurtenances necessary to manufacture a product as highly engineered as an aero-engine, all had to be found. Production engineers, rate-fixers and technicians were a scarce commodity in the North Midlands of the UK, and had to be attracted to Crewe, or trained as quickly as possible. As distributors, salesmen, service and installation engineers also did not grow on trees, it needs little imagination to grasp the time and travel involved to set up an almost world-wide network of distributors. Eventually, there were fifty-one dealers operating on behalf of Rolls-Royce Light Aircraft Division, covering seventy-eight countries. Obviously this did not happen overnight, as the minutes of the main board make clear. An entry for September

1963 tersely states that 'the Light Aircraft project would take longer than expected to reach profitability'.

NEW ENGINES

Following our detour along the by-paths of extra-curricular activities, we must return to the manufacture of cars. After the introduction of the Silver Cloud and S type Bentley to loud acclaim in 1955, the production line was extremely busy, as this range of cars soon gained admirers and customers in many countries. A slight hiccup in production occurred during the winter months of 1956/7, when the working week was reduced to four days, after Anthony Eden ordered British troops into Egypt in retaliation for the nationalisation of the Suez Canal under President Nasser. The short war that followed resulted in a severe shortage of petrol, causing the price of a gallon to rise by around 25 per cent, and resulting in preparations for petrol rationing. Many customers cancelled their orders for new cars, bringing rumours of redundancies among the workforce.

Fortunately, by the spring there was an upturn, as the international situation was resolved, and May 1957 saw production return to normal. A few months later the local paper carried the news that there was now a waiting list of four years for the Silver Cloud, with the export market taking priority. A totally unrelated event, in the spring of 1956, was the entry of ITV into the homes of south Cheshire, breaking the hegemony of the BBC forever.

The company had a policy of continual improvement on production models, as features of misbehaviour or aspects that could be improved were revealed. The technical production department was located in 21 test bed, and although Fred Hardy and Charlie Dix did much of the development, credit for its inception, in 1950, must be given to Tony Martindale, an engineer of the first rank in the true tradition of Rolls-Royce. According to Charlie Dix, two of the early tasks they were given were to reduce the weight of the Bentley by around 120lb, and a considerable amount of investigative work on adhesives. Dix was mainly responsible for setting up the department from scratch in a vacated test bed, scrounging a lathe and whatever other tools were needed. When Martindale was given other development responsibilities, Fred Hardy took control, until handing it on to Mike Parsons, with Ian Rimmer as technical assistant. A few sentences from Hardy's obituary notice in the *Crewe Chronicle* could not be bettered as a summary of his character: 'One of his outstanding achievements was his re-engineering of the Cromwell tank. As a technical production engineer his remit was to resolve any problems with Rolls-Royce cars, which he did with due consideration and expertise. He was a man of massive intellect coupled with huge practical abilities, but for all that a kind and gentle soul with a good sense of humour. He was a true perfectionist.' At his home in Westfield Drive in Wistaston, near Crewe, he had a magnificent workshop, a model of which is to be created at Paulerspury.

It was also true that once a model was well into its development stages, the minds of the designers turned to the contingent cars. A few months before the S series was offered for sale the experimental department was concerned with a prototype Continental. Many problems, which took months to rectify, were

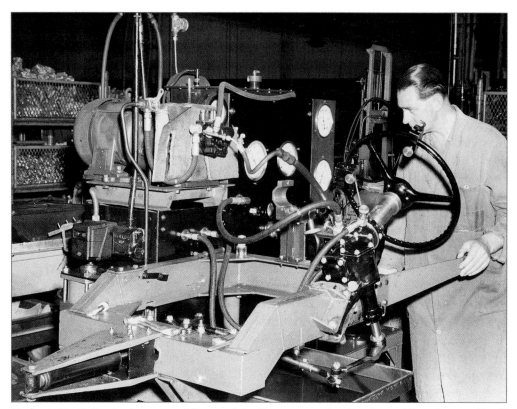

Herbert (Bert) Farrington assembling and testing power steering for an S series car. Geoff Bastow did much of the development on power steering. The fitter taught ballroom dancing in his spare time. *(Rolls-Royce Enthusiasts' Club)*

revealed on its first road test in the spring of 1955. Unfortunately, a longer spell of testing on the continent was curtailed when the car was involved in an accident, severely injuring Walter Lea and John Knapper, two of a team of four drivers.

In the years after its launch further modifications and improvements were made to the S series. For instance, LS reported to the main board in January 1956 that a power-assisted steering system was undergoing extensive trials, begun in 1954 with the refit of chassis 20-B after a crash in the summer of the previous year. Geoff Bastow, who published an informative article about power-assisted steering in the *Rolls-Royce News* of February 1958, led the design team responsible for this. Road testing was continued for two years by the drivers of experimental garage, and by 1957 power-assisted steering had been refined to the exacting standards of the RR development team, allowing it to be made available as an optional extra.

Four years after the introduction of the S series new versions, the Silver Cloud II and Bentley S2, were formally presented to the public at Bray on Thames, where Grylls made some remarks about the process of design: 'We are continually making changes to improve the car, in fact our works manager believes that we never make two cars alike. These changes are quite small in themselves and in no way constitute a new model. As a result of them, however, there was a very noticeable improvement for the better if one compared two cars manufactured twelve months apart.' The works manager mentioned here was Fred Stafford, one of the old school, who knew how to operate many of the machine-tools that filled the main machine shop, had occupied the office for about six years and was to remain for another twelve. Production of the Silver Shadow in the 1960s tested him, as it tested the mettle of every senior manager at Pym's Lane. A fair judgement would be that they emerged with honours.

Another model revealed at the same time was the Phantom V limousine chassis, which would be trimmed by one of the luxury coach-builders. These coach-builders were not as plentiful in 1955 as they had been in pre-war days, when such firms as Freestone and Webb, Brewster, Salmons, Mulliners and Rippon could mount a body on a Rolls-Royce chassis. If the prospective owner chose Park Ward, in 1955, to construct a body on a Phantom V chassis, the whole deal cost nearly £9,000.

The main change to the new models was the abandonment of the six-cylinder engine, owing to its having reached the limit of its development. That it was only just being superseded after a history of forty-six years speaks much for the original design in Sir Henry Royce's era. Over that time the horsepower had been increased in excess of four times the original figure. The new engine, a V8, was initiated as a design project in the early 1950s under the jurisdiction of Bill Hardy, the chief designer. Vivian Stanbury assumed responsibility when he arrived in 1956, but Jack Phillips carried the main design responsibility. Another reason why the straight six was abandoned was that a V8 was more acceptable to American drivers.

As the production engineers required a lead-in time of over two years, preliminary planning for machining and production of the V8 engine began in 1957. Walter Dazeley was in titular control of these operations and had been since his return from Argentina, in 1950. Much of the credit for day-to-day functioning must be given, however, to Freddie Green and Roy Jackson, working in the large open office, filled with desks and drawing boards, above the canteen. New machine-tools to the tune of nearly £250,000 were installed in the main shop in the twelve months preceding the introduction of the Bentley S2 and Silver Cloud II. One of the production changes was a camshaft cast from iron instead of being turned from solid bar, yet machined in ninety minutes to the same fine tolerances. As Sir Henry Royce had abhorred chain drives, the camshafts were driven by fine pitch gears, all made in the factory.

In addition to the modifications and improvements that the development team was introducing into current production models, the senior engineers were concerning themselves with design schemes to replace the S series. In the decade following the ending of the war, motor car design had advanced dramatically, and a body-mounted chassis was becoming a rarity on new cars wherever they were made. Even before hostilities began in 1939 Vauxhall and Morris had produced monocoque, or chassisless, cars, with Ford and Austin following suit in the early 1950s.

By the middle 1950s Harry Grylls, Ray Dorey and LS were majoring on the possibility of constructing a Rolls-Royce without a chassis, with Blatchley, but especially the veteran designer Ivan Evernden, privy to all discussions. By 1958 this project, code-named Tibet for the Rolls-Royce, and Burma for the Bentley, was exercising the minds and skills of the design office. Interestingly, an internal memo generated by Grylls, dated 6 January 1954, states that Tibet was to be a small Bentley, although, as it happened, the project evolved along different lines. The privilege of taking the prototype out for its first run went to Tony Martindale, the respected chief of the development team. Sadly, this talented man was to die of cancer within a year, leaving the project to be finished by others.

Despite the fact that only two experimental cars in the Tibet/Burma project had been built, Llewellyn-Smith considered that matters had advanced sufficiently for him to recommend to the board, in May 1959, a production target of eighty cars a week, a figure that seemed optimistic, considering the usual throughput was fifty cars a week. For a cluster of reasons, much water was to pass under the bridge before the Burma project was taken to production in 1965, and nearly twenty years were to pass before LS's target of eighty cars in one week was achieved, and then only with much overtime.

To the surprise of some, and the indifference of others, a shared project with BMC was made public early in 1962. This was the ill-fated venture of making a jointly-produced car, first mentioned at a meeting of the directors late in 1961, as a means of using idle capacity. That meant, one presumes, that the board wanted to increase revenue, which restates the importance and relevance of Robotham's desire for a smaller car. The basis of the collaboration, which took about thirty months to settle, was a Vanden Plas car with a Rolls-Royce aluminium-alloy engine, known in the factory as the FB 60.

In an unpublished paper delivered to the Belper Historical Society, Reg Spencer detailed the genesis of this engine:

In the early 1960s I was called upon by Harry Grylls, the Chief Engineer of the Motor Car Division, to produce an estimate for the torsional stiffness of a six cylinder in line petrol engine that I had been project designing for use as a military engine in a light weight tank, and which Mr Issigonis, the famous designer of the Mini became interested in, to re-engine the Vanden Plas Princess-R. I was given 24 hours to produce the figures.

In those days all our calculations were carried out using seven figure logarithmic tables, and a considerable amount of future business hung on achieving these objectives. Alex Issigonis was notorious for wanting results yesterday.

I had retained the guidance given by Charlie Jenner and used his empirical formula to produce an estimated set of results. On the basis of these figures Rolls-Royce were requested to proceed with the detailed design of this engine for the British Motor Corporation, and I was charged with the task of carrying this out.

We subsequently produced a prototype engine, which made its maiden run on the test-bed having a torsiograph fitted to the front end of the crankshaft, and accompanied with a lot of trepidation. Imagine our relief when the results of this first test showed the torsional stiffness was within 2% of the estimated figure.

From this account it can be grasped that the FB 60 was originally intended for a light tank, at the request of the Fighting Vehicle Research and Development Establishment at Chobham. The detail draughtsmen who worked with Reg Spencer were Len Sargeant and Ron Biggins, who later became a designer. Incidentally, the first design scheme for this engine, dated May 1959, was given the code-name 'Snippet' by Ivan Evernden.

The book *Hives' Turbulent Barons* suggests that Ray Dorey was the power behind this project, leaving him open to criticism when it eventually failed. This is unfair, as it was LS who took the scheme to the main board, where it was approved and capital was allocated. Alec Harvey-Bailey, in *Hives' Turbulent Barons*, states that the directors of RR Ltd were very enthusiastic at the time. When the project did fail, it was not through any fault with the engine element of the project. Another short-lived enterprise that was intended to be part of the liaison with BMC was the John Astbury-designed G60 engine with twin overhead camshafts.

The wraps came off the new £1,650 Vanden Plas at Longbridge on 29 July 1964, and, despite the initial optimism, only about 6,500 cars were made, half a year's production target if the figures of the BMC chairman are used. The production line and tooling, prepared at Pym's Lane at a cost of nearly £1 million, were located near the existing crankshaft machining department. Ted Bishop, head of production planning for the FB 60, purchased a state-of-the art Archdale drilling machine that accepted rough crankcases at one end, and ejected them at the other with all holes drilled.

SHORTAGE OF SKILLS

With all the projects that were on the drawing boards in the late 1950s and early '60s, Crewe RR was consistently and desperately seeking both design and detail draughtsmen, as were other engineering firms in the Cheshire/Staffordshire region, such as Hawker Siddeley at Chester and English Electric at Kidsgrove. To overcome the extreme shortage, the factory was combed for suitable apprentices or young tradesmen who could be trained in the drawing school by Bob Wildgoose, an ex-Clan draughtsman. The crash course lasted about six or seven months, turning out detailers and jig and tool draughtsmen. At that stage no women were trained for drawing office work, other than tracing. Harold Peak, the chief of the detail office, went on a virtually fruitless recruiting tour of Merseyside, south Lancashire and Ireland, coming back with two employees.

As it seemed easier to take the work to the workers, rather than to persuade people with scarce skills to travel to Pym's Lane, it was decided in the spring of 1960 to set up a design office in Manchester, with Joe Ion as section leader. Another, smaller office had been established in 1957 at Burslem, a town in the nearby city of Stoke-on-Trent. Arthur Mobberley, its section leader, and a couple of draughtsmen commuted to Crewe when the office was closed in the early 1960s. The experiment at Manchester was only a short-term solution, for that too folded around the same time, when Joe Ion returned to the detail drawing office at Pym's Lane.

These years also witnessed the retirement of some long-serving members of the design team. The chief designer, W.G. (Bill) Hardy, went in August 1956, to be replaced by Vivian Stanbury, formerly chief project engineer at Hawker Aircraft. Hardy had started working for Rolls-Royce thirty-six years before, after service with the Royal Navy Air Service, as an aero inspector at Derby, and later with the Clement Talbot Motor Company. One-third of his RR time was spent at West Wittering, under the eagle eye of the master, specialising in transmission and brakes.

Stanbury's appointment signified a sea-change in the policy of selecting senior design personnel, for he was the first outsider to be appointed to a top design post in the motor car division of Rolls-Royce. Reg Davis, chief of electrical design, went in 1963, after forty-four years' service. Two years earlier, Ivan Evernden, senior project engineer, decided to call it a day, having served the company well since he started, forty-five years before, as a junior draughtsman at 30s a week. Needless to say, his final salary was considerably more; even so, he felt the need to supplement his pension by drawing plans for jobbing builders, or so he claimed in a letter to Grylls.

Gee, Walker & Slater, the contractors for the original building, had retained a presence on the site from 1938 and were responsible for the alterations and new building that went on at this time. After Jack Valentine retired at Christmas 1960 Sid Torr occupied the office of equipment engineer and his first project, the new paint-shop, answered a long-felt need. Costing over £345,000, it was needed to cope with the extra work that a chassisless car would cause the body department. The new paint-shop was sited in the old 18 shop, recently vacated by the technical services department, which had decamped to the bungalow behind the main office block. To complete this merry-go-round of moves the purchase and accounts

Spraying an S series Bentley with its final finish, *c.* 1960. Masks were not required in those less-regulated days. *(Rolls-Royce Enthusiasts' Club)*

The wet deck, *c.* 1964. Rubbing down by hand between coats of filler and colour, surely one of the w●
jobs at Pym's Lane. *(Rolls-Royce Enthusiasts' Club)*

Princess Margaret
visited the factory i●
1962. Mrs Stafford,
wife of Fred Staffor●
works manager and
member of the car
division board, is
greeting her. Harry
Grylls is in the centr●
looking on. A visit t●
Pym's Lane by roya●
was not an unusual
occurrence.
(B. Fishburne)

departments, the former occupants of the bungalow, went to offices in the north-west portion of the ex-Kelvinator site.

One event that graced the early 1960s was the visit to the factory of Princess Margaret on 28 June 1962, and the itinerary for the visit, prepared by Eric Moore, still makes interesting reading. Pearson and LS of the main board escorted the Princess; Ray Dorey accompanied Lord Snowdon, and Fred Stafford attended the Mayor of Crewe. Among those to be presented to the royal party, in addition to the directors and their wives, were Bill Harvey, Alan Brogden, George Eardley VC, Pat Fulham the convenor, Ted Crouch and, if there was time, Ronnie Dyson. On the memo attached to the itinerary is the comment that 'there is no need to curtsey or bow to Lord Snowdon'.

COSTS AND CASH FLOW

The desire to reduce repair costs caused by driver error brought a new concept to Pym's Lane known as 'farmerisation'. In 1962 James Farmer, a former driving instructor to the Lancashire Police Service, was charged with the responsibility of checking and improving the driving standards of all who were accredited to drive the company's cars. Initially he was viewed with caution, even hostility, by some of the drivers and testers. Fortunately his diplomacy and skill won over the majority of the drivers very quickly, and he was so successful that the repair bill fell by 98 per cent, or to put it another way, the accident rate improved to one every 168,000 miles. To place that in perspective, the national average was one accident every 33,000 miles. Incidentally, one employee who came out with a near faultless performance from the first group of drivers assessed by Farmer was Jim Arrowsmith, who eventually became service manager.

As Farmer had nearly worked himself out of a job by 1969, security and fire prevention duties were added to his responsibilities. Perhaps, had he been employed a couple of years earlier, he could have prevented a labourer from driving himself home in a manager's Bentley. Needless to say, the labourer did not return to the factory, either in the car or on his bike.

One enterprise that was being designed and developed at Crewe during the 1950s was the K range, where three types of engines would be built: K40 (four cylinders), K50 (five cylinders) and K60 (six cylinders). These were two-stroke, opposed cylinders power units, operating on kerosene, diesel, petrol, or even, so the myth ran, peanut butter or creosote. The first mention of the project in the main board minutes was in January 1959, fifteen months before it went on test at Crewe, although Jack Phillips and his design team had begun preliminary work on the engine in 1953. The first major customer was the British Army in 1962, when it was decided to fit the K range into the Trojan Personnel Carrier. One year after this Sweden ordered some units to power tanks for its armed forces. Late in 1969 the Industrial Reorganisation Council criticised the project, stating that it was burdensome to the company, a claim that could never be levied against the B range engines.

Such a surfeit of projects, along with the cut in the working week from forty-four hours to forty-two in the spring of 1960, strained the finances of the motor division, especially when the estimate of over £1 million for Burma body tooling was placed before the main board. In the summer of 1961 the Burma/Tibet project was amended and restructured, owing in part to a drop in sales that left the motor division woefully short of revenue. A factor in this was the government's introduction of a price limit on business cars, which removed the company's models from the taxable allowance columns of British businesses. Also, the dated appearance of the Silver Cloud range must have hindered sales, making matters so bad that the *Crewe Chronicle* speculated that the Pym's Lane factory might have to close. It did not close, but poor cash flow meant that RR cancelled the Christmas bonus that was tradition-ally given to all workers – with the result that weekly staff lost an extra two weeks' wages.

As a short-term palliative for the decline in sales, the engineering department sought to improve the existing range of cars by lowering the radiator shell and introducing four sealed beam headlights, mounted in pairs. Minor changes were made to the interior and to the engine; nevertheless, as all alterations were subject to the financial crisis, nothing that called for major capital commitment was attempted. Thus the case can be argued that the genesis of the Silver Cloud III and the Bentley S3 lay in an urgent need to generate extra revenue through an improved model, without the massive outlay that the Burma/Tibet project eventually required.

At this time, and for the same reasons, the Burma and Tibet projects were merged, as the financial implications of introducing two separate cars onto the

A Silver Cloud III being inspected on the car assembly line by Alf Daniels, *c.* 1964. (*Rolls-Royce Enthusiasts' Club*)

market were way beyond the resources of the car division, even when subsidised from Derby. The tooling costs alone for the new body were around £1,400,000. Add to this the exponential increase in wages that began in the 1960s, hitting Rolls-Royce Car Division harder than high volume car makers, and a gap in finance of gargantuan proportions became apparent. For 1962 the loss was immense. In the sales brochure issued at flotation the profit and loss account of the car division – revealed for the first time – indicated that in the decade before 1972 Crewe RR drained over £2.5 million from the company's coffers, making a loss in seven out of ten years.

It was as a result of this seemingly insoluble financial impasse that Geoffrey Fawn was parachuted into Crewe at the behest of the main board. He had joined RR at Derby, in 1942, working his way ever upwards via gas turbines, nuclear submarines and aero-engine spares. That he was unwelcome to some at Pym's Lane was obvious to anyone who worked there at the time. Despite his brief to make Crewe profitable, he was not averse to organising the manufacture of a 'one-off' wooden steering wheel for his personal car. By the crude test of examining the figures on the sales brochure it could be judged that Fawn was successful in turning the car division around, for a loss of over £1 million in 1966 went to a profit of nearly £1.5 million five years later. To judge on figures alone would not be fair to Smith, Dorey and Grylls for by the early 1970s, the Silver Shadow was beginning to make its presence felt in the luxury market – which it would have done regardless of Fawn's presence at Pym's Lane. Perhaps the directors should have used the financial acumen of a machine operator in the main shop at Crewe who regularly raffled his unopened wage packet; he never went home with less than double his original stake, and paid no tax either.

Fawn's presence at Pym's Lane was seen as a kick in the teeth from the board to the erstwhile motor division hierarchy. If the chairman of the company was convinced that senior management was incompetent, he should have sacked those whom he thought to be responsible. Plastow had the virility to do this to leading names in 1982. Instead, Fawn's presence humiliated a quartet of engineers who had provided the motor division with a car that would not be replaced, in its entirety, for at least three decades. When one considers the financial and engineering chaos for which Derby was heading, it was rather rich that anyone should have been sent to 'sort Crewe out'. That having been said, Fawn did quicken the pace of the return to profit by gingering the lax attitudes and upsetting the cosiness apparent in some departments, and by simplifying the manufacture of the Shadow through removing the hydraulic levelling system from the front of the car.

As we have just seen, the car division in the late 1960s was traversing a particularly lean period while various revenue-earning schemes gestated. By the time these came to fruition some of the long-serving senior managers had decided to retire. One was the general manager, Raymond Dorey, who went at the age of sixty-one, having worked for the firm all his life. By anyone's judgement he was a colourful character and a fine engineer, in the early wartime years creating, on his own initiative, the immensely important scheme at Hucknall for repairing Merlin engines from damaged fighters. He was also responsible for the installation of the Whittle/Rover jet engine into a Wellington in 1942, and for fitting the Merlin engine

Fred Stafford and the works committee, *c. 1967*. Left to right: F. Stafford, Mrs Stafford, Bill Taylor, Bill Cartwright and Les Gallimore. The occasion was Stafford's retirement, owing to ill health. *(B. Fishburne)*

Definitely not in the factory or in working time. Left to right: Stan Smith, Alan Brogden, Eric James and Ted Crouch, March 1964. *(D. Pointon)*

into the American Mustang. That Geoff Fawn shadowed him in the closing years of his career must have been irksome to the point of desperation. Other senior managers who retired in these Fawn years were Harry Grylls, Fred Stafford and John Blatchley, the latter still at the height of his creative powers, which he felt were not appreciated.

This is not to say that all the personnel who took their pensions at this time went because of Geoff Fawn or other Derby implants. The passage of time had brought many of the Merlin workshop men to the end of their working lives, as each edition of the *Rolls-*

B-RANGE ENGINES

B 80 eight-cylinder petrol engine

ROLLS-ROYCE B-range of four-, six- and eight-cylinder petrol engines for military wheeled combat vehicles and commercial vehicles are produced at the Crewe factory.

The engines have a common bore and stroke of 3⅜ in by 4½ in, with the exception of the B.61, B.81 and B.81 S.V. which have a bore and stroke of 3⅝ in by 4½ in. Other principal details of the B-range engines:

	HP	Capacity	Compression ratio	Weight
B40 (four-cylinder)	82	173 cu. in. (2,835 cc)	6.4 to 1	650 lb
B60 (six-cylinder)	130	260 cu. in. (4,260 cc)	6.4 to 1	820 lb
B61 (six-cylinder)	168	298 cu. in. (4,887 cc)	7.25 to 1	815 lb
B80 (eight-cylinder)	170	346 cu. in.	6.4 to 1	1,000 lb
B81 (eight-cylinder)	194	398 cu. in.	6.4 to 1	1,010 lb
B81 S.V. (eight-cylinder)	236	398 cu. in.	7.25 to 1	1,010 lb

Power ratings: Some 3,750 rpm, some 4,000 rpm.
Power take-offs, optional drives and automatic and two-speed transfer gearboxes for B-range engines are also produced at Crewe.

MULTI-FUEL ENGINES

ROLLS-ROYCE multi-fuel engines — the K-range — are being developed by the Motor Car Division for the Fighting Vehicles Research and Development Establishment of the War Office.

K-range engines are twin opposed piston two-stroke compression ignition type capable of working on a variety of fuels, including petrol, diesel oil and aviation kerosene. The development is being undertaken to provide a range of multi-fuel engines suitable for replacing the Rolls-Royce B-range of petrol engines in British military vehicles. They have been designed to be interchangeable with the B-range, and are therefore light and compact in relation to other compression ignition engines.

Engines of four, five and six cylinders (K40, K50, K60) are to be built, rated at 160, 200 and 240 bhp respectively.

K 60 multi-fuel engine

RAILWAY TRACTION

THE Railway Traction Department supplies complete power installations for railcars and locomotives. The department is administered from the Shrewsbury factory where the engines, R-R C-range diesels, are built. The transmission systems, including torque converters, are produced at the Motor Car Division Crewe factory.

Horizontal engines

The following horizontal engines are supplied for railcars — C6N, C8N, C6S, C8S, C6T, C8T; and the following vertical engines for locomotives — C4N, C6N, C8N, C4S, C6S, C8S, C6T, C8T.

DFR torque converters are supplied for railcars, and CF, CFR and CO converters for locomotives.

Other rail transmissions are referred to under the heading 'Transmission Systems' in page 5.

CONTINENTAL ENGINES

A LICENCE agreement has recently been made with the Continental Motors Corporation of Muskegon, Michigan, USA. Under this agreement Rolls-Royce will produce Continental piston engines for light aircraft at the Crewe factory. Continental engines are air-cooled horizontally opposed four- and six-cylinder types, ranging in power from 65 hp to 400 hp. Three British light aircraft will shortly be flying with these engines.

ROCKET PROPULSION MOTORS

THE RZ-12 propulsion unit comprising two RZ-2 rocket motors for the de Havilland Blue Streak vehicle has been developed and built by Rolls-Royce. The motor is based on the S-3 series of engines of the Rocketdyne Division of North American Aviation Inc., with whom Rolls-Royce have a licence agreement.

Fuel mixture

The RZ-2 motor operates on a liquid oxygen/kerosene mixture and employs turbo-pumps for feeding the propellants to the combustion chamber. The turbine driving the pumps is energized by gases from a separate gas generator which burns a fuel-rich mixture of the propellants. The combustion chamber is of tubular construction and is regeneratively cooled. The thrust developed by each RZ-2 is 137,000 lb at sea-level. Development is under way to uprate this to 150,000 lb.

Part of a page of *Rolls-Royce News* dated 16 August 1961, showing some of the products manufactured at Pym's Lane. *(Author's collection)*

Royce News recorded. Three examples of the exit of the pre-war intake are Ern Potts, charge hand in the steel stores, P. Cowap, a truck driver with the millwrights and Cliff Thomason, an inspector. They are typical of the many skilled and semi-skilled workers who were retiring during this era but who must remain anonymous. Bob Child, gaffer in the electrical laboratory since it had been set up in 1951, went in the spring of 1966, two years after Stan Smith, a near neighbour in the factory. Death removed Ike Whitehouse in 1966, as it had Jack Edmunds, a fellow foreman, a few years before and as it did Frank Hallows a few years later. Again, these are examples of the silent changes that were taking place in the ranks of middle and lower management.

Before moving on to consider the late 1960s and '70s, it is worth a glance at the achievements of the Smith, Dorey, Grylls, Stafford and Blatchley era. They had developed an economy at Crewe that manufactured the Silver Shadow four-door saloon; the Shadow two-door saloon; the Shadow drophead coupé; the Phantom VI limousine; the Bentley T series four-door saloon; Bentley two-door saloon and the Bentley drophead coupé. In addition there were six types of B range engines and three marques of the K60 engine. Also in production were the Continental C90, 0-200 and 0-300 light aero-engines and the TX 200 six-speed torque converter transmission, along with the products of the investment foundry. These non-car products produced about 40 per cent of the turnover of the car division. Notwithstanding that the Bentley and Rolls-Royce cars were identical, it was not a bad inheritance for those who followed the aforementioned quintet of engineers.

Chapter Five

Floating on the Shadow

The Directors did not anticipate that as many changes as those that occurred on the Silver Shadow would ever happen again.
RR Motors Sale Brochure, 1973

The Silver Shadow and the Bentley T series were introduced to the public in the autumn of 1965. Only two cars had been made off production tools and the first few months of actual manufacture were problematic for planners, fitters and management alike. Again, these cars will not be described here in any detail, except to state that many innovative features had been engineered into the models, making them leaders in their field. The whole project was a major exercise requiring courage and commitment, as many problems, in the fields of technical and production engineering, had to be faced and overcome. The cost was tremendous, yet, in the long run, very worthwhile. Some idea of the stress involved for the senior management can be gauged from LS's comment that he was glad that he would never have to go through it again.

Blatchley's exercise had been to incorporate more than a tinge of modernity into the traditional elegance of a Rolls-Royce, and, judging by the sales figures over the next fifteen years or so, all the design teams must have got it right. Instantaneously, the new cars captured the eye of many that viewed them at the Paris and British motor shows of 1965. By the end of October, firm orders had reached the 3,000 mark – representing a waiting period of eighteen months for the would-be owner. This was typical of the luxury car market in the UK at that time, when senior executives considered the waiting list a sign of a successful company, rather than a symptom of inefficiency. For instance, Bill Lyons of Jaguar favoured a long order book, with its consequential long delivery dates, because it helped in planning production schedules. With such cavalier attitudes it is little wonder that the British share of the car market declined so drastically in these years.

About a year after the introduction of the Silver Shadow, Crewe Rolls-Royce cooperated in the Quality and Reliability Scheme sponsored by the British Production Council. Three working parties endeavoured to produce a quality and reliability programme and posters, reminiscent of wartime slogans, were placed at strategic points around the factory, urging workers to 'Give waste the sack' or 'Support our sales, they support You'. Along with these measures the existing quality system was examined and tightened up. Later in 1967 advertisements for quality engineers in the local paper claimed they would be 'identifying and solving manufacturing problems in the workshop and car assembly areas', and this was when Ian Rimmer arrived at Pym's Lane. By such strategies was the quality of the product improved.

There was an aspect of quality that was peculiar to Rolls-Royce, as Stanley Bull pointed out at his retirement in 1969:

> . . . the Motor Car Division is unique in that every purchaser of a Rolls-Royce car is a different human being with his own likes and dislikes; his own appreciation of the value of money; his own personality; his own domestic and business life; and his own profession. They have one thing in common. They pay thousands of pounds for a motor car and they expect perfection, as indeed they have every right to do. Criticisms and complaints are an everyday fact of life with any commodity. A service department of some sort or other has to deal with the customer. It is the way the service department behaves which reflects the image of the manufacturer. This is the crux of the situation. Because of the price bracket of a Rolls-Royce car, owners frequently complain about things they wouldn't even mention on a lower priced car, even though the component in question might be identical. Some owners make a frightful fuss about things we think are trivial. One big lesson I have learned is not to think too much in engineering terms as nobody is interested in being blinded by science. I try to look at the owner's personality or his wife's or even his Chairman's point of view. Thus one slowly changes from being an engineer to being a psychologist and a diplomat.

It is fair to conclude that the attitude detected beneath the surface of these remarks altered after 1971, when Plastow reorganised the marketing and service departments, and became more professional in the process.

An urgent problem, partly caused by the launch of a model incorporating a great deal of technical change and innovation, was the large number of teething troubles. As a counter to this, John Hollings, appointed director of quality in 1965, was brought from Dounray, along with Don Simmons, with the specific brief of improving quality. No doubt there was a large dose of Fawn's influence in Hollings's coming to Crewe – and it has been said that the waves of farewell from Dounray were more vigorous than the handshakes of welcome from the existing engineering staff at Pym's Lane.

One immediate action of Hollings was to establish a quality department under the control of Simmons as chief inspector, who six years later was moved sideways to make way for Reg Spencer. In the middle 1970s Spencer was promoted again, being given the title of manager of quality control and inspection, reporting to Nelson, with Mick Roberts and Graham Lovatt also being enrolled as managers into Nelson's empire. At the same time Mike Parsons was moved from car repair and given responsibility for quality engineering, replacing Andrew Bee, who had been senior quality engineer since 1967. One of Spencer's first administrative changes was to put Reg Marsden in charge of the standards room, with the brief to computerise the system; the effect was to remove 30,000 extraneous gauges, meaning that for the first time in many years it was possible to locate every gauge in use. The standards room, which had been established in pre-war days, was kept at a constant temperature of 20°C, and on average 1,500 gauges were recalibrated every week by a staff of nine inspectors.

Not all of the quality problems emanated from parts manufactured at Pym's Lane. Tony Flood remembers that one of the first recall situations that he worked on was in November 1969, when a problem with the hydraulic hose that fed the braking and levelling system resulted in a host of complaints. Apparently a union into which the hose was screwed would burst when the pressure mounted during use, releasing a spray of oil that had a very deleterious effect on the bodywork. After much investigation, involving the use of the investment foundry's X-ray apparatus, it was discovered that the union had been drilled off-centre, leaving only a very thin skin of metal at a critical point, which could not be detected by an external examination. Needless to say, a redesign was initiated.

The introduction of the Silver Shadow series exacerbated the perennial problem of the shortage of skilled labour. To counter this, the personnel department, under Ronnie Dyson, ran advertisements for both manual and technical staff for the whole of the spring and summer of 1966. The local employment office also held interviews, in Manchester, and offered council houses as an inducement for suitable recruits to move permanently to Crewe – although this was not as altruistic towards RR as first might appear, for Crewe was, at the time, the site for a Manchester 'overspill' scheme. In addition, a programme of training for mature machinists was initiated in the enlarged apprentices' school. Thus, by various means, including overtime, the ever-present skill shortage was addressed.

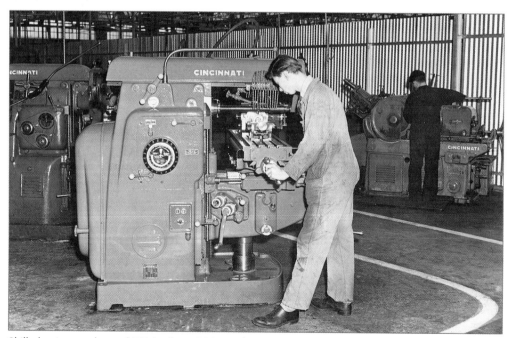

Skill shortages plagued RR in the 1950s and '60s. Here a Cincinnati milling machine can be seen in 250 department workshop (experimental). *(Rolls-Royce Enthusiasts' Club)*

One model that did not tax the Cheshire labour market was the replacement for the Phantom. The assistant chief engineer in the 1960s, J. Macraith Fisher, stated in a special edition of *Queste* that a 9in longer Silver Shadow was proposed to replace the celebrated limousine, only for it to be rejected by Geoffrey Fawn, now the managing director, owing to the car's not having the 'necessary impressiveness and prestige'. To obey these strictures far more interior space was necessary, which in turn brought problems of torsional stiffness. By June 1969 the design team at Pym's Lane had schemed a new Phantom by lengthening a Shadow under-frame by 27in. This car, with the project title 'Beta', was mocked-up in London, but never went into full-scale production.

Another event that generated departmental changes in the middle 1960s was the retirement of Jack Scott from his position as sales director at Conduit Street, and the departure of Stoddart for pastures new. Conduit Street had been the prestigious headquarters for sales from the time of Charles Rolls, with Crewe as the branch office from 1946 onwards. Now the position was reversed, as Plastow rationalised car sales into marketing by bringing all the products made at Pym's Lane under one umbrella, with such men as Harry Bell and Peter Hunt in charge of military engines and cars respectively, and Melvyn Reynolds overseeing publicity.

The late 1960s saw increasing austerity, instigated by the main board directors at Derby. They had colossal worries of their own, and so tended to keep the Motor Division on a tight rein, although another justification was the large deficit that Crewe had generated while the Silver Shadow was tooled up. One example of this financial rigour was the axing of a much needed ventilation scheme, costing less than £2,000, in the experimental department. Other capital schemes were capped as well, even to the extent of not painting the central spares stores in the former County Clothes building. Money was so tight that the payment of sick pay by registered mail was also stopped, meaning that employees who were absent from work owing to illness had to collect their wages from the cashier's office in Pym's Lane. The one exception to the capping of capital projects was the renovation in 1968 of the oil stores on the eastern rim of the site, primarily because a 23-year-old employee had been found dead at the bottom of a sump used for storing swarf. The ensuing inquest concluded that the cause of death was asphyxia induced by fumes.

Shortage of cash did not preclude the planning and development of a mark 2 version of the Silver Shadow, coded SY 270, as well as various other experimental models detailed in Ian Rimmer's definitive work on the firm's experimental projects. These plans for the future should not mask recognition of the continued improvements to the Silver Shadow all through its product life. Two such modifications, within the first two years, were a higher steering ratio and alterations to the sensitivity settings of the brakes.

The decision to fit the GM 400 three-speed gearbox to all models from the summer of 1968 brought an end to car gearbox production at Crewe. Previously this box had only been fitted to left-hand drive cars, with the 'Gryllsaway' gearbox used on right-hand drive models. This latter, a General Motors box with modifications designed by Grylls, had been fitted to 2,289 cars before giving way to the GM 400.

In 1971 the tool-room was relocated to the former gearbox shop, along with experimental machining and 219 department, the latter having until then been based in a Nissen-type hut near to the Chester railway line. Brian Dickson was made superintendent of the enlarged department, named the tool and prototype department, whereas Jimmy Rozell, the erstwhile boss of the tool-room, was left to oversee the machine-tool fitters. Geoff Moreton was transferred, at this time, to the aero shop, a move that eventually led to his promotion as manager of machining in the main shop.

DESIGN BY LEGISLATION

May 1966 saw critical charges levelled at Rolls-Royce cars by Ralph Nader in the USA. He had published a seminal book, entitled *Unsafe at Any Speed*, that censured the motor industry in general, and the American manufacturers in particular, for lack of built-in safety features. Over 100,000 words long, and replete with pertinent observations on current models, Nader's book must be among the few published volumes that radically influenced western society in the latter half of the twentieth century. It is difficult now to understand the lethargy that pervaded the motor industry with regard to designed-in safety, although RR claimed that it had always concentrated on primary safety features. By this was meant incorporation of such things as dual hydro-mechanical braking systems in 1946, and electrical rear window demisting five years later.

Crewe's local paper reported Nader's sensational claim that the doors, bonnet and boot of a Rolls-Royce would burst open in a collision at 20mph. There were other strictures in *Unsafe at Any Speed* that caused the whole of the motor industry to pay far more attention to safety and to exhaust pollution than previously. One repercussion of all this was Jock Knight's appointment as car safety development engineer. Geoff Bastow, who retired in 1972, was also involved, in his latter years, with the development programme that was driven by international safety legislation.

Around this time the United States Congress began to pass stringent safety and environmental measures that had serious implications for Rolls-Royce, as a large percentage of its cars was exported to the USA. In response to US safety legislation, modifications were made when all bodies were built to accord with Federal standards. The picnic tray was removed and padding was added to the seats and the instrument panel, but the most well-known alteration, as far as the general public was concerned, was the collapse on impact of the 'Spirit of Ecstasy' mascot.

Further legislation demanded that the design and development engineers implement around twenty-four modifications to the cars between 1965 and 1970, although not all were directly accountable to the US legislation. Changes in workshop practice can be traced to this environmental concern, for early in 1969 a computer was introduced into the test department to provide a monitoring facility for exhaust gases. The electrical laboratory technicians, led by John Coyle, built the interface that linked the computer to the analyser, and Rolls-Royce claimed that it was the first motor manufacturer in the UK to automate analysis of exhaust gas to check for compliance with American standards.

As so many of the cars were exported, the engineering department had to ensure that each one met the regulations of the receiving country. By 1978 there were well over 300 separate regulations, over 200 tests and nearly 250 forms and reports to be made out. The increasing bureaucracy made life difficult for John Hollings, the chief engineer, as he struggled to reconcile a finite budget with the massive assignment of developing and improving the current models, as well as coping with the demands of the legislators. A report in *Autocar* highlighted the absurdity of the need for two separate tail light assemblies for EEC countries and the USA. In 1973, Sweden became the first country to demand headlight wipers and, although the exports to that country were not great, RR still had to comply. There was a desperate and urgent necessity for the various countries and states to reconcile their demands, as even the colour of lights was not standardised across the continent of Europe. It is a remarkable and important, but often forgotten, feature of the Shadow that it could be adapted to cope with the flood of legislation that was not thought of when it was first designed.

Another 1960s innovation that was an omen for the future was the increased use of computers. Their first mention in the board minutes was in March 1955, with the laconic entry of 'agreement in principle to continue investigations into electronic computers'. Data processing of a primitive form was introduced into the Crewe factory as early as 1942, but progress and development demanded the most recent improved version, and the 1969 computer was the fourth to be installed at Crewe. In the summer of 1969 A.F. Kelley, an executive director of the company, officially opened a new computer block, built on land at the north-western edge of the site that was known to many as 'the ponderosa', from *Bonanza*, the popular television western of the era.

The new computer centre housed an IBM 360 capable of performing routine tasks such as pay-roll calculations, the analysis of stock and material purchases and the compilation of spare parts price lists. As time went on, further tasks were added, such as product assembly breakdowns, scheduling of parts and material for production, control of spares and a variety of engineering problems. As the 1960s moved into the 1970s the computer required a staff of almost forty to service it, among which were six programmers and twenty-eight operators.

INDEPENDENCE

As the 'swinging sixties' ended the will of the people swept Harold Wilson's government away, to be replaced by the Conservative administration led by Edward Heath. The relentless march of time wrought manifold changes of personnel in the seats of power at Pym's Lane. John Hollings replaced Grylls as chief engineer; the post of chief stylist, vacated by Blatchley's early retirement, was, somewhat surprisingly, given to the engineer Fritz Feller, who had, apparently, secretly lobbied for it. His first major achievement was to increase the styling staff by 100 per cent. J.E. Scott, sales director, and mainly resident at Conduit Street, retired in 1967, as did E.P. Armitage, manager of the main machine shop, Nurse Hillier of the ambulance room, Currall, the first boss of assembly trim, and Frank Dodd, chief quality engineer and Royce's former chauffeur. Darby, chief inspector

This was taken shortly before the retirement of Edward Armitage (second from left), for over twenty-five years manager of the main machine shop, *c.* 1966. On his right is Mike Hoffman, while on his left are Bob Banks and Vic Masefield. Armitage also served as chairman of Wistaston Parish Council for many years. Mike Hoffman eventually became CEO of Massey Fergusson. *(Roger Bolton)*

and one of the investigators into the malfunctioning Merlins in 1942, received his retirement gifts in January 1969, only to die four months later. Stanley Bull, service director, and Walter Holmes, sales manager, went at more or less the same time. Joe Williamson, head of the service station, or car repair as it was known, departed, in company with Bill Harvey, the works manager. Fred Stafford went to his grave in 1970, having retired three years earlier, and Freddie Green, the chief of jig and tool, died in the autumn of 1969.

The list of grey-haired men now retiring, who had started to work at Pym's Lane before the Second World War, has many names. It includes the author's father and uncles, all of whom occupied more humble positions than the above persons, yet were proud of their skills. On average, between eighty and a hundred workers a year reached retiring age. Every employee who achieved twenty-five years with the firm was invited to a celebration dinner, where a commemorative book was presented – replaced after a few years by a Flying Lady ashtray. As these proved to be more desirable the works committee made a request, in 1980, that all long-serving employees who had received a book should be given an ashtray retrospectively. The request was refused, perhaps because the management guessed that many would soon end up on the thriving second-hand market of RR memorabilia. One man who did receive a silver Flying Lady, having purchased a fleet of eight Silver Shadows, was a Hong Kong hotel owner. Unfortunately he was not really satisfied, as he had light-heartedly requested a discount. Incidentally this man made many purchases, including eight Shadows in 1970, another eight in 1976, a similar number of Spirits in 1987, and nine in 1993.

Another on the list of retirees was O.G. Valentine, the chief fire officer, who had joined RR in 1941 as a counter-measure to any further wartime bombing. When he retired in 1969 it was decided to amalgamate the fire service with the works policemen. For some time management had been concerned with the loss of materials and equipment through petty theft, consequently, James Farmer, a former policeman and the firm's driving instructor, was given overall control of the new security department, meaning that the firemen and policemen were retrained and designated security officers. Farmer, by walking around the firm's car park in Pym's Lane and externally examining the workers' cars, achieved one early success in his new job. From this examination he identified six cars with RR fittings and parts, meaning that, after a court appearance and a fine, six employees were discharged from the factory. He was similarly successful in his fire prevention duties, for when he took over an average of forty-five fires occurred at Pym's Lane annually, mainly caused by cigarette ends, whereas by 1978 this had been reduced to three.

Retirement of two members of the machine-tool maintenance department, Jack Caine and Joe Jordan, c. 1959. A clock was a frequent retirement gift despite its being a depreciating asset for the recipient. Others in the picture are Harold Hassall, Jack Dickson, Reuben Gibbons, Ken Brown and, on the extreme right, the author. (Author's collection)

Some of the staff of the car repair department marking the retirement of Charlie Gibbs in 1976. Front row, left to right: Austin Whitehead, Jim Ellrington, Bill Batterbee, Wally Hind, Bernard Preston, Charlie Gibbs, Arthur Ellam, Brian Lea, Tom Blainey, Roy Basford, Norman Vickerman, unidentified and Peter Griffith. *(Bernard Preston)*

The major figure to emerge from the management changes at the end of the 1960s was David Plastow. In some ways he was not typical material for a Rolls-Royce higher management post, having neither graduated from university nor served the company from his early years. He was promoted to sales manager in 1960, a couple of years after joining Rolls-Royce. Seven years later he was promoted again, this time to marketing director. From then on he dominated the hierarchy of the Motor Division, or Rolls-Royce Motors as it became in March 1971. It could be argued that Plastow, a manager to his finger-tips, was one of the most significant figures ever to work at Pym's Lane, as an article in *Town and Country Magazine* suggested, using phrases like 'a master of delegation', 'fine instinct for removing deadwood', 'increased profitability under his management'. The *Guardian* certainly thought Plastow's vision and energy were succeeding at Crewe, for that newspaper named him Young Businessman of the Year in 1976.

He was also largely responsible for the decline of the traditional RR management structure, where managers were always promoted from within. Whether this was good in the long term for Rolls-Royce Motors depends upon one's point of view. While Plastow remained close to Crewe, he exercised a shrewd and diligent control. When others, with less feel for the traditions of RR and of engineering, were at the helm, the ship was sometimes steered by charts other than those used by Sir Henry.

The debacle of 1971, when Rolls-Royce Ltd went into receivership, could have daunted a lesser man than Plastow. Fawn had only just been recalled to Derby, where he displayed an attitude that earned him a red card from the chairman Sir Kenneth Keith. The Conservative government of Edward Heath had appointed Keith as chief at Derby, so he was an all-powerful newcomer, a position not easily comprehended by the erstwhile boss at Crewe. Whereas it might be churlish to state that faint cheers could be heard from various offices and desks at Pym's Lane when it was learned of Fawn's fate, it would be none the less true. It is interesting to speculate on the consequences for the Car Division had Fawn been at Crewe in February 1971. Would he have been as successful in guiding and motivating the Car Division as was Plastow? Thankfully, historians do not deal with 'ifs'.

Plastow skilfully led the division through the fenestra of flotation, always having a vision of what independence could bring; not an easy task, for the car side of the business had often relied upon Derby to assist in difficult times. Excepting a short period when he had the wise counsel and experience of LS to assist him, Plastow was the lone senior figure. In addition to Wedgwood Benn's hovering threat to nationalise the concern at the first opportunity, he had to contend with Lucas Girling's notorious unreliability in providing parts, prolonged strikes at Mulliner Park Ward and statutory price controls. To further complicate matters, the oil crisis of the early 1970s cast a glowering shadow over the long-term future of petrol-

Retirement in 1976 of Neville Sadler, a pre-war employee (see pages 9–10) and Jack Wrighton (technical services), who moved to Crewe from Hythe Road in the 1950s. Left to right: George Telford, Wendy Fry, Jack Wrighton, Neville Sadler, Vince McDonagh, and Ian Nelson. *(Neville Sadler)*

thirsty cars. Consequently the first years of the new leader at Pym's Lane were fraught with a multitude of problems.

If the information in *Who's Who* is studied, it will be seen that Plastow had a far greater spread of interests than LS, who was a fine engineer in the Rolls-Royce management tradition, deeply concerned with car manufacturing and mechanical engineering. Although he was always considered aloof, it was not unknown for Llewellyn-Smith to reward office boys or mail girls with a sweet, if the inner door to his office was open, when they delivered the information he was waiting for. Plastow had the inclination to be involved in other than commercial matters and, to give but two examples, he served as Patron to the Samaritans and President of Crewe Alexandra Football Club. In contrast to the shy and private LS he was far more rounded and approachable than 'Doc' Smith ever was, but that is not to gainsay LS's extensive engineering expertise.

It is well known that the development of the giant RB211 engine at Derby plunged Rolls-Royce into the anguish of receivership, and it was fortunate for Plastow, indeed for all of the directors and workforce at Crewe, that it did not

Production staff assembled in 1979 for the retirement of Ron Bingsley, one of the early employees of RR Crewe, having first served an apprenticeship in the LMS workshops. Ron is holding the tankard. Others the group are Jack Waring, Stuart Wright, Peter Cable, Frank Crawford, Paul Dyer and George Cornes. B Ward, another early employee, is next to Ron in the front row. The lady in the centre is Diane Dyer. Jo Moore, a senior production engineer, is on the right of the picture, wearing a sweater. *(Diane Dyer)*

occur a few years earlier. By 1971 the Silver Shadow series was generating much-needed revenue for the Car Division, gilding flotation with a golden sheen. Peter Pugh records, in *The Magic of a Name*, that return on capital was over 10 per cent, a yield far ahead of most other British car builders, affording Plastow the luxury of being able to plan for the future without having to wrestle with massive losses.

The news of the bankruptcy was announced to the workforce at Pym's Lane over the company's public address system, meaning that at certain places in the factory an interpreter was needed to pass on the bad news. Among those present that day was Tony Flood, who, over thirty years later, recalled the occasion quite clearly:

> I well remember arriving for work at just after 7.30 a.m. on Thursday 4 February in readiness for the start of the day's work at 7.55 a.m. For the two or three days previous the whole of the Crewe site was awash with rumours of the serious problems at Derby with the RB211 engine that was to power the Lockheed Tristar airbus; in fact rumours had been circulating since the late months of 1970. Everybody on site on 4 February knew something was about to happen and at approximately 9.30 a.m. all directors had been summoned to the board room and told the bad news that bankruptcy of the Company had been announced. Relevant managers were summoned and told to inform all staff that Rolls-Royce Ltd was in receivership. Employees on receiving the news were physically 'shell-shocked' and some could not take in the news, finding it impossible to accept what had happened. Later that day David Plastow spoke to all employees over the Company inter-com system. He seemed emotional but composed during his speech and ended by saying he sincerely hoped the receiver appointed would look favourably on the Car Division. Employees stood silently during this speech, one could hear a pin drop. It lasted about ten minutes, but seemed a lot longer. After he finished every one tried to return to their relevant jobs and carry on as normal although still in a daze. On returning to mine I well remember one comedian saying, 'Well I feel we will always sell our cars but I'm not sure whether Lockheed will be able to sell their gliders'. Somehow humour always follows adversity!

It was said by others that Plastow's voice seemed to show evidence of strain and emotion; all agree that he also offered more than a sprig of hope that the car business would continue. If one sign of a good leader is to maintain morale, then Plastow succeeded that Thursday morning.

Some of the effects of administration spawned moments of high farce. In part two of Peter Pugh's previously cited work it is recorded that Tom Neville had to sell scrap metal to a local dealer to raise sufficient cash to feed the apprentices. At the same time the Water Board threatened to cut off the supply to the factory because of an unpaid bill of £8,000, even sending a nine-man team with pneumatic drills, hammers and road signs. Fortunately matters were resolved before the pipes were capped. Bankruptcy also brought an end to *Rolls-Royce News*, the company's in-house newspaper. Published by Derby RR at a price of 2 or 3 old pence, it contained very little about Pym's Lane. Four years passed before Crewe began producing its own newspaper in the spring of 1975, initially called *RR Motors Magazine*, and re-titled *Voice* after twelve issues.

Administration also brought an outburst of frenetic activity from interested, if impotent, persons. At a public meeting in the Lyceum Theatre on 7 March 1971 Crewe's MP, Sydney Scholefield Allen, called for the firm to be nationalised. Sir

A few cuttings from the local paper detailing some of the events that affected the lives of RR employees

Grant Ferris, the member for Nantwich, initiated moves to get an all-party group of MPs to visit Crewe RR on a fact-finding mission. He was involved because about 2,000 of the employees at Pym's Lane lived in Nantwich. Regarding this visit, Frank Culley stated that he was appalled at the lack of detailed knowledge among MPs, for few of them knew that almost every major fire brigade in Britain depended on Crewe RR for engines and spares.

It was only when Rupert Nicholson, the Receiver, announced that a new company, Rolls-Royce Motors Ltd, would be formed, that the business ceased to be the lead story in the local paper. The chairman of the new company, for the first few months, was the 62-year-old Llewellyn-Smith, who was still living at Barthomley, about 5 miles from the factory – unlike his successor Ian Fraser, who never lived anywhere near the town of Crewe. Other directors were John Craig, Dick Garner, Ian Nelson, John Hollings and G. Lewis. Tom Neville, the financial director and a member on the main board, had arrived at Crewe from Derby in 1962 as chief accountant, and Craig, transferred from London in 1967, was responsible for marketing. There is an interesting account of Plastow's management strategy in *How to Manage*, published in 1982.

When RR Motors was offered to the public in 1973, around two hundred employees bought shares in the new company, despite Wedgwood Benn's threat that it would be nationalised with no compensation. Les Gallimore, chairman of the shop stewards, summed up the workers' attitude to Mr Benn when he used a phrase containing (among others) the words 'mouth' and 'shut'. Surprisingly, Plastow also uttered a note of caution, in an article summarised in the local paper in which he was reported as advising workers not to invest in a company they worked for, because, if everything went pear-shaped, the worker would only lose his wages.

One positive result of the Receiver's negotiations was that RR Motors purchased the factory site in Pym's Lane and the sports ground in Minshull New Road when contracts were exchanged with the government for the freehold for £2.5 million, payable by instalments. One million pounds was due when the contracts were exchanged, another £750,000 in March 1974, and the remaining £750,000 one year after that. Until 1973 RR had been paying rent of £91,000 a year. The sale brochure pertaining to the flotation also recorded that the directors had authorised £1.75 million for re-equipping the factory with computer-controlled machines, an expenditure that was to be repeated for a number of years. Another paragraph stated that no future model would contain as many changes as had the Silver Shadow, a comment charged with as much significance for the past as for the future.

PRODUCTION PROBLEMS

Car building and other production went on apace, despite the negotiations in the financial world. Three major factors that bedevilled the production targets were labour relations, especially in the trim and body-build department, shortages and scarcity of labour. The first of these is the subject of a separate section, so suffice it to say that often, in the joint works committee meeting, management would accuse the union representatives of not doing enough to control their members.

This raised a counter-claim that the cause of failure to meet build targets was the continued shortage of parts, and that was the fault of management. That there was a consistent chronic shortage of certain parts is beyond argument. In February 1969 the shortage was, on average, sixteen items per car. A few years later the problem still persisted in such proportions that George Fenn and Ian Nelson, two senior executives, devoted a considerable amount of their time to analysing the problem, meeting each day to deal with immediate shortages. By the autumn of 1973 the situation was improving to the extent that only 150 minutes of manpower per car were devoted to rectifying shortages, rather than the twenty-seven hours it had taken previously.

The stewards and the convenor on the works committee were concerned that management's increased production target, of 10 per cent a year, might exacerbate the shortage problem. Their reasoning was that if there were shortages building sixty cars a week what would sixty-six occasion? Management's partial answer was new and more efficient machine-tools and an enlarged workforce. Roy Jackson, responsible for production machining, reported in the autumn of 1973 that three new Hepworth automatic capstan lathes, three B and S bar autos and one vibratory finishing machine had recently been installed, while two Wickman automatic lathes and four bar automatics were on order.

Reorganisation of space was another method of improving the flow of parts from production to assembly. By the time of the formation of RR Motors the production and plant engineers had taken over all the available floor space released by the departure of County Clothes and Kelvinator. Extra floor space was urgently needed.

After the successful flotation the board had the power to build new premises without referring all requests to either Derby or the Receiver for approval. The extra space could be built when capital was available. The precursor for any new building was the removal of Hill 60, the mound of clay left from the wartime building, as this covered the only land available for factory expansion. Fortunately the town council needed soil to cover the refuse tip that was rapidly filling the valley of the Leighton Brook on the north side of Pym's Lane. A deal was done between the contractor and the council, enabling the hill to be moved in the early months of 1974. Its removal also meant the end of the helicopter-landing site, as this was where they touched down. From 1974 onwards those who wished to be ferried to Pym's Lane by helicopter had to make do with the sports field, about half a mile away in Minshull New Road. Martin Bourne, of the styling office, acted as helicopter movements officer.

Increasing the workforce was not as easily accomplished as ordering new machines or clearing a site. The personnel department, now in the hands of Brian Dorey (Ray's son), ran a long series of job advertisements in the local paper. There was such a shortage of labour in the south Cheshire region that these adverts were just part of four and a half pages of broadsheet replete with similar appeals. During 1974, 900 employees were recruited, making a net gain of 300 after retirements and natural wastage had taken their toll. Most of the vacancies were to fill the enduring gaps in the ranks of the body line workers. An agreement had been negotiated with the National Union of Vehicle Builders in 1971, to allow fitters to do the work of coach-builders, and was uneasily adhered to for most of the decade, only to capsize on the rock of union intransigence in 1979, when the accord became discord. The stewards countered with the argument that if RR paid the skilled body workers the rate current in the Midlands, personnel would not leave and the problem would not arise.

As a panacea to meet skill shortage, the craft apprentice intake was increased by 50 per cent in two years, until it reached its practical limit of about ninety places. Around 900 applications were received annually for training places, only for many to be rejected for lack of basic educational attainment, especially in mathematics. It was also in the middle 1970s that Pym's Lane indentured its first female for craft training, Annette Jones, a local teenage girl, who later attended a reception at Downing Street to mark International Women's Year. About a year after this she had to attend the local hospital when she lost part of a finger while operating a vertical spindle woodworking machine.

The increase in training did not alleviate the pressing need for skilled and semi-skilled body workers, as numbers of job vacancies remained high throughout the 1970s. Local recruiting was a spasmodic event, so in ever-increasing circles other geographical areas were covered, until Scotland was being tapped. The impediment to attracting workers from long distances was the perennial lack of affordable rented accommodation, despite an improvement from the licence-wracked days of the immediate postwar era. Private housing was available for those with a deposit and mortgage status. Unfortunately, about 10 per cent of prospective employees wanted local authority housing, and well into the 1970s the town council minutes record requests from the personnel department for a quota of houses. Just as often the request was turned down, or an insignificant number offered.

One propitious event for council tenants was the replacement by link-houses of the despised wartime flats at Totty's Hall, and the area was renamed Leighton Park to remove the stigma generated by its former name. Good news, it might seem, for all on the waiting list, including workers at RR. Not so, as the hapless town planners had omitted to provide a means of access to the rear of some of the houses. A few tenants had to countenance the window cleaner carrying his ladders through their homes, and one keen gardener with a long-suffering wife even barrowed topsoil through his dwelling in order to make his rear garden grow.

That the car plant executives did not take umbrage at the council's refusal to grant them a steady supply of houses is signalled by the action they took in March 1975. For around fifteen years Crewe Municipal Borough (by 1975 Crewe and Nantwich Borough) had operated as the mayoral limousine a Silver Wraith that had, unfortunately, broken down a couple of times when on civic duties. A special arrangement, inspired by a letter to the borough's chief executive from Craig, the marketing director, led to a Phantom VI replacing the Silver Wraith. This was termed 'a magnanimous and unique offer' by the grateful council. The terms were kept private, but it was certainly less than the annual estimate of £1,600 that the Wraith was costing.

In discussing the need for factory expansion, it must be emphasised that cars were not the only items manufactured at Pym's Lane. In the 1970s K range engines were still in production, as were the B range. One interesting development of the B range engine was the substitution of liquefied petroleum gas for petrol as a fuel. Light aircraft engines, nozzle guide vanes for at least five different types of aero-engines, heads for golf clubs, sub-contract work for Alvis, Massey Ferguson and Linotype were just some of the components in the flow of work planned by the production department. Neither did either management or local unions carry all the responsibility for the many shortages that plagued the production line, as over 1,000 items a week were delivered from outside suppliers. An annual total of 71,000 items was purchased from about 4,000 suppliers, consequently RR was often at the mercy of other firms, who frequently let it down.

LABOUR RELATIONS

The years following the introduction of the Silver Shadow should have been a period of harmonious working throughout the factory, in order to maximise production; instead they were one of niggling labour relations. A cost-of-living bonus, granted at Derby, was delayed at Crewe through management indecision. As Fawn had been sent to Crewe to introduce savings, perhaps this was down to him. Critical feelings were also aired in letters to the local paper, one claiming that the supervisory staff would not allow food to be eaten during the mid-morning unofficial break. Again, perhaps the fear of Fawn produced a clamp-down on unauthorised practices, as he was apt to appear in any department at any time. Later in the year the wage freeze introduced by Harold Wilson's Labour government was responsible for further unrest. Consequently, the production target of forty cars a week by December 1966 was not achieved until the summer of 1968.

In the middle 1960s there was also a meeting between management and unions to discuss the employment of coloured persons. Crewe had not been a centre for large-scale inward migration of West Indians or Asians, as had others of the Midland car towns. Consequently, there was only a small pool of black workers, most of whom found employment in the railway works or the motive power sheds. At this meeting, in August 1964, senior management emphatically denied that it was operating a colour bar, the personnel department claiming that coloured applicants lacked the skills necessary to fill the vacancies. Despite the vehemence of the denial it was a rather weak excuse that would certainly not be tolerated today. Another practice, symptomatic of an attitude held by some in the personnel department, was the circumvention of the regulations of the 1944 Act compelling a firm to have 3 per cent of its pay-roll as registered disabled persons. It was not unknown for an existing employee with a hernia to be asked to register as disabled in order for the firm to reach the required percentage, a practice against the spirit of the legislation.

Indicative of the deteriorating labour relations in the 1960s was the succession of convenors elected to represent the many trades unions at Pym's Lane. Charlie Elson had lost the position when he became of Mayor of Crewe in 1959. Elson, despite his militancy, was now part of the local establishment, and gone were the days when the management received a warning from Whitehall about his political leanings. He was unjustly thrown out of the local Labour Party in the 1980s, because he ignored a collective decision of the Labour group. Although he was by now an old man, his

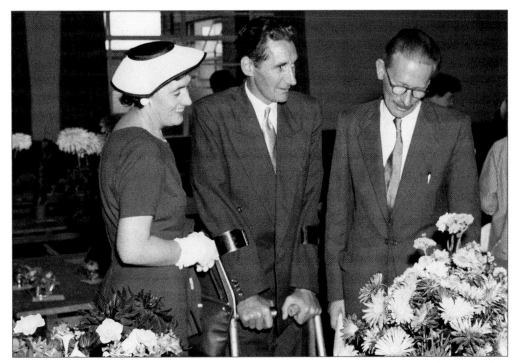

Charlie Elson and his wife Eileen. For nearly twenty years Elson, formerly a tool-room miller, was the works convenor. His wife worked in experimental stores. The man on arm crutches in the centre is Roland Bridges, an experimental test driver, who was just recovering from a very serious road accident while driving along King Street, Middlewich. *(Author's collection)*

views remained well to the left of his erstwhile council colleagues, so much so that the local Methodist minister, who had been Elson's chaplain during his second mayoral year, arranged for 'The Red Flag' to be played at his funeral in 2001. It was during Elson's first tenure as Mayor that the town began to use a 1958 Silver Wraith, registration CMB 1, as the Corporation's limousine.

The judgement on Elson's long tenure of the convenor's office must be that he served the men well and sensibly. He occupied the post for nearly two decades, including the difficult wartime years, and led, rather than followed, the men he represented. In accord with his character, he did not accept his replacement with good grace, for he felt that Ernie Roberts, a fitter from the pre-war intake, had usurped him. There is some evidence that Elson had lost the confidence of some of the more militant newcomers in the workforce, but what cannot be denied is that the next twenty years brought more industrial strife than had the previous twenty. One year after the election of Roberts a younger man took over, only to resign suddenly after a couple of years.

There was an obvious rift between the full-time union officials and the workers at Pym's Lane, that deepened as the 1960s progressed. Previously, improvements in pay and working conditions had been negotiated nationally, and action only affected the local scene when the national officials of the Confederation of Shipbuilding and Engineering Unions called for token strikes to support wage claims. During the

1960s the context of the engineering industry was rapidly changing, owing to many factors. One of these, the microchip, was the reason for Harold Wilson's famous phrase in which he called for amended attitudes that must be forged in the 'white heat of technological change'. It was at this time that the Draughtsmen's Union changed its name to the Draughtsmen and Allied Technicians Union, to cater for the increase in technicians generated by that technological change. To alter working practices and expectations was not so easy as to rename a trade association.

With the active cooperation of the unions, it had been decided at senior management level to introduce a simplified wage scale, and management, under Fawn, organised working parties to explain the scheme to groups of manual workers. Unfortunately unofficial leaders among the workers sought to dislocate these efforts wherever possible, even reaching the columns of the local paper, where it was reported that notices were appearing in the factory advising workers not to cooperate.

In May 1969 some of the stewards called for an unofficial strike against the government's 'In Place of Strife' Bill. This was ignored by the rest of the workers – unlike an incident two months later, in which fifty men from the paint-shop downed tools in support of a colleague suspended for horseplay. The convenor's snarled response to this unofficial action was that it was 'time they grew up', and such incidents illustrate the gap between factory union representatives and the organisers of lightning strikes. Undoubtedly the 1960s developed a greater tinge of militancy, meaning that Billy Taylor, the incumbent of the convenor's office, earned his salary. From anecdotal evidence it would seem that a factor in the increased militancy was the enlargement of the workforce, following the success of the Silver Shadow in the autumn of 1965. This was when a few freshly hired workers emerged as militant stewards to muddy the employment pool at Pym's Lane.

When the record of the various convenors is examined it can be confidently claimed that Rolls-Royce was saved from more serious stoppages. Michael Edwardes suggests in his book *Back From the Brink* that British Leyland was consistently badly served by a convenor capable of fomenting trouble and manipulating opinions, who constantly misled and misinformed the workers at Longbridge. The convenors at Crewe RR constantly sought common sense solutions, rather than stir up trouble.

Not all of the unrest can be laid at the door of either management or the unions, as the 1960s were a period of wage restraint, imposed by a Labour government that was running into difficulties in maintaining the parity of the pound. Fred Catherwood, the Director-General of the National Development Council in the 1960s and '70s, claimed that the growth of shop floor power had a negative influence on the effectiveness of the devaluation of the pound in 1967. Although never assuming the proportions that were manifest in other car plants, it has to be admitted that wildcat strikes were present at Pym's Lane during these years. Some of the stoppages were a technique whereby skilled craftsmen sought to recover wage differentials that were withering, following uniform pay awards.

Early in 1969 the clerks and administrative workers were in dispute over a salary claim, leading to an overtime ban and a threat to work to rule. At the same time the national union officials called for a work to rule and overtime ban, to express sympathy with workers who were being made redundant at other RR plants. All of the manual workers, and the majority of the white-collar salaried staff, reluctantly obeyed the request.

The next month, following a management refusal to increase a bonus offer, the so-called non-productive skilled workers stopped work, ignoring the pleas of Bill Taylor and Ron Bartlett, respectively convenor and chief shop steward, to resume. A ballot confirmed the strike mandate by a small majority, and Taylor had to report deadlock with the management. At the same time local RR workers, without national union approval, called off the sympathy action, only to be met with a management refusal to sanction a return to overtime, as a reprisal for introducing the ban. It is, perhaps, ironic that Fawn's 1969 new year address to the town, via the *Crewe Chronicle*, contained the hope that cooperation between management and staff would be on the same excellent level as had been enjoyed in 1968. The works committee minutes tell a different tale.

Staff status did not preclude militancy, for early in 1970 the draughtsmen downed pencils in protest at the slow pace of their wage negotiations. This took the form of a short meeting and demonstration on the lawn fronting the detail drawing office, before they were persuaded to return to work by the canny and straight-talking Joe Tapley, a union representative and an acknowledged self-taught expert on the minutiae of the staff pension scheme.

A few weeks earlier Billy Taylor was involved in trying to solve the details of a bonus dispute in the transmission department, where over fifty men had walked off the job. Almost at the same moment the maintenance electricians were out for a short time. Part of the reason why factory union officials were against wildcat strikes was that they undermined their authority, so perhaps Mr Taylor was not sorry to hand over the keys to his office in February 1970, when Harold Jones took over as convenor – the sixth man to hold the position since Charlie Elson's ejection ten years previously.

This type of industrial action was typical of the 1960s and '70s in the motor car industry. Part of the trouble, as has already been noted, was the prolonged wage restraint of the Wilson government, which had been introduced with the tacit approval of the trades unions in 1965. It was renewed the following year when Denis Healey, the Chancellor, cobbled together a package of measures in a fruitless attempt to save the pound. After devaluation, in the autumn of 1967, there was another period when the unions were promised 'jam tomorrow', leading to further unofficial action and increased militancy. Compared to BL with its thirty-four plants and around 200,000 workers and 200 militant stewards, Pym's Lane was a peaceful haven.

That having been said, there were certain departments of the factory where trouble was more likely to break out at any time. One of these was the paint-shop, where stoppages occurred with monotonous regularity. In April 1970 the supervisor there posted a notice complaining that malicious damage was being caused to cars proceeding down the line. Management suggested that such damage was a ploy to create overtime, so, predictably, the response was a lightning strike.

Three months later there was a dispute in the machine shop over the dismissal of a steward who had acted beyond his authority. It all centred on a rate-fixing valuation, and when the convenor and the chairman of the works committee tried to adjudicate they were accused of being in collusion with management, because they would not sanction an all-out strike. The negotiating skills of the AEU district officials were required before the strife could be resolved.

Even the cataclysmic event of February 1971 did not stop the agitation for higher wages. In May of that year the foremen were demanding a wage increase to bring them into line with other motor manufacturers, claiming that senior foremen at Austin Morris were on £2,700 a year, and at Vauxhall on £2,600, whereas at Crewe Rolls-Royce they were only being paid £1,700. In the mid-1970s the monthly staff representatives started negotiations for overtime payments, as traditionally they received a set salary. It took about eighteen months of hard bargaining to successfully conclude an agreement. One of the chief and most able negotiators on the staff side was the previously mentioned Irishman, Joe Tapley, a senior designer, who was never wrong-footed by any management negotiating team.

Over the next nine years stoppages at Pym's Lane that were serious enough to reach the columns of the local paper totalled up to twenty-seven – not many, perhaps, when compared with the Midland car plants, but quite dramatic when placed against the absence of action in the 1950s.

In a positive effort to improve industrial relations, the management endeavoured to involve workers in the outer fringes of car production when Ronnie Dyson, the personnel manager, introduced the employees' suggestion scheme in 1966. The awards ranged from £1 to £500, and in April R. Bartlett, of the body-spraying department, was the first Crewe employee to be rewarded under the scheme, when he won £50; the highest award in the first two years, £150, was gained by Derek Precious, an auto electrician. By 1989 the scheme, renamed 'Inspirations', was paying out over £45,000. That year two employees, Mike Warner and Andy Billington, shared £5,000 for a joint suggestion. When all the winning ideas were incorporated into production, the firm gained by saving around £150,000 per annum.

A conference was arranged for May 1972, when a proposal to introduce a single grade for all skilled workers was discussed by the works committee. The first stirrings of this proposal can be traced to August 1967, when Ian Nelson engaged P&A Consultants to ascertain the feasibility of job grading. Further meetings generated enough material to construct serious proposals for consideration by the works committee, although the discussions dragged on for a considerable time. Eventually a scheme was worked out and the graduated rates for a variety of skills were replaced by a single rate, supplemented with a bonus.

Feelings of 'them and us' were always widely manifest at Pym's Lane, with 'them' being the staff and 'us' being the workers on hourly pay, and this was a potent factor in many of the discussions during the period of increased militancy. One example, in 1976, was the difference in treatment over unpunctuality, when blue-collar workers lost money, yet staff did not. All through the 1970s the shop stewards used the differences in working conditions between themselves and the

Winners of the 'Inspirations' suggestions scheme in March 1988 grouped around the staircase of the main offices. The stairs lead up to the board room and senior executives' offices. Ken Lea, director of manufacturing, is shaking hands with Bill Consterdine of the tool and prototype department. Others pictured are Bernard Wharton, Miles Colclough, Dave Proudlove, Clive Barnett, Dave Simcock and Peter Wood. *(W. Consterdine)*

staff as a lever to improve their own circumstances. In an effort to ameliorate the atmosphere Plastow introduced monthly briefings and discussions by line managers, when production would be shut down for about an hour. Another similar device was a weekend away at a resort, such as Llandudno, for senior union representatives and section leaders, organised by Alisdair MacKenzie of the industrial relations department. Any tool that could improve the bond between management and unions was important, for Plastow reported in 1980 that disputes were costing around £5 million.

That workers did not always welcome new technology was shown in 1975, when a more efficient machine was installed in the main machine shop, raising the complaint that there was already insufficient work in the department affected. Rennie Steele, of the Precision Components Division, faced down similar criticism with the observation that the alternative to a new machine was a workshop full of milling machines. Components formerly made at Pym's Lane, such as exhaust systems, could be purchased more cheaply from Germany, much to the unions' chagrin. To report this is not to criticise the stewards, for their task was to watch out for their members' jobs. They were not Luddites, as industrial action was never organised against new production methods, although there was a determination that the hourly paid employees would share in any savings.

In the middle 1970s, when some hourly paid workers were granted works staff status, it was noted that, within two years the works staff absentee rate was running at 13 per cent, compared with 7 per cent for other manual workers and 5 per cent for weekly staff. This had even deeper implications for the company's coffers than is first apparent, because staff status brought paid sick leave. Critical comments were made at a works committee meeting in 1977 that a minority of the 900 manual staff were abusing the system, because it was running at four times the estimated cost. When all the mitigating factors are considered, such as the advancing age of many of the manual staff, and the physical demands of a blue-collar job, as compared to that of an office worker, there still remains the suspicion that a considerable amount of malingering was engineered by a few.

It was around this time that a measure leading to free cigarettes was organised. To counter the unsanctioned private enterprise shops that were located in personal lockers around the factory, the management introduced cigarette vending machines at strategic points. Not many hours passed before some enterprising centre lathe turners, on night shift, manufactured blank 'coins' that operated the machines, releasing packets of twenty cigarettes into grateful hands. Needless to say, the flow soon dried up.

For those that worked on the shop floor there was always the feeling already described as 'them and us'. The differing canteens, working hours, 'clocking' practices, and even the style of address on the clock card, were tokens of a class attitude. Mr or Mrs always preceded the names of the staff, whereas hourly paid workers simply had their surname, job title and clock number. This might not appear to be a great difference, but it was indicative of a mind-set and was a source of grievance, at least as far as the hourly paid employees were concerned.

The dilapidated condition of the toilet blocks was a matter of perennial concern for the works committee, and as these lavatories were of pre-war vintage the complaints were quite justified. Unfortunately there never seemed to be money available for a root and branch solution. For instance, the excuse offered in March 1980 was that a series of national two-day strikes by the engineering unions in the previous year had affected the financial position, as had the drop in sales in anticipation of a model change.

Disputes over job times also generated friction between management and workers. As a badly timed job could lose money for the company, or cut the bonus of the employee, there were many opportunities for argument. A typical case happened in the summer of 1981, when a conflict occurred between a rate-fixer and a coach trimmer over the method of performing a particular task. A more efficient way was suggested by the work-study engineer, which reduced the time taken from sixteen minutes to eleven minutes, only for the operator to reject it. Eventually, the study was curtailed when the engineer claimed that the coach trimmer 'lacked effort'.

It could be imagined that the three-monthly joint meetings between management and unions were extended sessions of corrosive conflicts. A glance at the agenda for August 1982 would counter such thoughts. This meeting, the last attended by Jim Farmer, discussed drinking fountains, pedestrian gates, painting, washing facilities, fork-lift truck training, asbestos, eye protection, noise levels, a report from the accident committee, fumes, safety policy, heating and the old favourite, toilets. At this time the factory was about to commence a three-day week, so great was the drop in demand for the company's products, and further redundancies were forecast. Despite this, over £2,000 was donated to the South Atlantic Fund via a collection organised by the works committee, the money going to support the troops in the Falkland War.

NEW MODELS

The years immediately following flotation were ones of encouragement, if the sales figure alone is used. From around 2,300 cars, the build increased by 26 per cent in three years, despite the chronic shortages and labour troubles that bedevilled industry in the 1970s. Two general elections in 1974 yielded an inconclusive verdict, leading to a period of political instability, combined with raging inflation that was caused in part by the hike in oil prices. Perhaps the secret of the increased production figures at Pym's Lane had something to do with a measure introduced in April 1973, when it was decided to canvass the younger members of the female staff for 'Pin Up Girl' of the month. Each proud winner had her image displayed on the factory's bulletin boards, and the first lady chosen was Pamela Anderson of the mail office. What a novel way to encourage the troops!

At Pym's Lane a new car was ready to be introduced to the public, almost before the Receiver had had a chance to study the figures. This was the 'Gamma' project, or Corniche, as it was called on introduction to the public. According to Ian Rimmer, it was the end result of a development project that had begun in 1970, when it was desired to increase the performance of the two-door version of the Silver Shadow. This was achieved by altering the valve timing, increasing the bore of the exhaust and fitting a superior air cleaner, in addition to redesigning the dashboard and seats. To do full justice to its rarefied name, the French Riviera was chosen to show it off, obviously a more suitable spot than Crewe in the dismal March days of Heath's blighted administration. There was a jaundiced comment about the town in *Barons*, one of America's leading financial journals, which stated that Crewe was a grimy town with a nondescript factory (Pym's Lane) not far from shunting diesels. No doubt this resonated with some, but not with the majority of the town's people.

In October 1973, after over a year of road trials, the local paper broke with tradition and printed the news that an experimental car was being tested in the locality, and also in France. Never before had the *Chronicle* hinted that a new car was in the offing, even if every editor worth his salt must have known when a new model was being developed. Loyalty to the factory meant that the secret was kept until revealed by the firm. The paper now stated that reports had been coming in for ten months of an experimental car that would cost over £20,000. The source must have been reliable as it quoted the design name 'Delta'.

The second of the six experimental Delta models went to the MIRA testing ground, to ascertain that all safety standards for cars involved in crashes had been met. By this date the standards demanded from the USA were quite rigorous, and crash testing, though expensive, was the only way, at that time, to prove that a model complied. A visit to the MIRA testing complex in the West Midlands was an interesting, even mildly exciting, experience and it was not unknown for some of the participants to privately film the wrecking process. They also received mementoes of the visits that still decorate not a few shelves in homes around Crewe and Nantwich.

Without argument, the most controversial design element of the Delta project was the choice of stylist. For the first time the in-house team of stylists, including Bill Allen and Martin Bourne, was passed over in favour of Pininfarina. Regardless of the expertise and esteem of the Italian designer, this has to be recognised as a slight to the team sitting at home. Bill Allen, one of nature's gentlemen, although approaching retirement, was still a very competent and formidable stylist. Of all the design schemes that he worked on in his forty years with RR the two-door Silver Shadow, introduced in 1966 and given the name Corniche in 1971, was his favourite. Allen's obituary notice, when he died in January 2000, touchingly recalled that he considered the Corniche a nice car that would never sell, as the coke-bottle wing line made it too old-fashioned. How wrong he was, for it continued in the sales list for twenty-four years, the second longest production run of any RR car.

The name on the door of the chief stylist was now that of Fritz Feller, who had taken over when Blatchley, still only in his fifties, retired in 1969. Feller, a Derby development engineer, moved to Crewe in 1951, along with all from Clan Foundry. After experience on the B and K range engines, he transferred his attention to the Wankel rotary diesel engine, a government-funded project for, it was hoped, military use. Most of the contemporary workers at Pym's Lane remember it for the thick clouds of exhaust that vomited from its nether regions, attributable to continuing trouble with seals. Walter Sexton was one of the main development engineers who worked with Fritz Feller on the Wankel engine and its installation. Sexton and others were convinced that the project had a future and that cancellation was premature, although Plastow, in an article in a *RRM Dealer Newsletter*, postulated that the oil crisis of the early 1970s was the final nail in the Wankel coffin.

The choice of an outside agency to style the Camargue must have been demoralising for the small team, now under new management, and such a move would not have been sanctioned by Blatchley outside of a resignation. Feller's opinion of the car can be gauged by an interview he gave to a motoring magazine on the launch of the Silver Spirit in 1980. Here, he suggested that the Spirit was much more of a Rolls-Royce than the Camargue. It has been claimed that Hollings, Plastow and Ward (of Mulliner Park Ward) fathered the approach to the Italian design house. One name, that of Geoff Fawn, is missing from that little list, and one can hardly imagine that, as senior executive at Crewe, he did not have a large input into the final decision. To keep the project reasonably secret it was put about that Pininfarina's contribution was for a one-off car for the firm. After its launch to the press in Sicily, in January 1975, a strong rumour began to circulate around the factory that the Mafia had requested, and received, a bribe to allow the occasion to be trouble-free. Perhaps, like many rumours, it has no basis in reality.

The Camargue, although styled in Italy, was built on the platform basic to the Corniche and the Shadow, and when offered for sale in March 1975 it was priced at £29,250, a third more than the local auctioneer, Peter Wilson, paid for his large auction rooms in the centre of Nantwich, twice the price of a Silver Shadow and three times that of a four-bedroom house in the town of Crewe. It certainly did not do much for the economy of the town, as most of the work was completed in London, and of its production run of 530 only one went out bearing the Bentley badge. Perhaps the final judgement can be found in the minutes of the works committee, where the 1992 management team, led by Peter Hill, described the Camargue as 'awful'.

One year before the Camargue was offered to the public a new division was formed, known as the RR Motors Export Services Division, with premises on the Weston Road industrial park in the south of Crewe. This land, originally designated as an airport, was in the late 1960s still being cited as a possible landing ground for helicopters. The new division offered support to the overseas marketing subsidiaries through a twenty-person team led by the Crewe-born George Reeves, recently returned from New Jersey. Most of the others, among whom were Salisbury-Jones, Alan Sutton, Cedric Browne and John Brown, were transfers from Pym's Lane. This latter Brown was apparently the last tenuous link with Cooke Street, being the son of a man who had worked with Henry Royce in Manchester.

One project that did not gain a lot of publicity in the early 1970s was the conversion of the Shadow into an armour-plated car by the technical production department, stationed in 21 test bed and then under the control of Ian Rimmer and Mike Parsons. The international scene was tending towards terrorism, and the UK government wished to protect its ambassadors as far as it was able. Once the first cars had been successfully converted under the guidance of Geoff Bastow, with Freddie Ikin writing the specification, the rest of the thirty or so cars were modified, when required, by car repair. Brazil and Canada received the first two, while in later years Peter Jay, the prime minister's son-in-law, received one when he was sent to Washington by Jim Callaghan. The armour-plated Shadow used in Argentina was the first of the marque to be seen in that country.

Although provision against terrorism could be engineered into the cars, there occurred an event, early in the new year of 1976, which could not be countered in its effects locally, or upon the continent. This was the great wind of 2 January, when gable ends, chimneys and sheds were blown away and much damage was caused in south Cheshire by gusts of wind that reached 100mph. At Pym's Lane car bodies stored in the yard were whisked up like ping-pong balls, along with other light articles and loose materials. At Hamburg docks, where about thirty-five Silver Shadows were garaged, awaiting distribution across Europe, a high tide, whipped even higher by the unusual weather, flooded the warehouse to a depth of around 3ft. Obviously, the cars had to be recalled for retrimming and for fitting of new exhaust systems and brakes.

EXTENDING THE PLANT

The availability of spacious units on the Weston Road industrial estate enabled the export division to house finished cars that were waiting to be shipped to the purchasing country. In effect, it was a car bond warehouse, with administrative offices to arrange sales and shipping. Until 1978 the car bond for the home market was located in the former Kelvinator block and was guarded for many years by Joe Hodnett who claimed to have driven more than 31,000 Rolls-Royce or Bentley cars.

Planned expansion also occurred at Pym's Lane, in the autumn of 1975, with a £25 million investment programme into new buildings, renovation and extension. An article in the *RRM Journal* of 1982 stated that these new buildings were the first since the Merlin engine had gone out of production. This is not quite correct, as we have seen, because the drawing office on Pym's Lane and the gearbox shop are but two examples of buildings erected earlier in the car years.

The first elements of this investment scheme were visible in the alteration and renovation of the receiving stores at the northern end of E block that included the area known as the cathedral. Next was a new emission test centre for investigating the exhaust fumes of up to twenty cars a day, built at the junction of First Street and Fifth Avenue. The company had thousands of pounds invested in equipment for testing and analysing fuel emissions under the control of Graham Starling, a development engineer, and Dave Preece, foreman of the unit.

Final valet of a Silver Shadow before it entered car bond, *c. 1970. (Rolls-Royce Enthusiasts' Club)*

This was the time when the hike in oil prices was beginning to bite, and another target on Ian Nelson's agenda was to reduce heating expenditure. A start was made when the planning office was fitted with false ceilings and, although they were a seemingly negligible expense when compared to the massive sums involved in designing and developing a car, it is sobering to realise that pre-1970 heating costs rose by approximately 13 per cent every ten years, whereas there was a ten-fold increase in the next decade.

The following year, 1977, brought the erection of a new engineering centre and an automated body store on the recently cleared site on the western edge of the factory. The former cost about £1 million and included a garage for the experimental department, capable of holding nearly thirty cars, while still having room for such unusual tasks as fitting gas engines into double-deck buses. An electrically operated door screened off from curious eyes the shape and identity of future projects. In addition, there were a wood shop, wood mill, styling studio, body-build area, stores, paraffin wash, indoor car-wash, oil store, chassis strip and rig testing facilities, copper-shop, sheet-metal benches and a suite of offices.

In the early 1980s, in what was possibly Ian Nelson's last major task, the engineering department was reorganised, with the long-serving Mac Fisher reporting to Hollings, the engineering director. Jock Knight served as general manager alongside E.P. Barrows, with the chief engineers N. Colbourne (body), D. Coulson (chassis) and John Astbury (engines) under his direction. Responsibility for building Rolls-Royce and Bentley prototype cars came under the remit of the experimental build department, managed by John Fox, who was assisted by Ernie Pointon. A new post for developing and installing computer aids to increase productivity and assist computer modelling was given to C.J. Cooke. By this date, Jock Knight was almost at the end of a career that had included wartime army service in the Far East, building roads and repairing bridges as the allies advanced against a retreating Japanese army.

The electrical laboratory, under its chief development engineer John Coyle, was also moved into the new building at the same time. He had taken over from Bob Child, who had migrated from Derby with the design staff in 1951, whereas Coyle was a local man. On the test benches in the electrical laboratory were electronic mock-ups of current and future electrical devices and circuitry, all tested to destruction or until sufficient information about efficiency and reliability was available. Most of the dozen or so electrical engineers who worked in the laboratory were qualified to at least HNC level and one of them, Fred Hawkesworth, had been responsible for developing the electrical actuator for the automatic gearbox. Two other electrical engineers who must be representative of many were John Epps and Ken Wade. At the time of the move intensive testing of microcomputers was in progress.

Until 1977, when the new building was completed, the experimental garage was in the middle of the finishing area, where it had been placed when this department was transferred to Crewe in the late 1940s. By the 1970s it hindered the production flow and its transfer to the new block released an area of around 48,000sq ft for manufacturing purposes. Somewhere in the region of 300

View of the electrical laboratory, *c.* 1980. The radio engineer at the front of the picture is Mike Gillitt, Stewart MacLeod (also a leading member of the RR cricket section) is on the right bending down, with Steve Fitzgerald just beyond him. Nick Gutton is on the left. *(Rolls-Royce Enthusiasts' Club)*

employees worked in this purpose-built engineering area, a number that included about ninety development or design engineers under John Hollings.

Although the bulk of the work by the engineering department concerned Rolls-Royce and Bentley cars, there were also assignments for the light aircraft and specialist engine division and the B range petrol engines, along with their derivative, the gas engine – a B range engine modified to run on either propane or natural gas. Research, design and development on this began in order to ascertain the modifications needed to maintain an enduring performance. Without being too simplistic, it would be true to say that most of the work centred on the inlet valves, although there were other areas, such as combustion and carburation, which needed careful investigation and modification.

The end result was an engine that, in the emissions-conscious world of the late 1970s, was advertised as 'solving one of today's major problems'. There were, in fact, two engines, the G61 and the G81, capable of delivering 145bhp and 210bhp respectively at an engine speed of 3,750rpm. One of the first installations of the G81 was in a Daimler Fleetline bus on Teesside. Others were installed in stand-by generators, milk tankers and skip lorries. There was also a fruitless attempt to persuade Crewe and Nantwich Borough Council to fit one into a refuse-collecting vehicle.

A tedious yet vitally necessary task for the engineering department was analysing the abundance of motoring legislation still flowing in from many countries. Car safety was a stimulus that provoked every government in the developed world, and because most of the cars exported from Crewe went to America, the greatest concentration of effort went into energy conservation, as powerful yet fuel-mean cars were now part of the American dream. This paradox exercised the minds of the development and design engineers for most of the 1970s, along with absorbing a large proportion of the budget.

For long periods nearly half of the experimental department's cars were devoted to emissions and energy conservation work. For example, the *Autocar* of April 1978 gave details of a fuel consumption test that involved a Shadow being driven continuously for four months, with lengthy checks every 1,000 miles. Most of John Hollings's working week must have been devoted to the many engineering problems raised by this mass of conservation legislation. It is somewhat ironic, therefore, that a letter was published in the local paper in December 1977, signed 'Wife of RR employee', which suggested that RR should design a smaller car capable of returning 20 mpg, exclaiming that it would sell well in America. If only Hollings had thought of that first! No doubt if she had appended her name and address she would have been approached to join the design team.

Following the prolonged discussion of the rehoused engineering department, we now return to the second of the 1977 new buildings, the body stores. This housed 300 'bodies in white', and was built at the south end of the factory site. Perhaps it ought to be explained that a 'body in white' was not the corpse of a bride on her wedding day, but simply an unpainted body shell. The plans submitted to the town council indicated that at a future date the space between the two new buildings would be filled with other workshops, forming a complete block running the whole length of the site. This piecemeal development is symbolic of the chronic lack of capital available to the board of Rolls-Royce Motors, whether as a division or as an independent body. For the entire second half of the twentieth century the Pym's Lane factory was run on a shoestring, comparatively speaking.

This building, completed in 1977, was officially opened in March 1978 by Eric Varley, Secretary of State for Industry, who, in Shrewsbury earlier that day, had opened a new factory for producing RR V12 diesel engines for the armed forces. The same year saw further building, when a new car bond appeared on the north-eastern fringe of the site. It was immediately behind the Girl Guides' hut on Pym's Lane, and agitated neighbours in the council houses opposite were soon pacified when the limited height of the new structure was explained. This large, low shed was for cars destined for the home market only.

A larger gate was constructed in Sunnybank Road during these years, allowing traffic to enter the factory with minimum disturbance to the neighbourhood. This was important because in August 1973 an articulated vehicle en route to RR with a load of body shells had been involved in a fatal accident in Crewe. A small boy was killed when the lorry mounted the pavement as it tried to negotiate the tight corners of the town centre. At that time the main roads of the town still followed the pattern of its pre-industrial lanes, and the Coroner suggested that all heavy goods traffic should use alternative routes to the factory, a formality that Crewe RR had been advising its suppliers to observe for a number of years. A new car park was also opened in 1973, to the west of Sunnybank Road, on land purchased in the years of Llewellyn-Smith.

Another project that opened during the years of independence, and which involved a high degree of capital expenditure, was the apprentices' school and training centre on the south-west corner of the site. There is no doubt that the erection of this two-storey building begot a modernised, structured apprentice training scheme at Pym's Lane. The ground floor was devoted to trades such as sheet-metal working, milling, planing, grinding, turning, coach-building and electronics. Each instructor was responsible for compiling his own teaching scheme, based on the syllabus of the Engineering Industry Training Board. Instructors were also charged with the responsibility of visiting schools to interview prospective apprentices. The intake in the early 1980s was around 120, a number that included one or two girls who were interested in learning a trade.

The upper storey was given over to administration, except for a few drawing boards where Eric Moss instructed trainee draughtsmen and technical apprentices in the intricacies of projection, sections and detail drawing generally. Vic Harris was in overall charge, and Eddie Swann, a skilled tool-maker and an even better ballroom dancer, was senior instructor. Unfortunately the advent of Vickers and a downturn in the fortunes of the company spelt the end of the training scheme as it had originally been envisaged. Some instructors were made redundant and a government-sponsored Youth Opportunities Scheme was substituted for apprenticeships.

The other venture, at a cost of £1 million, was a new spares store that backed onto Sunnybank Road, with the front facing Fifth Avenue. This new warehouse, together with the apprentices' school and a new vacuum casting facility for the Precision Components Division (PCD) (formerly the investment foundry), represented considerable capital investment.

To make room for a two-tier prefabricated construction, known later as the Elliott building, erected for the PCD in this south-west corner, a 15ft square brick-built holding tank, filled with water, had to be demolished. When the work of demolition began it was discovered that it contained a large quantity of fish, such as carp and tench, which had been fed by an endless succession of unknown workers for quite a few years. Four members of the firm's angling section had the happy task of netting the fish in order to add them to the stock of the town's park lake.

An indication that the pot of investment capital was limited is gained from the difficulty the works committee had in persuading the management to release funds for refurbishing the toilet blocks, as we have noticed previously. Even though the estimated cost was only £7,000, resources were allocated to modernise just one block a year. Much to the annoyance of the unions, money was found to pay for signs on every road into the town, announcing that Crewe and Nantwich was the home of the best car in the world. Perhaps it came out of the advertising budget?

NEW DIRECTORS, NEW MODELS

As the 1970s waned, Plastow brought new blood onto the board of RRM. This was the last period when all the promotions came from within the company, for Plastow's long-term management strategy included attracting personnel from other firms. His contribution to a book on management techniques, published in 1982, emphasised the benefit of senior managers being exposed to a wider range of management expertise, as compared to working for only one company. This was a complete departure from the previous route to higher management at Pym's Lane and, without any shadow of a doubt, it altered the family ambience, where all long-term employees knew most of the managers, having watched them rise through the ranks.

Part of the justification for the board changes was the retirement of Dick Garner. Joining RR in 1924, Garner traversed a wandering but interesting path, which took him to the Schneider Trophy, riding mechanic for Kaye Don in Miss England, senior development engineer, chief inspector, materials manager and materials director. Plastow took over as group MD and Tom Barlow, a pre-war Crewe employee, moved from the Diesel Division to occupy Plastow's former seat for about a year until he became chairman of the Car Division board in 1976.

One of the youngest members, appointed to replace Garner as materials director in 1975, was the tall, dark and handsome Vincent McDonagh. He had arrived in south Cheshire in 1939 as an evacuee, and his rise was meteoric by RR standards. Commencing as a clerk in the progress office in 1956, soon he moved into the purchase office, becoming a buyer in 1964, and was promoted to manager in 1968. Sadly, he was killed in July 1980 while landscaping his garden. Peter Jones, a chartered accountant and an RR employee for six years, took his place, with George Fenn, Ian Nelson, John Carpenter, John Hollings, John Romer and Roy Jackson completing the board. The latter, a local man, served an apprenticeship with RR before rising, via the production planning office, to works manager after Bill Harvey's retirement. Further changes occurred about four years later, when Roy Jackson was made director for personnel, and Ron Ashley took Jackson's post of director of manufacturing. Ashley, a product of the local grammar school, started at Pym's Lane in 1951 as an engineering apprentice.

In addition to the Corniche and Camargue, both introduced in the 1970s as we have seen, the Shadow was continually improved. In 1972 eleven modifications were introduced, including the major change of fitting radial tyres, a more difficult exercise than might appear to the uninitiated in motor engineering. There is an interesting article in *RR Motors Journal*, vol. 1, no. 16, in which Derek Coulson, the chief development engineer (chassis) and P. Harding, steering and suspension section leader, discuss the problems that tyres can cause for a car's suspension.

Alongside official modifications, it was also possible for special requests from purchasers to be incorporated into new cars as they were being made. One such request, raised by Hollings for a manufacturing friend, was for an extremely accurate speedometer and a pad on the door for the driver to rest his knee. The electrical laboratory dealt with the first of these, with the trim department coping with the pad, even requesting that the client come to the factory for a 'fitting'. Such requests were usually treated on an ad hoc basis, until a small department known as special features regularised proceedings.

Initially much of the work on the Camargue was completed at London, but a perusal of the works committee minutes reveals that a board decision was made, late in 1976, to complete much more of its manufacture at Crewe, because of labour disputes at Mulliners. Some stewards suggested that it was a move that

The last Camargue built at Pym's Lane, photographed on 3 March 1986 at 2 p.m. Some of those pictured are Barry Corbett, Dave Green, Alan Ellis, Norman Evanson, Brian Stockton, Syd Wright, Derek Cornes, Phil Wright, Bob James, Lester Boyd, Alan Yearsley and Harry Alban. *(Brian Stockton)*

cheered the hearts of the Mulliner Park Ward personnel, as they wanted to get rid of it, and it certainly had a mixed reception from the workforce at Crewe. Many of the coach trimmers were against it, unless further financial reward was forthcoming; others were glad that Crewe was gaining more work. When it was phased out in 1986 only about two dozen workers of varying skills were affected.

The whole Camargue venture, known to many at Pym's Lane as 'Plastow's baby', raised some strange issues. Ian Nelson's opinion was that it was the company's flagship, because it generated interest in the whole product range. Another director claimed that it was like having a flash car in the showroom window, as a prospective purchaser would enquire, out of curiosity, only to buy a cheaper model. Do the rich and powerful buy their cars according to that philosophy? It was even asserted that it enabled Rolls-Royce International to increase the price of the other models by more than would otherwise have been possible. The sales logic seems devastating!

Two years after the Camargue was offered for sale the RR Silver Shadow II was revealed to the world, along with the Bentley T2. This revision of the marque sold well for the rest of the decade, helping to break all previous sales records, for the 1970s were years when production usually increased annually. From 2,473 cars in

1972, the sales rose to 3,347 in 1978. Among the improvements were new bumpers, altered radiator shell, twin exhausts, split level air conditioning and modified suspension. Probably the major change was the rack and pinion steering in place of the recirculating ball, a modification that marked the definite demise of the Grylls 'sneeze factor'. Malaga, in southern Spain, was the chosen spot for the launch, and a party of RR engineers including Fenn, Hollings, Carpenter, Mac Fisher, Feller and David Plastow were there to answer any queries raised by the world's press. No doubt they all eagerly embraced the opportunity to leave Crewe in February, for a few days in the Spanish sun.

Following the release of the Shadow II series, the Silver Wraith II was added to the company's list of cars, after nearly two decades' absence. It was to all intents and purposes the long wheelbase Shadow proudly bearing a pedigree name. This was the last of the new models to grace the sales department's brochures before the years of independence ended. (While mentioning brochures, it is interesting to note that a thriving second-hand market exists for RR and Bentley ephemera such as sales leaflets and booklets.) The 1970s was also the decade when the Bentley all but disappeared from the company's balance sheet, as by 1980 only around 3 per cent of the cars sold bore the winged 'B'. As there was virtually no difference between the two models, even as to the price, it is little wonder that the Bentley was ignored in favour of the better known Rolls-Royce.

As the 1970s drew to a close it was obvious that all was not well with Rolls-Royce Motors. George Fenn broadcast to the workers over the tannoy system, warning that the company was losing money, imputed in part to a series of two-day strikes organised by the CSEU in support of a national wage claim and a cut in hours. At this date wages and salaries were 37 per cent of the company's total expenditure, the same percentage of costs as materials.

Pickets were placed on the gates to seek to persuade fellow trades unionists not to make deliveries to the plant. These strikes, organised for the first two days of each week and involving all of the 4,000 hourly paid workers, were called off after four weeks to allow negotiations to resume. So far as the men were concerned these were successful, for the hours of work were reduced in stages to thirty-nine, meaning that by 1981 the normal working week was amended to four full days and Friday morning only.

At this time 350 car assembly workers were laid off, along with some in the Precision Components Division, because there was no work for them. Perversely, other sections of the factory were short of labour, as was indicated by the advertisements in the local paper for sheet-metal workers and machine-tool setters. In defence of Fenn and the board, it must be pointed out that, compared with other countries, the UK's inflation rate was horrendous. In the last five years of the 1970s the cost of living rose by 16 per cent in Germany, 35 per cent in the USA and 66 per cent in the UK. The Shadow was now four times the price of a Cadillac.

Further turmoil must have been caused in the accountant's office when the Shah fled from Iran in 1979, along with his order for 1,000 tanks. As the Diesel Division of RRM at Shrewsbury would have provided these with engines it was a massive blow to the company. Added to this were the costs of developing the next model, code-named SZ. At around £30 million these were not huge by other car makers' standards, yet combined with all the other costs, it was a heavy burden. All of these factors dipped the profit for 1979, down by 49 per cent on the previous year.

One of the costs that constantly ate into the profitability of the company was that of warranty expenditure. The 1977 outlay was 40 per cent up on the previous year, and by 1978 the annual payments accountable to guarantee pledges were over £1 million, and much of this was laid at the door of the paint-shop. The two major causes of manufacturing complaints, at the start of 1979, were poor detail finish on the paint-work when the owner took delivery, and micro-blistering that developed after a period of use. For a variety of reasons the assembly line and paint-shop had been a source of concern from the late 1940s, when car production was established. The minutes of the works committee contain examples of the management's concern for improvement in workmanship and efficiency. Lack of investment and scarcity of traditional skills in body building and vehicle painting, in the south Cheshire area, were largely to blame. Unlike machining, where investment was slowly replacing the artisan's skills, much of the Crewe RR paint-shop was still reliant on the manual work.

Chapter Six

Merged with Vickers

*One of the things that I could not fail to notice was the family
feeling that exists at Crewe.*

George Fenn, *R-RMC Journal*, no. 17

An announcement in the financial press on 25 June 1980, and also over the
public address system at Pym's Lane, that Rolls-Royce Motors had merged
with Vickers was greeted with mixed feelings. That the workforce had
recognised the grave financial position of the firm was indicated by its acceptance
of a wage rise well below the rate of inflation. Whether the majority accepted the
wisdom of the merger is open to doubt. Perhaps the *Crewe Chronicle* best summed
up local feelings when it suggested that it was a marriage of convenience because
the car firm urgently needed cash, although it was not lost on some in Crewe (such
as Frank Culley) that Plastow had been a non-executive director of Vickers from
1975. Job preservation was a major component influencing attitudes on the shop
floor, as a rash of redundancies swept across south Cheshire when BREL cut back
the workforce in the railway workshops and Foden, the Sandbach truck makers,
went into receivership.

Two months after the merger the SZ project matured when, in October, the
Silver Spirit series went on sale. This replacement for the Shadow had become a
project in the design office barely a year after the firm came to financial grief in
1971. It was designed and developed during years of continuing drama, when
nationally there were strikes, political instability and industrial unrest, along with
high inflation. Oil prices rose massively during the 1970s, increases that must have
occasioned grave uncertainty in the boardrooms of the manufacturers of expensive
cars. There is not the slightest doubt that the directors of RRM also had
reservations about the viability of the SZ project. Thankfully for the workers at
Crewe, their nerve held and the SZ eventually went into production.

Ian Rimmer's work on experimental projects informs us that the first of the
prototype SZ cars was ready to be driven out of the factory in April 1975, by which
date the decision to manufacture the model had been made. It was based upon the
Shadow's underpan and running gear, with a redesigned body. By late autumn
1977 the shape and specification had been sufficiently developed for the fourth
prototype to be sent for endurance testing in France, where test drivers based at
Blois took the mileage to around 40,000 before the car came back to Pym's Lane.
Ten prototype cars were built, with the first one being the subject of crash tests at
MIRA, and the last one dedicated for training two teams of workers in pre-
production build, under the supervision of Charlie Dix. An interesting comment,

pregnant with meaning, was made about the Spirit in a report in the magazine *Motor*, where it was claimed that at last Rolls-Royce had a car that truly reflected its reputation.

Fritz Feller had charged Graham Hull and Ron Maddocks, along with Martin Bourne, Ryan Lewis and Norman Webster, to style the new car lower and wider than its predecessor. Feller's claimed desire, according to one report, was that the new car should not look out of place at the head of a cavalcade. He also made another declaration, quoted in many journals, denigrating any product that was average and mean as being dull and miserable. Sadly, for most of the hourly paid production workers on repetitive jobs, where the skill was built into the machine, it was difficult to view their work with the excitement that motivated Fritz Feller.

The same month that the Silver Spirit was released it was resolved by the board to stop building light aircraft engines, as the division had been losing substantial amounts of money for about two years. As discussed in an earlier chapter, this project had begun with great expectations in the early 1960s. By 1974 it had been combined with petrol and gas engine manufacture to form a separate profit centre, known as the Specialist and Light Aircraft Engine Division. John Craig was chairman and Graham Williams, who had commenced employment at RR in 1951

Graham Hull and Ron Maddocks of the styling department working out clearances, *c.* 1977. *(Rolls-Royce Enthusiasts' Club)*

as an engineering apprentice, was appointed managing director. A valiant, if unavailing, effort was made by Tony Cleaver, the light aircraft sales manager and an ex-draughtsman, to drum up interest at the 1979 Paris Air Show. Sales did not increase and the decision was taken to terminate the agreement between RRM and Teledyne Continental Motors on the last day of 1980. As a consequence of this forty-eight employees were made redundant.

The Precision Components Division was also feeling the pinch when the early months of 1981 brought a sharp decline in orders for new castings, especially for aero-engines such as the Dart, Conway and Avon. By the year's end only 76 per cent of the profit plan had been realised, making it obvious that fresh markets were urgently needed. Workers in the foundry and machine shop were placed on a four-day week, but the only realistic remedy for the fall-off in orders was a programme of redundancies. At the same time the fabrication section of the division was transferred to Shrewsbury. The only visible sign that Vickers had taken over the PCD was the appointment to the board of Noel Lewis, a Vickers nominee.

The constant search for new work was successful, to some degree, for the early months of 1984 brought an 8 per cent increase in the numbers employed. Further investment of £2 million enabled two new vacuum furnaces and a computer-controlled twin-spindled form grinder to be purchased. Half a million pounds was spent on installing a new computer system, under the control of Bob Wilkinson, which was directly linked with the fabrication section at Shrewsbury. Vickers Precision Components now numbered among its clients Allison, Fiat, Singapore Aerospace, Pratt & Whitney, Smiths Industries, Burnley Engineering, as well as RR divisions at Derby, Bristol and Leavesdon. To put matters another way, products were exported to Italy, Belgium, Switzerland, Germany, France and the USA.

RETRENCHMENT AND THE STRIKE

Nationally, a policy of strident monetarism was being followed by the Conservative government of Margaret Thatcher elected in 1979; a policy that was bringing more than a whiff of unemployment to south Cheshire. Advertisements for situations vacant disappeared from the pages of the local paper. Crewe clothing firms were shedding labour, as were the railway works, Metal Box and ICL. The *Crewe Chronicle* reported rumours of a large cull of workers at Pym's Lane, only for them to be denied by RR officials. One month later, in February 1981, the rumours became reality, with 5.8 per cent of the workforce being declared redundant, and the apprentice intake being trimmed by 50 per cent. Money was so tight that even the receptionist in the front office was dispensed with. By the summer local unemployment figures were the highest since the temporary blip following the winding down of Merlin production.

It was hoped that the Silver Spirit would bring an increase in sales sufficient to lay the spectre of depression. Things did not work out that way, for, although sales increased in 1980 as compared to 1979, profit was down by 17 per cent to £8.7 million. By the end of the following year sales had collapsed to 1,551 cars, with a consequential devastating effect on profits. As usual, the answer was a reduction in costs through the blunt instrument of short-time working and redundancies. In

June 1982 the hourly paid workforce, or blue-collar workers, were on a four-day week. Midland Rollmakers, at the south end of Crewe, was also enduring the same phenomenon. Things went from bad to worse at RR, for the working week was reduced to three days.

At the end of the year another 750 workers were docked from the pay-roll, some walking through the gates having accepted voluntary redundancy. Those who had been forced out of work took it badly, with some long-serving staff employees, such as 'Tim' Friesner and H. Whittaker, being escorted off the factory after less than an hour's notice. Seven foremen who had been sacked in this purge unsuccessfully prosecuted the company for unfair dismissal. Among the casualties from the higher echelons of management were John Hollings, Ian Nelson and John Carpenter. Some of the union representatives can still recall the atmosphere at a meeting on 14 October 1982, where George Fenn read out a list of management changes. Roy Jackson, the former director of manufacturing, was not one of these, for he retired a few months later after forty-three years of good and faithful service. It could be thought amusing that the afore-mentioned Ian Nelson was reported in *Voice*, in the autumn of 1981, as saying that 'I am a confirmed believer that there is always a better way of doing things'. Fenn must have been of the same mind when he handed him the sack twelve months later.

Locally the economy was crumbling, with further job losses at British Rail Engineering Ltd, General Relays Ltd and McCorquodale Security Printers. At RR an extra week was added to the annual summer holidays, as the company confessed that sales were not as high as anticipated. Crewe's unemployment figures had seen a 300 per cent increase in two years and the local MP called upon Mrs Thatcher to visit Crewe and explain to the men where their jobs had gone.

It was in this sullen and acrimonious climate that the worst strike in the history of Crewe RR occurred late in October 1983. A pay dispute was at its centre, although as usual there was a multiplicity of causes. The strange spectacle of an entrenched picket line outside the Pym's Lane gates is explained by the previous months of festering relations between management and unions. Negotiations had taken place against a background of falling sales and straitened company revenue. Even such mundane consumables as paper towels in the works toilets had been costed at 8 pence per person per week. Peter Hill, the personnel director, was concerned over the cost of installing new hand-drying facilities at a time when the company's financial state was critical. Although the rate of increase in the cost of living was falling, it had averaged 12 per cent per annum over the previous three years. When the company adamantly refused to raise the pay offer above 4 per cent the scenario for a bitter industrial conflict was set. At this impasse the union officials walked out of the conference, blaming Richard Perry, the MD, for displaying a 'macho' attitude, for it was claimed that, as it was his first pay round, he was determined to prove his masculinity. The suspicion that the company was not averse to having a strike at a time of its choosing has long lingered in the industrial air of Crewe.

The first day of the dispute saw an overwhelming show of support, with over 1,000 persons demonstrating outside the factory. The works committee organised the permitted picket and the pattern was set for the next five weeks. After a fortnight, Perry sent a letter to the homes of all the striking workers outlining the proffered terms – a tactic used by Michael Edwardes at Longbridge during the nadir of industrial relations at British Leyland. His move backfired when nearly 400 of the letters were brought to Pym's Lane to be burnt on a ceremonial bonfire, accompanied by the cry of 'Perry out'.

That this was a bitter dispute by a workforce that had not entered into a mass strike for forty-four years is stating the obvious, and it was almost unbelievable that there was an industrial conflict involving the whole workforce. Moves were made by some, at the time, to suggest that there was coercion by the strike leaders to keep the men out. A letter to the local paper stated that the writer knew that all the workers were against prolonging the contest. There is no doubt that in a traditionally docile and non-militant workforce there were some who wanted it to end quickly. After about four weeks it was put to a works gate vote, where a large majority decided to carry on. It is also true that the management did not want a few trickling back to work, with the inevitable consequences for industrial relations when it was completely ended.

All the anecdotal and documentary evidence would suggest that this was not a dispute fostered by a few industrial hotheads. The *Crewe Chronicle*, neutral in such matters, reported that it believed there was overwhelming support for the strike. This is further indicated by the rejection, after a month, of a resolution to return to work, despite a recommendation to accept by the national executives of the unions involved. The strike was eventually ended on 25 November, when the works committee placed further improvements in money and conditions to a mass meeting on the company's Pym's Lane car park. Credit for keeping the strike firm and sensibly controlled goes to George Ellis and John Edwards, as it never required more than a token police presence, unlike the contemporary one at a print works in Warrington, where very ugly scenes were manifest and the cost of policing was huge.

Although there was no improvement on the basic rise of 4 per cent, there was harmonisation between staff and works, various technical points in the bonus scheme were improved, all increases were back-dated to July and a basic £2 was added to all grades. The glaring discrepancies between hourly paid and staff, a long-standing bone of contention, were partially addressed by allowing the hourly paid workers to abandon the clocking on and off system. Management gave many warnings later, that it might have to be reintroduced if abuse by a minority did not cease.

At the start of the dispute George Ellis, the convenor, claimed that the management was class conscious and was totally unconcerned about the wages and conditions of the shop floor workers. He also claimed knowledge of a memo given by management to the representatives of white-collar unions promising that any improvements would automatically be awarded to the salaried staff. It is an informative, although unconnected, fact that the same week that the dispute was concluded members of parliament voted themselves a pay rise of 28 per cent.

Once the factory was back to its normal working patterns, it was decided by senior management to offer every employee a 40-mile ride in a Rolls-Royce. To give everybody the privilege took eighteen months at fifty persons a week. There is no record that arguments ever took place as to who should sit by the driver, for on most occasions the passengers changed places every 15 miles. One of the first employees to benefit from this offer was Frank Dale, a power train section leader in the detail drawing office.

MORE CHANGES

Following the Plastow-inspired purge of some of the top managers in 1982, new faces appeared in the offices fronting Pym's Lane, most brought in from elsewhere. Among these were the 47-year-old Mike Dunn, the replacement for Hollings, Ken Lea, production director (from 1986) and Peter Ward, still in his thirties, yet the first man ever to be given world-wide responsibility for marketing and sales of RR and Bentley cars. Richard Perry was an exception to the 'outsiders rule', as he migrated, at Fenn's behest, from the RR-owned Park Ward. Two experienced members of the engineering team who made their own decisions to take their pensions at this time were Jock Knight and Mac Fisher, although the former did not completely sever his links with Pym's Lane, assuming responsibility, on a consultancy basis, for stretched limousines.

Perry became chief executive, on Fenn's retirement in May 1984, and immediately exercised his powers in somewhat unorthodox ways in attempts to overcome shortages, or similar interruptions in production. One example was the rectification of the leak of oil past the piston of the brake pump on the car. The context for this was the change from moisture-absorbing brake fluid, which tended to produce traces of rust in the master cylinder, to mineral oil – but the lubricity of mineral oil caused it to leak past the piston, a fault that proved difficult to counter. Perry called a meeting of interested parties, including Bernard Preston and Adrian Hill, to the machining area to discuss the progress of the modifications that it was hoped would rectify the situation. The foreman of the department, Bob Tomkinson, happened to remark that when his father worked in the local locomotive works, grooves were machined into the pistons to prevent egress of steam. Perry immediately seized on this, and ordered it to be tried on the pistons of the brake system. And so a cure was effected, the paperwork being left to catch up at a later date.

The board now comprised Perry, Ron Ashley (production), M. Dunn (engineering), P. Hill (personnel), J. Stephenson (product planning), J. Symonds (Mulliner Park Ward) and Peter Ward (sales and marketing). By the new year it had changed yet again, when Ashley left and Symonds took his seat. Compared with the previous years, the R-RMC board in the 1980s and '90s took on the complexion of musical chairs, so frequent were the changes as the country's management firmament was searched for bright stars that could make RR and Bentley cars saleable again. It was not before time, where the latter name was concerned, for by 1980 Bentley had almost disappeared from the revenue-raised column of the balance sheet. Faint streaks of a new dawn for the Bentley could be detected with the arrival of the Mulsanne, the Bentley-badged Silver Spirit.

It would not be a travesty of the truth to suggest that the arrival of Peter Ward accelerated the tendency, commenced by Plastow, for marketing and salesmen to manipulate the levers of power, for he charted a marketing strategy that dominated the engineering staff. Ward is on record as criticising the dichotomy between the sales, production and engineering teams that was evident when he arrived at Crewe. It could be claimed that it was a long-time feature of RR for the engineering department to develop a car and leave the sales team to sell it. It is surprising how quickly Ward found his feet, stating in *Voice* of September 1983: 'In the past, engineers have gone ahead and done what they thought was right. Now they have to check with sales and marketing to make sure it's right, before they even commence.'

Another of Ward's early actions was to promote Tom Purves from sales manager with RR International to director of UK sales operations. Also upwardly mobile was Bernard Preston, who, in addition to product assurance functions, was group service executive, until appointed as director of product planning in 1985, when Stephenson resigned owing to a disagreement over a future project. This promotion for Preston completed the journey he had begun as an office boy in the progress department in 1953, meaning that he covered a greater distance up the greasy pole than any other Crewe apprentice, excepting Vince McDonagh and Roy Jackson.

That Ward and Dunn produced a sea-change is obvious from what followed in the next ten years. Many local people claim that, following the changes initiated by this duo, RR was not what it had been, yet a very good case can be made that without them things could have been very much worse. It was only natural that Dunn faced suspicion from established engineers when he arrived at Crewe. That he thought the engineering department lacked leadership is obvious from the tone of an internal memorandum dated 21 February 1983, where he wrote that he was conscious that engineering had missed its dates in the past and his wish was to re-establish its reputation.

One positive example of Dunn's period as engineering director was the further attention given to Jack Phillips's engine, where, according to Ward, more development was initiated in the three years after Dunn's arrival than in the previous twenty-two years. This V8 engine, nearly thirty years into its cycle, was now producing 22 per cent more power, yet with a decrease in fuel consumption. The number of parts was also reduced.

Another new feature was a more efficient method of stock control, where parts were kept in a wire enclosure, with entry gained by means of a swipe card. In previous years it had been possible for anybody to gain access to the finished parts stores by simply walking through the doors when the storekeeper was not looking.

As we noticed above, the Silver Spirit did not storm the luxury car market when it was introduced in 1980, owing to another hike in oil prices and the downward spiral of the world economy. There was also the respectful rejection of the car as past its sell-by date. What was needed was a vehicle as radical as that introduced in the days of Smith, Grylls and Dorey, when they released the Shadow onto the market, but there was no way that sufficient capital would be available to bring an entirely new car to fruition.

The Spirit also had troubles of its own making. A news item in the local paper early in 1983 commented on the number of cars being returned because of large numbers of faults. One example quoted had eighty-four defects, despite having completed only 2,000 miles. Reports from the road test department regularly criticised the rear axle assembly, rejecting the cars for excessive noise. Post-sales warranty costs were increasing, chargeable mainly to poor paint-work – poor that is, according to the exacting standards of the owners of luxury cars. Criticisms from owners were doubly distressing, following the advance into the luxury car market of Mercedes and BMW. No longer was the Crewe car maker the lone provider in this niche market.

One who worked on procedures that would protect the cars from corrosion was Tom Creer, the laboratory manager. He was awarded the prestigious Crompton-Lanchester Medal when, in a paper delivered at the Institute of Mechanical Engineers in 1983, he summarised the methods that the company employed to combat rust. Each and every car body, along with doors, boot-lid and bonnet, was subjected to rigorous anti-corrosion treatment, involving zinc coating. Spot-weld surfaces were treated with thick zinc primer. The body itself underwent a six-stage phosphating pre-treatment, followed by twenty-six separate operations that included total immersion in primer, two further coats of epoxy primer, stoving, three colour coats and two final finish coats. All of this was interspersed with rubbing down and inspections.

The complaints about the paint-work on some of the finished cars were long-standing, as we have seen in a previous chapter. In an attempt to remedy them, a new final paint finishing shop, costing £2 million, was constructed in a vacated building at the south end of the one-time Kelvinator section, and adjacent to the body line. Although the new paint-shop arrested the level of complaints regarding external finish to some extent, there were other areas that troubled the warranty.

A drive for perfection was the company's antidote to the errors in the system. In one attempt to decrease them, the Japanese-inspired quality improvement circles were introduced, where small groups of workers from particular sections met to review their operations. Reg Spencer first heard about quality circles from Jim Rooney of Derby RR, and mentioned them to George Fenn. As a reward, Spencer was given responsibility for establishing them at Crewe, which he did so successfully that he went on to become a founder member of the National Society of Quality Circles. According to the *Rolls-Royce Motors Journal*, the ultimate aim of the Quality Improvement Groups (QIGs) was savings in costs, new production methods and creation of a better working environment – the aims of the many other training schemes introduced, at much greater cost, over the next two decades. Interestingly, a neck-tie was designed to publicise the merits of quality circles; unfortunately the abbreviation 'QIG' was often read as 'PIG' by the short-sighted, an error that did not do much to encourage wearing of the ties.

The works committee mistrusted the whole project and authorised the stewards to organise a policy of non-cooperation. In the poisoned atmosphere of the early 1980s it was easy for the hourly paid workers to see ulterior motives whenever management came up with anything new. Eventually Spencer, through diplomacy and tact, persuaded enough workers to get the quality circles project functioning. To further increase the improvement of quality, a campaign was initiated under the slogan 'Right First Time'. This was supposed to motivate all employees diligently to consider every action and to view any changes in a positive light.

Spencer's other resolve was to reduce the number of inspectors through natural wastage. Large numbers of inspectors had been essential during the war years, when inspection had to cope with the vagaries of a very mixed workforce, even to employing time-served joiners as skilled inspectors. By the 1980s inspection was becoming a home for the halt and the lame and Spencer reckoned that the time was ripe for the workforce to self-check, with a reduced inspection department performing sampling, rather than 100 per cent checks. It must be said that such sentiments were a reflection of the truth, for the number of workers in the inspection department decreased from nearly 500 to 250, without any noticeable increase in the rate of recorded scrap.

Another rationalisation feature of 1983 was the transfer of the chauffeurs' school from Hythe Road to Pym's Lane. The school had begun at Alvaston, near to Derby, in 1919, before being transferred to the metropolis six years later. Most courses lasted for five or ten days, with the successful candidates being awarded a cap badge and a certificate. Under Peter Perris, its first principal at Crewe, it was located in a partitioned area of the training centre, with sufficient space for a workshop that would accommodate three cars.

Bentley Revival

Perhaps the most striking feature of this period was the dramatic increase in the sales of the Bentley, as it moved from 5 per cent of units produced in 1978 to 28 per cent by the early months of 1985. Overall, 2,603 units were sold the following year, just under half of them going to the USA. Four years later Bentley production outstripped RR for the first time and, although the years leading up to the end of the century brought a severe trade depression, the brand that had started life at Cricklewood forged ahead regardless. Whether this would have happened without Ward and Dunn being at Crewe is a moot point, as the car was given a new image before they arrived, yet full credit must be given to them in that they continued to develop the Bentley.

The suggestion that Plastow should have re-invigorated the Bentley after 1971 ignores the immense difficulties faced by the nascent car firm in the immediate aftermath of bankruptcy. That the Bentley survived to enjoy a renaissance, when similar high performance cars with pedigree names disappeared, is a matter for congratulations. Perhaps this was all down to the faithful enthusiasts who supported the sales during a period when it could have entered oblivion.

The Bentley Mulsanne Turbo was launched in 1982, priced at £58,612, and proved to be the remedy of new life for which the Bentley badge was waiting; indeed, for many enthusiasts it was the first car that merited the name Bentley since the R type Continental in 1952. Along with the Bentley Eight that went on sale in the summer of 1984, it was the prime cause of a dramatic surge in the sales figures. (Incidentally the wire-mesh grille sported by the Bentley Eight was the last innovation by Fritz Feller, who retired shortly afterwards.) Some critics have claimed that it was only RR tunnel-vision of previous years that took the Bentley sales figures down to the dismal levels of the 1970s and early 1980s. We have noted in a previous chapter, however, that the company claimed it was a deliberate decision to merge the cars, rather than neglect of the Bentley name, that led to the single car syndrome.

The genesis of the turbocharged engine was a suggestion from Plastow to John Hollings three or four years after the bankruptcy, with the thought that it should be fitted into the Camargue. Commercial sense, however, demanded that it should go into a car with the probability of higher sales, so it was soon earmarked for the Bentley. The specialist firm of Broadspeed Engineering was commissioned to turbocharge a car on a one-off basis, leaving an in-house development team, led by Jack Read, to develop it to perfection. This they continued to do through the fat years of record production and the lean years of the trade depression, which meant that the time span for development was extensive, even by Rolls-Royce standards. Despite this, overtime had to be worked in the prototype department in the months immediately before the car's unveiling, at the Geneva Motor Show, early in 1982. Building this car was the last assignment of Charlie Dix, alongside of the production fitters, before he retired after many years of excellent and highly skilled service.

By the end of 1984 the car firm was supplying over 40 per cent of the declared profit of Vickers, due in part to the changes introduced by Dunn and Ward, but not forgetting that the Mulsanne Turbo was on sale before they arrived. On offer was a range of cars that included the Corniche, Camargue, Silver Spirit, Silver Spur, Bentley Eight and the Bentley Turbo R. The Camargue was removed from the list early in 1986, when its cost to the customer was over £80,000. The decision to cease production had been taken three years earlier, those at Pym's Lane who needed to know being informed in a memorandum dated 6 December 1982.

A few months after the Mulsanne Turbo's appearance, the dealer network was reorganised in an effort to increase the efficiency of the marketing of the cars. It was a sign of the times that Rolls-Royce needed to pay keen attention to what would have been considered vulgar in former years. Perry sent Bernard Preston and Nigel Cornelius, two of the senior members of the sales and marketing team, on a retreat for about three weeks to concentrate their minds on the task of constructing a network of dealers with the capability of selling over 1,000 cars a year, and to service 26,000 Rolls-Royce and Bentley cars. They were able to identify the location of all existing owners by extrapolating statistics from the government's vehicle licensing centre at Swansea, and when they emerged from their sojourn the number of distributors had been cut from seventy-one to thirty-eight, with nineteen authorised service dealers. It is a significant and salient comment that Ford had reorganised its dealerships in 1963, twenty years before Rolls-Royce.

An attempt on the One-Hour National Endurance record in September 1986 finally proved that the Bentley Turbo was an exceptional car. The rationale behind this was to seek a device that would demonstrate the worth of the car without involving a great outlay of capital. A standard production Turbo R, C891 MMA, was taken to Millbrook Proving Ground (owned by General Motors) and, from a standing start, Derek Rowland covered just over 140 miles in one hour. By any index this was a tremendous achievement for both driver and car, and signalled the excellence and reliability of the car and the supreme skill of a Rolls-Royce experimental department driver. It could be argued that not sufficient publicity was generated from this fine performance.

North American launch of the Bentley Turbo R in 1989. Left to right: Mick Hill, Mark Simmon, Walter Lea, Malcolm Hart, Jim Armstrong, Steve Hughes, Barry Taylor. *(Walter Lea)*

While we are considering endurance tests, mention must be made of a production management scheme that was introduced into the Crewe car plant in the middle 1980s, when the MRP 11 project was commenced. It had been bought, at great expense, from Oliver Wight Enterprises of America as a cure-all for the production woes at Pym's Lane. The book that outlines the methodology of MRP contains some comments that are worthy of emphasis. On page 5 of the 1984 revised edition of *Manufacturing Resource Planning*, Denis Healey and Rupert Murdoch condemned the attitude, prevalent in Britain, of denigrating manufacturing as a career and stating that well-educated and intelligent young people from the best universities would never consider dirtying their hands in industry. This attitude still persists a quarter of a century after the book was first published.

At its most basic, MRP was a method of coordinating production with sales through the use of computers. Purchasing, inventories, cashflow, marketing, manufacturing and financial planning would all be involved, along with team-work and reduction of conflict in the workplace. Never again would there be shortages, or hold-ups on the assembly line, as the Manufacturing Resource Programme would ensure trouble-free manufacturing. Geoff Moreton was given the thankless task of heading the committee responsible for its introduction in 1988, and it was not long before some wag at Pym's Lane attached the epithet 'Moreton's Recovery Programme' to the initials MRP. Overall, the cynical judgement seems to have been that it achieved very little, other than substituting new phrases for old. For instance 'list of parts' became 'bill of material' and 'start date' was renamed 'cut over'. Besides being subject to the rigours of MRP 11, the employees had to attend regular briefings in the Starlight Room, where it was not unknown for some older employees to fall asleep as soon as the room was darkened for the presentation.

CELEBRATIONS

One significant event at this time was the completion of the one hundred thousandth car in August 1985, marked by a pageant organised by John Foster's marketing operations department. Hundreds of employees, with their families, gathered in Pym's Lane on a cool August day to watch a procession led by the Regimental Band of the Scots Guards. Noel Edmonds, a contemporary TV personality, who had arrived by helicopter on the company's sports ground, provided the commentary. One of the cars on view was a 1901 Decauville, a type that had inspired Henry Royce to make his first motor car in 1904.

Members of the Rolls-Royce Enthusiasts' Club proudly drove fine examples of the many cars manufactured at Crewe or Derby over the years. Regarding the two centres of production, it is a pertinent fact that three-quarters of the 100,000 cars were made in the Cheshire town. Together with the cars paraded were an armoured Silver Ghost used in the wars that marred the twentieth century and a Phantom I, originally built for Otto Oppenheim, the diamond millionaire. The high point of the parade was the entrance of the 100,000th car, a Silver Spur Centenary special edition, accompanied by the company's original demonstrator, a 1907 Silver Ghost, as well as five mounted policemen. Proudly seated inside the Silver Spur were two long-serving employees, Jack Goodwin and Margaret Green, and it was from their hands that Richard Perry received the ignition keys, an act that symbolised the permanent adoption of this car by the company. A further twenty-five examples of the Centenary Silver Spur were manufactured, and rapidly snapped up by eager clients. Around the time of these celebrations employees were asked to submit names suitable for future models. The list was never made public.

Two years later the company's Silver Ghost was on duty again, when Queen Elizabeth, accompanied by the Duke of Edinburgh, visited Crewe to attend the celebrations marking the 150th anniversary of the first steam train passing through the district. Charles Elson, the former convenor at Pym's Lane, then serving his second spell as Mayor, met the royal party at the station. One of the Queen's many engagements that day was a visit to Pym's Lane, where the 1907 Silver Ghost was waiting to drive her through the gates. Unfortunately, after moving a few feet, the car lost forward motion. David Preston of the publicity department, one of the few employees allowed to drive this valuable vehicle, displayed remarkable aplomb by restarting it with a swing of the starting handle and continuing the journey. Some onlookers swore there was the ghost of a smile upon a regal face. The royal party found the experience of looking around the factory so interesting that it was recommended to the Princess Royal, who visited in a private capacity the following year.

Europe's 1985 Motor Show at Geneva was the occasion for a preview of things to come, when Rolls-Royce and Bentley Motors displayed Project 90. This was an exclusive sporting Bentley reminiscent of the 1952 Continental. With restyled suspension and alloy wheels, it attracted many to the stand, where the public's reaction was analysed. Evidently the results of the exercise were satisfactory, for it was the harbinger of the highly successful Continental R introduced in the 1990s. As was traditional, the whole design and development of Project 90 was given an

Asian name, 'Nepal'. Six prototypes were built, and tested in the heat of California's Death Valley and the arctic cold of northern Sweden, in addition to the more scenic lands of Germany and Italy. At the conclusion, the company had an attractive car that could accelerate from 0 to 60mph in just over six seconds, and with a selling price of £166,000. It was also a further nail in the coffin of traditional RR methods, for partial responsibility for design had been commissioned to an independent styling house.

The Plastow-induced practice of appointing non-RR persons as managers continued apace. It must be emphasised once more that this was an alien practice, so far as concerned Pym's Lane, where, for most of the firm's half-century in the town, promotions had come from inside. Quite often 'inside' had meant Derby, much to the disgust of some long-serving Crewe employees. One achievement of the Plastow doctrine was the complete elimination of the traditional RR management ethos, where every senior manager in the top team was a Rolls-Royce man through and through. John Blatchley is reported as having stated in 2005 that he was never a car man, just a Rolls-Royce man. That says it all.

Perry and Ward also supported the use of as wide a base as possible from which to draw executives and managers, as they too wished to avoid 'inbreeding'. Some examples of their selections are Malcolm Hart from BL, John Bodie (British Coal), Charles Matthews (Nabisco Group), Keith Sanders (Toyota) and Christine Gaskell from Fisons at Holmes Chapel. The last five years of the 1980s also saw the deaths of many of the stalwarts from the wartime years. Jack Valentine, E.P. Armitage, George King, Eric Moore and 'Doc' Smith are just a few of the many well-known figures who died in the late 1980s.

The new year of 1985 also brought management changes at Vickers Precision Components (VPC), with Chris Dawe appointed as general manager, Mike Dale, head of machining and Terry Walley promoted to marketing director. The rest of the workforce was offered a ride in a Rolls-Royce, provided that this was in their own time and they had been employed for no less than five years. The context for this was an offer by the management of R-RMC to its employees at Pym's Lane of a similar treat, the difference being that it was given during working hours. The works committee expressed its disgust by registering a fruitless complaint of partiality.

Another device to increase turnover in VPC was to extend the maintenance facility. In 1984 component repairs had yielded under £100,000, whereas the 1985 projection was £500,000. The increase was to be achieved by servicing nozzle guide vanes and turbine blades, rather than replacing them, and was supposed to yield a 25 per cent saving over new parts. It was hoped, under normal conditions, to increase the repair revenue to around £2 million by 1990. As it happened, things did not work out as planned, because that year brought large-scale redundancies, followed by the permanent closure of the investment foundry early in 1991. This had implications for the manufacture of the 'Flying Lady' mascot that until then had been cast in the foundry. From 1991 it was made in the Southampton area.

The immediate reason for the foundry's closure was the loss of orders, amounting to £3.5 million; the cause was creeping, uneconomic business. The company briefing, issued in February 1991, clarified the grounds of closure as a complex mix of work, unacceptable scrap rate, excessive operating costs, archaic working practices, high rental from the host (R-RMC) and the decision by RR plc to cancel contracts. A detailed breakdown of some of these reasons illustrates the type of problems faced by the foundry. The work mix involved the manufacture of 112 different castings, some dating back to 1956, being spares for older engines such as Dart, Avon and Spey. As most of the plant operated via tunnel furnaces rather than the more economic and up-to-date rotary furnaces, costs were higher than they needed to be. It is ironic, though typical of Crewe RR, that rotary furnaces were in the 1994 business plan – in other words, too little, too late – for as usual insufficient funds were available to replace plant and machinery when necessary. Regarding the rental, R-RMC charged Vickers PCD almost £1 million per annum for the foundry. When it closed, approximately 180 workers joined Crewe's lengthening dole queue.

An increase of 7 per cent in car sales in 1987 did not mean that the town's economy was buoyant. The other large employer of labour, British Rail Workshops, renamed BREL Ltd as a precursor to privatisation, was rapidly reducing its workforce. As part of the Thatcher government's economic miracle many acres of the former LMS's giant workshops were being sold off, inspiring John Paton, a junior minister in the government, on a visit to Crewe in December 1987, to outline a brilliant idea to counter the loss of local employment. His novel suggestion was that Rolls-Royce should become a tourist attraction, a suggestion not enthusiastically received by the company. A far better idea, and one supported by the now retired Frank Culley, was for a section of the redundant rail workshops to be converted into a transport museum.

Perhaps the leading technical accomplishment of 1988 was overcoming the stringent demands of yet more legislation regarding emissions. In order to achieve this, catalytic converter equipment was engineered into the Turbo R, an exercise that occupied the development team for many months. Not the least of the problems was to find sufficient accommodation beneath the bonnet. Another was to eliminate back-pressure, which had a deleterious effect on engine performance – not what the turbo had been developed for in the first place.

Further investment in 1989 saw the commencement of a completely new paint-shop, planned by Jim Symonds, director of manufacturing, which eventually filled the remaining space on the western fringe of the site. Costing £10 million, with a capacity for seventy bodies-in-white a week, it brought the body preparation process at Pym's Lane into the late twentieth century. One of the main additions to the previous methods was electro-phoretic priming of the bodies, in simplistic terms, immersion of the body in a vat of anti-corrosive electropaint while an electrical current was passed through the tank. Apparently the end result was a coat of primer reaching into the recesses that other primers could not reach. Lord Young of Graffham officially opened the paint-shop on 24 July. It was managed by Peter O'Rourke.

Replacing outdated machines was a continuing process on a tight budget, which meant installation of new equipment was a red-letter occasion, usually the subject of a report in *Voice*. The 1990 spring edition recorded the latest advance in the modernisation of the machine-tool stock, comprising the addition of two machines, a numerically-controlled polishing machine and a Buderous grinder. Geoff Moreton, manager of machining and the Special Engine Division, claimed that this modernisation would reduce unit costs, improve safety and create cleaner working conditions. The same year the first Flexible Manufacturing System or FMS at Pym's Lane was finally commissioned. One part had been in place for nearly twelve months but, typical of R-RMC, the completion of the investment of £900,000 had to wait until more capital was available. The FMS was made up of two Huller Hille 150 machining centres, linked by a linear pallet system, which could machine a wide variety of parts, including rear axle casings, exhaust manifolds, cross members and air intakes.

Bill Roche of the TGWU was reported as saying that the Midland car makers were ten years behind Renault and Fiat. The probability is that Pym's Lane was even further behind, as most of the machines were decades old. When the new owners examined the factory in the late 1990s the fixtures and fittings did not impress them. If the march of progress was measured by investment in new machines, then it seemed that the rest of the motoring world had left R-RMC far behind, for a worker who retired in the 1950s would not have been fazed if he had returned in the early 1990s, as the scenery of the main shop and most of the other departments would have been instantly recognisable.

Before the installation of these new tools the relatively antiquated machines still had to obtain the tolerances demanded by design and detail draughtsmen. Machining parts at Pym's Lane always required the skill to work to fine tolerances. In November 2003 there was a series of letters in the *Daily Telegraph* regarding the tolerances that Ford worked to when manufacturing wartime Merlins. To engage in that debate in this volume would be invidious, yet a claim that 'RR blue prints had to be redrawn to the more demanding Ford standards of accuracy at Dagenham', has to be vigorously repudiated if it is meant to suggest that RR was incapable of fine limits. Such propositions must have had Sir Henry rolling in his grave, for it is certain that Ford had to redraw the drawings in line with its mass production methods. Packard performed the same exercise when it began Merlin production, for the same reason and also owing to lack of international standards for engineering drawings, as an article in *Archive*, No. 67, the newsletter of the Rolls-Royce Heritage Trust, makes clear.

Machines in the main shop at Pym's Lane had to be operated to tolerances of tenths of a thousandth of an inch. For example, the final bore of the cylinders in the crankcase had a limit of 0.0005in. The crankshaft of the V8 had a test piece removed for analysis in the laboratory; if the tensile strength were correct the webs, bearings and crank-pins would be turned and both ends drilled, along with the oil and sludge holes. After being balanced and hardened by the nitriding process, it would be finished by grinding to a tolerance of 0.0005in. Other parts called for still finer limits. Such demands meant high skills, especially from machine-tool setters. It would be no travesty of the truth to maintain that Pym's Lane contained craftsmen whose traditional skills could stand up to comparison with those present in any motor car plant in the world. This was because many of the techniques still

Plating shop, 1939. *(B. Fishburne)*

lay in human hands and not in the machine, as investment had not kept pace with changes elsewhere.

In an attempt to improve the local unemployment figures, Rolls-Royce joined in a 'Make it in the Locality' campaign. It was organised and publicised by the Crewe Development Agency, but as Peter Ward was the chairman of that body it was to all intents and purposes controlled from the Pym's Lane office block. The rationale behind this was that as RR bought in parts to the tune of £85 million, some of this sum could be spent locally. Brian Dickie, the director of purchasing, arranged an exhibition in the Starlight Room, where castings, forgings, springs and other items were displayed that could be made locally, or so it was proposed. Over two days some 1,500 enquiries were received, and although nothing dramatic was achieved in reducing the unemployment figure, the directors were demonstrating a concern for the local economy.

To mark the golden jubilee of Rolls-Royce and Bentley Motors settling in the town, an open day was held, and over 80,000 persons walked through the gates on 18 September 1988 to celebrate fifty years in Crewe. Many more were able to

ating shop, c. 1988. The growth of clutter needs no comment as the picture powerfully indicates what fferences fifty years can bring. *(Rolls-Royce Enthusiasts' Club)*

witness the ten-minute flying display by a Spitfire that, for many of the onlookers, brought back nostalgic memories of the Merlin years. A more permanent memorial was a plaque presented to the borough council by Peter Ward on behalf of R-RMC.

Another event, in a far more majestic setting, was the launch of the new models in June of the same year, although as each was nominated as the second in the series it would be more correct to term these cars as revisions. This grand affair was arranged for the distributor network in the august surroundings of Blenheim Palace, where three of the directors welcomed the guests to a dinner, a dance and a display of the 1989 models. Perhaps these cars were responsible for the 1980s ending on a high, with the sales figures showing a 16 per cent increase, the last good news for the best part of the next decade. What followed were rumours of redundancies, and more rumours that the firm was for sale. Early in 1990 Sir Ron Brierley, the New Zealand investment speculator, was the first to make a bid for R-RMC. Plastow's attitude to Brierley's bid was that when R-RMC had been

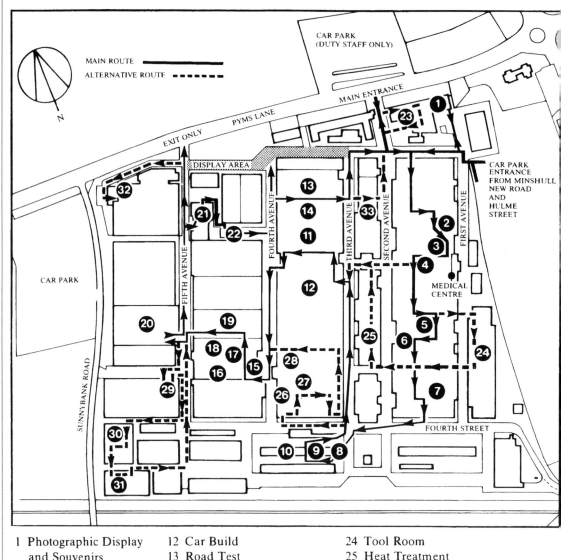

1 Photographic Display
   and Souvenirs
2 Clean Room
3 Gears
4 Swedturns
5 Crankshaft
6 Strip Inspection
7 Engine-Line
8 Test Bed 9
9 Test Bed 11
10 Test Bed 12
11 Car Build

12 Car Build
13 Road Test
14 Road Test
15 Wood Shop
16 White Line
17 Unit Dash Build
18 Production Electrical
19 Trim and Upholstery
20 New Finishing Shop
21 Emission Test
22 Anechoic Chamber
23 Canteen

24 Tool Room
25 Heat Treatment
26 Wax Room
27 Shell Room
28 Vickers Precision Components
29 Parts Distribution Centre
30 Training School
31 FD12 Unit Build
32 Shaker Rig
33 Laboratory

A programme of special events including a 'Flypast' by a Spitfire was arranged to celebrate fifty years of Rolls
Royce in Crewe on 18 September 1988. Pictured here is the route of the factory tour. Other attractions
included the Band of the Life Guards and a cavalcade of Crewe-built motor cars. *(Author's collection)*

independent in the 1970s it could not thrive alone, being vulnerable to the vagaries of the currency market and fluctuations in demand. Another statement claimed that the management and employees were better off within the Vickers group, a statement that returned to haunt the employees time and again in the 1990s. Brierley's bid was rejected at the Vickers AGM in the spring of 1990, with only 33 per cent in favour.

Chapter Seven

The End of the Road

. . . the Flying Lady is being primed for the unwanted attention of German wooers.

Gareth Walsh, *Crewe Chronicle*, 28 December 1994

The late 1980s and early '90s brought a determined attempt by the management to reassert its authority over the workforce. In 1989 efforts made by Peter Hill and Charles Matthews to deal with the practice of unofficial breaks were only partially successful. A tea break of fifteen minutes in the forenoon, and one of ten minutes in the afternoon, had become the accepted norm, but these had been extended by the men in some departments to well over the acceptable length. Loose timing of piecework was at the root of the problem, for this meant that a day's target could be reached with the minimum of effort. Such a statement is not meant to apportion blame, for such practices grew over the years, owing to a combination of weak management, opportunistic employees and some inept timing of jobs. The notion of custom and practice was a jealously guarded one so far as the shop floor unions were concerned.

With regard to custom and practice, there had always been an acknowledgement that only skilled workers who had served a recognised apprenticeship in an engineering trade could perform certain jobs. The company gave tacit approval to this in that it provided an apprentice training scheme. As the end of the twentieth century approached the demand for traditional skills was declining, leading to a corresponding decline in the negotiating power of the stewards. A further lever that worked against the unions was the increase in effectiveness and efficiency of work study. There had always been an undeclared battle between the skilled man and the rate-fixer, with the operator trying to manipulate the time allowed in his favour. If he was successful, it meant a more relaxed pace of working and the opportunity for regular overtime. In September 1989 the company-inspired document 'Working Time Disciplines' became one of the opening shots in a campaign to tackle what management considered was trade union opposition to change.

It was against this background that the workers' representatives received a bombshell when they met management off-site for the annual pay negotiations in December 1990. In the late 1980s they had accepted the introduction of cashless pay from the beginning of 1991, and so were hoping for a quiescent meeting. Instead of the expected figures and percentages, the union side was presented with a package of measures that demanded an end to demarcation, an introduction of team-working and a new disputes procedure. Any increase in pay depended on acceptance of the proposals in what became known as the Green Book. It is possible to see the first gleams of this book in Peter Ward's seemingly innocent statement reported in the issue of *Voice* dated March 1990: '. . . we must be determined about increasing our productivity to below 1,000 hours per car in order to meet the profit targets necessary to pay for our future'. It was by blunt instrument methods, such as the Green Book, that productivity was tackled.

The Green Book had been compiled by an executive caucus, consisting of Charles Matthews, Chris Brookes, Ron Pearce and three senior managers, and was an 'ideal world' scenario, so far as management was concerned. When the union side strenuously protested, it was informed that it could be implemented, if necessary, by giving six weeks' notice. As a precursor to the introduction of an imposed 'disputes procedure' the company had resigned from the Engineering Employer's Federation in October 1990, so that it would no longer be bound by the national status quo. What Matthews wanted was flexible working practices to harmonise with the wage grade structure introduced in 1988. To achieve this, the Green Book proposed: 'It is agreed that all Unions party to this agreement, agree to end all restrictions and demarcations based on union spheres of influence. . . . Accordingly, employees will undertake any work which is within their capabilities irrespective of trade or grade, any where within Crewe site and undertake any training necessary to achieve this.' Matthews claimed that the accent had to be on maximum accountability and responsibility, right down to the shop floor.

This drive for flexibility smashed the departmental system that had been operating at Pym's Lane since 1938, in which every department had a foreman and a charge hand. Under the new regime the factory was divided into eighteen zones, with each zone having a manager and ten teams. A team consisted of a leader and ten workers. For instance, zone one was located at the north end of the main shop and consisted of the former departments numbered 101, 102, 103, 104 and 121. Basically, these covered capstan and bar auto lathes, milling and drilling. Owing to the worsening economic climate, both locally and nationally, the unions had little option other than to sign up to the measures thrust at them, and this they did on 18 March 1991, despatching half a century of industrial administration into oblivion.

DRASTIC DECLINE

By October it was not only the autumn leaves that were being blown away from Pym's Lane, for the winds of recession were becoming a gale in the UK. Various factors, such as the tax on luxury cars in the USA, events in the Persian Gulf and the fiscal policies of Nigel Lawson in the late 1980s, were blamed for this. Lending for mortgages and personal consumption grew at just under 20 per cent a year, until September 1990. Nigel Lawson, the Chancellor in Thatcher's third administration, asserted that any misjudgements he might have made were compounded by the mistakes of the private sector in general and the banks in particular. In the event interest rates moved up sharply and negative equity was the burden that far too many owner-occupiers had to live with. Unfortunately many could not afford to do so, and nationally 36,610 homes were repossessed between June and September 1991.

By the end of 1991 the consequences of the recession for R-RMC were horrific. Sales did not dip, they dropped as a stone down a mineshaft, if a mineshaft could have been found. Car production fell from over 3,300 to 1,723, a cut of nearly 50 per cent. Overtime was drastically curtailed, leading to speculation that further redundancies would follow. In a determined attempt to curb such speculation, a chimerical statement was issued to each employee at Pym's Lane in October 1990, boldly claiming that there was no reason to fear for the future. Within four months the axe had fallen on 15 per cent of the pay-roll.

The whole of the workforce now began to fear for their jobs. In previous recessions many of the skilled tradesmen had been confident that they would be kept on even if the lazy, the late and the agitators received their notice to quit. This time, with the constant drip of redundancies feeding apprehension into every department, distress was apparent in all corners. Mike Dunn was also in the stream that flowed out through the Pym's Lane gate in 1992, although his exit was announced months earlier and he went voluntarily, with the good wishes of the majority of the Crewe car makers. The consensus locally is that he did a good job during a difficult decade. That he was never replaced is indicative of the low regard for engineers at Pym's Lane in the 1990s.

A three-day week was introduced in July 1991, scheduled to last until the new year. Local anguish and resentment were not mollified when it was reported that Plastow, chairman of Vickers, had received a salary increase of £1,900 a week. Although this rise was related to the profit that Vickers had made in the previous year, it was especially galling when it was announced six months later that Vickers had made a loss of £4.3 million in the first half of 1991. Such news served to gild his salary increase with further ironic tints.

John Major's Conservative government was now ensnared in a maelstrom of economic muddle that culminated in the so-called 'Black Wednesday', 16 September 1992, when the UK fled the ERM in ignominious circumstances. Manufacturing output declined continuously between August 1990 and March 1992, when the bank rate was always in double figures, and in the south Cheshire region unemployment doubled in a few months. The pharmaceutical firm known as the Wellcome Foundation and the Sandbach truck makers ERF were shedding labour, as were the local rail workshops and the Royal Ordnance factory at nearby Radway Green. Ogihara, the Japanese car component manufacturer that had planned to open a huge factory on the town's industrial estate, to be its European headquarters, cancelled the project. As has already been noted, the foundry of Vickers Precision Components Division was closed down, along with the Mulliner Park Ward plant in London, though the activities of the latter were recommenced at Crewe.

Industrial relations between groups of workers deteriorated to rock bottom. At a meeting of the works committee in September, a manager was alleged to have said that he was fed up with shop floor workers moaning about having to struggle on a three-day week. More complaints were aired, in union meetings, that management did not communicate with the hourly paid employees. The autumn of 1991 saw further job losses and a two-week lay off, causing Gwyneth Dunwoody, MP for Crewe and Nantwich, to make a long speech in Parliament likening the Crewe RR management to Victorian bosses of the worst kind. She also said that RR believed that, 'because the workforce was pliable and helpful, it could impose whatever work conditions it chooses'.

Three weeks before Christmas 260 workers were sacked, although not on the 'last in, first out' principle. The selection criteria were skills, experience, flexibility, special qualifications, employment record and work performance. Dunwoody said that management was initiating a reign of terror, as it deliberately sought confrontation. Tony Blair, as shadow employment minister, visited Crewe to examine the unions' alternative options to redundancy, an examination that led to a request for the management to think again, only for John Bodie, speaking for management, to reject the request. In this context it is significant that Bodie had worked with Ian McGregor during the miners' strike.

Faced with deteriorating markets, the company had very little option than to down-size, for by January 1992 the order-book was virtually empty. It could be argued – and argued vigorously – that the fashion in which the down-sizing was done was incompetent and deliberately provocative. Some notices were delivered at night by a courier on a motor cycle; one was delivered to the wrong address, and not received by the addressee for some days. Another man marked out for the sack even had to pay a surcharge to the postman because his notice was sent in an under-stamped envelope. In total 1,500 jobs disappeared in 1991. Seven of the dismissed employees sued the company for unfair dismissal and won their case, receiving three months' salary as compensation. The tribunal's judgement was that 'individual consultations were carried out in a hasty, intimidatory, inadequate, and chaotic fashion'. Incidentally, this has become a classic case in worker/management relations, even being cited by Amicus as 'Case Study 1' in a booklet on redundancy. The tribunal's verdict was not received with a glad shout in the boardroom at Pym's Lane. There can be little doubt that the reputation for responsible and caring management vanished from Rolls-Royce, Crewe, in 1991.

In the autumn of that year United Research (UR), an international management consultancy, was engaged to reverse the horrendous losses and to initiate change. The UR personnel worked alongside teams of employees, altering and amending working practices in such areas as future projects, engineering effectiveness, manufacturing improvement, quality, marketing strategy, bought-out items, management and communications. In the second issue of *Reach*, an extra in-house newspaper distributed to all employees, the benefits that would result were outlined, being stated as better quality engineering, reduced costs, fewer unnecessary design changes, improved level of engineering output and shorter engineering lead times. Altogether there were around twenty teams involving about a hundred persons, including eight from R-RMC, for just over a year. Whether the exercise had any substantial long-term effect upon the company's financial position is debatable. What is beyond argument is that it had its own technical language. With such titles as RAMP, RAT, WIP, ZEST and JIT the lexicon of acronyms was certainly expanded.

At the same time Vickers made it known that the company was for sale, stimulating rumours that BMW, Toyota, Mercedes Benz, Ford and Peugeot were interested parties. Speculation was rife, with Vickers supposedly seeking £200 million for RR from Toyota, against BMW's offer of £120 million, a massive sum, in the middle of a trade depression, for a car manufacturer that had just declared a loss of £60 million and, as the local paper pointed out, with no rights to its own logo.

Amid this redundancy, overtime was a strange phenomenon at Pym's Lane, yet it did exist. That is, until the unions banned it in a successful effort to force the management to consult with the representatives of the workforce.

GLEAMS AMONG THE GLOOM

Despite all of the turmoil three new models were introduced within a period of eighteen months. The first was the Bentley Continental R, which has already been mentioned as the fulfilment of Project 90. It is supposed to have caused a sensation when unveiled at Geneva, in March 1991. Priced at £168,000, it broke a ten-year famine of new models and was the first two-door Bentley to be manufactured at Crewe since 1950. The second, a Silver Spur II touring limousine, made its appearance seven months later at the Frankfurt Motor Show, and to ensure exclusivity it was planned to build just twenty-five cars a year. The last of the new models was the £91,000 Bentley Brooklands that proudly made its debut in September 1992 at Brooklands in Weybridge, Surrey. Ian Kay, the marketing director, expressed hopes that it would attract more customers. Obviously, for else why was it made? The latter appellation had also been attached to the refurbished Pym's Lane canteen, which was now known as 'Brooklands Restaurant'.

In addition to these cars, the company manufactured a weather vane for the extension to Crewe's Municipal Buildings. The original building, dating from 1903, had on its roof a model of Stephenson's *Rocket*, manufactured in Crewe railway workshops. The weather vane for the extension was a model of a Silver Cloud, made by apprentices at Pym's Lane. The firm also became the first motor car design and manufacturing company to be awarded international standard ISO 9001 for its Quality Management Systems, an award that was necessary for competitive tendering for Ministry of Defence contracts.

Not all changes in the models sold from Pym's Lane were so obvious that they needed to be announced as new. Many changes could involve minor alterations such as modifying the size of a hole, or varying the material of a component. Eric James had regulated these changes by virtue of the 'engineering change department', with Denis Irwin, Brian Salisbury, and 'Jolly' Jack Jolley organising them through the aptly titled 'modifications section'. By the late 1980s these changes could generate about 2 million pieces of paper a year, in order that they could be tracked by all the personnel with a need to know. In any one week engineering could be dealing with up to forty items, so in 1990 a computer system known as integrated product change management was developed. This reduced the amount of paper used and eased the task of John Fleet and the engineering change coordination department.

Further computer systems were developed as they were needed: for example, one that more efficiently halted the flow of non-conforming materials and another that gave the shop floor greater access to information on manufacturing layouts. The distribution resource planning system, which revealed the world-wide stock situation and allowed a proper balance to be kept, was controlled through an IBM AS/400 computer, apparently a totally new machine for the Crewe site, and data could be accessed within seconds of the technicians putting it through the computer terminals.

Driven by the overall business plan, the training and development department was reorganised in the early 1990s into two main sections under the control of Ron Pearce, formerly employee relations manager. The workshop training was amended so that the needs of adult manual workers were included as well as those of the apprentices, with the aim of producing a more flexible workforce. The other branch of the department was for management and supervisory training, as well as language tutorials in French and German for those with a business need for such coaching. Over 500 employees a year used the various courses and facilities of this department, in addition to its being an agency for the Conservative government's Youth Training Scheme, or YTS as it was known.

Rolls-Royce Motor Cars also made a token gesture, in the 1990s, at saving the planet, when it produced a policy statement committing the company to protection of the environment, both in its own operations and in the day-to-day activities of the employees. We have seen earlier in this book that emissions legislation in the

Despite lack of capital, the management was always conscious of its environmental responsibility. This is a panoramic view of the interceptor built to filter water and waste discharged from the factory. The brook into which it drains runs through the fields on the north side of Pym's Lane before emptying into the River Weaver. (Rolls-Royce Enthusiasts' Club)

USA and elsewhere brought a vigorous response from the company when it affected the sales of its product. As RR had, in 1969, installed a plant to deal with the industrial effluent at a cost of nearly £250,000, the firm could not be accused of dereliction of duty, for surface water drainage, waste and air pollution were already tightly controlled. In 1992 Mike Parsons was given the additional title of environmental coordinator, with the brief to initiate a policy statement. To help him, a steering committee consisting of Tom Creer, Vic Harris and Mike Brookes was set up, with the objectives of forming a training plan, a vendor policy and a plan for the minimisation of waste.

ROCK BOTTOM

Within a month of the Bentley Brooklands being offered for sale, information of the worst kind was a hot topic in the financial pages of various newspapers. Further drastic job losses were intimated and, although initially the firm denied the rumours, within a few days the information was confirmed as correct. This was a body-blow to the remaining employees, for a special issue of *Voice*, in March 1992, had suggested that the worst was over. Something in the region of a third of the workforce had to be released, meaning that hundreds of jobs disappeared. The criteria used by the board to arrive at the figure were a reduction of capacity to match anticipated sales, out-sourcing of a number of components and extending a new departmental structure into a much leaner organisation. This latter phrase, 'leaner organisation', was the fashionable economic nostrum of the time. What it meant in practice was the disappearance of the bar auto lathes, copper-smiths, sheet-metal working (except for radiator manufacture), exhaust and welding, styling, jig and tool design, design and detail drawing offices. The tool-room and the prototype departments were reduced in size to the point where Pym's Lane could no longer make experimental cars. The demise of these departments, and their replacement by buying-in of parts and services, meant that the plant could operate with a pay-roll of about 2,100, enabling a break-even production figure of 1,500 cars a year.

The date when the redundant employees left the factory had to be brought forward rapidly, owing to serious damage done to a few cars by a disgruntled worker or workers. Regarding this period, Peter Hill said that no group of managers and union representatives had ever faced anything so serious in the history of Rolls-Royce cars. At the meeting early in October where these matters were discussed were the aforementioned Hill, M. Brookes, Phil Harding and John Spackman, the union representatives being (among others) John Rhodes, Tony Flood and John Edwards. The workforce of 2,100 was left under no illusion that it would have to do the work of 2,800, even to the point of working overtime for standard rates.

Locally there was much frenetic action. Peter Kent, the council leader, along with Gwyneth Dunwoody, met Neil Hamilton, a junior minister at the Trade and Industry department, to lobby for Assisted Area Status, which would have meant Crewe getting government help. Nothing was granted, despite the unemployment rate's increasing by seven percentage points to 11.5 per cent in less than two years. All the local ministers of religion were invited to a special meeting, held at the

Salvation Army Citadel, to coordinate a response in prayer and action. The *Crewe Chronicle* printed a prayer, by courtesy of the Industrial Chaplain, that requested that the hearts of the workers might be saved from bitterness. Not to be outdone, the commercial representatives on the Chamber of Trade suggested that the time had arrived to abolish the fees at Crewe's public car parks. An ameliorating factor, provided by the Company, was a job club entitled 'Pathfinder', where redundant employees were instructed in the art of compiling a CV and showered with financial advice.

Feelings regarding the management can be gauged by the comment of a regular columnist of the local paper, suggesting that better bosses for RR could be provided from the ape house at Chester Zoo. The same source went on to write, with some prescience, that a viable future could only be guaranteed by the current management being replaced with executives from Germany or Japan. Most people in the south Cheshire area did not, at that time, realise the full extent of the trauma that the R-RMC board faced as it tried to run a firm that was bleeding to death. Warburg Securities, a prestigious international merchant bank, suggested that Vickers should divest its self of R-RMC in order to remain in business. Many of the national tabloids were horrified by this proposal, especially when it was rumoured that R-RMC might slip into German hands. It still remains a source of congratulation to all at Pym's Lane that R-RMC at least broke even in 1993, although most of the credit must be given to the bizarre buying habits of Prince Jefri of Brunei.

A concomitant factor that further depressed the beleaguered employees was the pledge by the management that there would be no pay review for the whole of 1993. As the cost of living rose by over 5 per cent in the two years following January 1992 this was akin to a wage cut, yet the cost stability must have been a contributing element in the return to profitability. By the end of 1993 a packet of measures had been negotiated that promised two years of job security for the remaining rump of the workforce, along with a 4.5 per cent wage rise spread over the next two years – still below the rate of inflation.

It was during 1993 that a £30 million revamping project, affecting every car that the company produced, was realised. The seventy changes that had been engineered into the cars, mainly by Mike Dunn before he left Crewe, helped to make them 'greener' than any previous models. The continued development of Jack Phillips's V8 engine brought an increase in mid-range power of approximately 20 per cent. The cheapest car was now the Bentley Brooklands, at £96,401, and the most expensive was the RR Limousine, costing not far short of £250,000.

A few months after this Graham Hull, the chief stylist, was given a design brief for styling a new model under the code P3000. Over the next three years this project brought innovations such as seats that were adjustable in four planes and a climate control system that allowed the temperature to be regulated on each side of the car. Eventually the new model was launched under the name of Silver Seraph.

Early in 1994 R-RMC became the largest British-owned car manufacturer, when BMW completed the purchase of Rover Cars. Richard Charlesworth, the public relations chief, said that such a sale was sad because the firm was no longer British. He was grateful that the maker of the best cars in the world was still

British-owned and stated that the nation should take great pride in that fact. Despite this, whispers abounded that R-RMC was up for sale, if the price was right, with BMW, Toyota and Mercedes being on the list of suitors.

DERBY KNOWS BEST

Later in the year Vickers proclaimed its intention to staunch the haemorrhage of capital at Pym's Lane. Apparently over £100 million had already been supplied to Crewe, yet still more would be necessary to develop a completely new engine to replace the V8. As collaboration with a wealthy partner was an attractive proposition for the main Vickers board, a hunt began for a foreign partner to supply a power pack suitable for the new millennium, a hunt that quickly resolved into a choice between BMW and Mercedes and two engines from North America. According to Tucker in *The Goodwood Phantom*, BMW was unaware that Ward was negotiating with Mercedes.

It is well documented that the R-RMC hierarchy preferred the new V12 engine being developed by Mercedes at Stuttgart. At a meeting in the autumn of 1994, held, for secrecy's sake, in the empty factory after the Friday morning shift had gone home, forty or so engineers, directors and senior managers discussed the various offers until early evening, before choosing the Mercedes V12. It is said that Peter Ward eventually shook hands with his opposite number at Mercedes as a signal that the deal was on. Deplorably, others had levers that could dismantle deals decided at Crewe, and RR plc, along with the board of Vickers, favoured BMW's engine.

It is on record that Sir Ralph Robins of RR plc threatened to prevent Vickers using the RR logo if it used the Mercedes engine. This is how Richard Feast, in his book *Kidnap of the Flying Lady*, describes the shuffling deal that resulted in the substitution of the BMW engine for that of the Mercedes: 'What might, outside the arms and aerospace industry, have been an uncomplicated automotive decision was defeated by behind-the-scenes Anglo-German power politcking by Robins and Pischetsrieder. They were destined to play the same double act to secure the ownership of Rolls-Royce Motor Cars for BMW three and a half years later.' The minutiae of the dealings that resulted in the decision need not concern us here. Suffice it to say that Peter Ward realised that his time at Rolls-Royce and Bentley Motors had run out, leaving him little option other than resignation, although severance pay of over £400,000 must have anointed his disappointment. It has to be stated that he derived more honour from his action than did some of the others involved in this cynical cabal.

Being the supplier of an engine for R-RMC placed BMW in pole position whenever the question of new owners of Rolls-Royce and Bentley was discussed. A link-up between RR and BMW was a lively topic in the town, where the *Crewe Chronicle*'s hope was that the partnership would mature as one between equals, and not to the point where BMW would dominate – for a wholesale take-over by the German car maker would be a tragedy. The same source contained an article with the prophetic words that the Flying Lady was being 'primed for the unwanted attention of German wooers'.

Buying in the power unit for the cars spelt the end of machining in the main shop. This was a momentous change, as the Pym's Lane factory had been built to manufacture engines, and for nearly sixty years this large area had throbbed with the clamour and din of machines, day and night, especially during six years of war. The skilled and semi-skilled machinists were offered retraining and were either content or desolate with the replacement jobs that were generally in body trim and the wood shop.

Meanwhile, for the other workers at Pym's Lane, life returned almost to normal after they resumed full-time working early in 1993. Homage was paid to one of the social issues of the decade when a no smoking policy was negotiated that allowed the dreadful weed to be enjoyed at limited times and in strictly demarcated places. A Company Council, comprised of five hourly paid employees and two staff, was installed in place of the works committee, and among its first members were John Edwards and Tony Flood. Employees were re-titled 'associates' and given special work-wear that included monogrammed navy blue sweatshirts. Previously attire was varied, with boiler suits, khaki smocks or cow-gowns and blue jeans being the most common workshop wear. In the 1950s there was an occasion when Ronnie Dyson admonished one rather colourfully dressed apprentice for looking as though he worked in a circus.

Added to the curriculum at Pym's Lane, in the spring of 1993, were training sessions on a 'Strive For Perfection' project, with the objective of increasing customer satisfaction, quality, sales, delivery, cost, warranty, inventory, planning and model year delivery and reducing non-conformance. To guide employees along the road of efficiency and proficiency a newspaper was published, aptly titled *Strive*.

In addition to the STRIVE project another scheme was introduced, called MOST (an acronym for Maynard Operational Sequence Technique), a variation on method time measurement that was used quite widely throughout the industry. It involved a video camera replacing the traditional stop-watch, so that an analysis of the number of movements taken to perform a particular task could be made and a time allocated to them. Initially it was given a trial run in the trim shop, when little consultation resulted in little cooperation. Steve Taylor, the convenor, went on a fact-finding mission to the Creda factory in Stoke-on-Trent to see MOST in action. This led to other stewards and workers being trained in its principles in order to be practitioners or applicators. A commentator on industrial affairs at Crewe RR made the pertinent observation that it was noticeable that no outright challenge was made regarding the use of the technique.

The demoralised workforce was now beginning to believe the company's oft-expressed mantra that they, the remaining workers, were lucky to have a job. Judging from contemporary comments, the MOST scheme's greatest success was in providing one or two days' training every week for a workforce desperate not to join the window-watchers at the local job centre. At least one day a week was spent in training each other in problem-solving.

There is an enigmatic thought regarding the multiplicity of training projects introduced into Pym's Lane, with monotonous regularity, in the last two decades of the twentieth century. Each one was trumpeted as the answer to the problem of quality or organisation, so the pliant and patient workforce went along to the training sessions expecting little, and never being disappointed. The journey that had begun with the appointment of John Hollings as director of quality, and that had run through Reg Spencer's quality circles in the 1980s, must be judged pointless if training schemes and quality monitoring systems were still necessary in the 1990s. It would appear to the casual observer that, every time a new executive or quality director was appointed, he introduced his favoured quality scheme into the production processes and by implication denigrated that which had gone before. Gazing at them from a distance, it is possible for the more cynical to see some of these schemes as caricatures of the real thing.

The success of the various courses, programmes and quality drives in the 1980s and '90s can be gauged by a comment from Graham Morris in the summer of 1997. He had been at Crewe for all of three months when he said that all employees showed a lack of understanding of business in the world market, and that R-RMC standards did not measure up to their key competitors. If such lamentable conditions existed a couple of years from the twenty-first century, then all of the other schemes must have failed. Morris then entered enthusiastically into the next bout of quality awareness under an appellation new to the works at Pym's Lane, namely 'A Place of Renown'. Under Vickers' ownership, a new slogan arrived every three or four years. Previously the workers had been cajoled with 'Right First Time', 'Strive for Perfection' and 'Together we will make Crewe the world's best workplace', to name but three.

A mark of the 1990s that was being taken up by schools, colleges and businesses, was the mission statement, so, not to be outdone, R-RMC produced its own which was 'To create the world's finest motoring experience'. This seems reminiscent of the slogan, 'The best car in the world', which Plastow had persuaded Crewe and Nantwich Borough Council to emblazon on its entry signs, adjacent to every major road in south Cheshire. Very few were unaware of this slogan. Very few were aware of the mission statement, even among the employees.

ALL CHANGE

In 1995 a fifty-year working practice was ended when it was decided that bodies would be made in-house rather than bought from a specialist supplier. As outlined in a previous chapter, Robotham started the car division's life in Crewe by approaching Pressed Steel to manufacture the first all-steel bodies, whereas the last contract for this work was given to Rover Cars. When body production commenced, the former Kelvinator section in the block adjacent to the paint-shop premises was fitted out with all the machinery necessary to produce bodies to the standard demanded by R-RMC.

Measurements to a fraction of a millimetre were a necessary part of the dimensional integrity of the RR and Bentley bodies, and computer-controlled checking ensured design compliance. No less than 6,500 spot-welds, using a technique known as plasma brazing, provided rigidity to the body, yet with almost invisible joints. This brazing was a new method of cool temperature welding that prevented distortion of the panels. The body of the Silver Seraph was the first to require the newly acquired skills of body assembly workers.

Further investment was made in the 1990s in other departments, including the wood shop and the reception area. A refurbished wood shop, under the management of Ian Kershaw, was able to reduce the time taken to produce the car's wood components from twenty-three days to sixteen. The reception area at the centre of the main office block had been the main entrance for important visitors ever since the factory opened, although there was an economy drive in the early 1980s that, for a short time, replaced the receptionist by a telephone. The artist's sketches showed the new reception area redesigned with a glass canopy, gravelled approach and silver birch trees. The intention was translated into reality, resulting in an impressive entrance, although the trees are cropped at regular intervals. The intention in reforming this area was to impress upon visitor and employee alike the vast heritage that the name Rolls-Royce embraced.

Another, more drastic and dramatic element of this modernisation programme was the introduction of a moving production line. Previously, all cars on the assembly line were physically pushed to the next station. If needed parts were missing, imputable to shortages, these would be fitted further up the line. Shortages were a consistent, perennial problem at Pym's Lane, regardless of who was in charge of production. Nobody seemed able to organise an assembly line that was not blighted by lack of parts.

Along with the £40 million programme to modernise the plant, there was a concerted effort by the board to re-brand the marques. The rationale behind this endeavour, according to Ian McKay, director of marketing, was to successfully position Rolls-Royce and Bentley for the next century. Every arm of the publicity department worked to change the way that the outside world perceived the cars by 'creating identities and retail environments that reflect the strength of the marques'. Over the 1997 winter the word 'new' in conjunction with RR or Bentley was used wherever possible. In one paragraph on page 6 of the 1998 spring edition of *Quest*, a magazine especially published for Rolls-Royce and Bentley owners, the word 'new' was used seven times in a description of the debut of the Silver Seraph. Perhaps it was the example of Tony Blair in successfully re-branding his party as 'New Labour' that provided the inspiration for this campaign.

The modernised assembly process is described in detail in the special 1998 summer edition of *Quest*. All extraneous walls and compartments had been removed from the build hall, creating a vast space (vast by RR build standards) in which the whole assembly, including trimming the car, took place. The assembly process consisted initially of overhead slings, attached to a raised monorail, onto which sub-assemblies could be built. At the same time the body was mounted onto the two sub-frames, travelling at a speed of 2.7cm a minute through the build hall, where all the sub-assemblies and other parts were fitted. The system, designed solely for Bentley Motor Cars – or so *Quest* maintained – allowed twenty hours for the car to be assembled. Testing had also been modernised, with the installation of a rolling road, a monsoon chamber and a shake rig, ensuring that every known road and weather condition could be replicated. Test engineers, sitting on any seat in the car, responded to computer prompts recording technical data as it arose, although road testing still continued, as any observer of Pym's Lane gates could tell.

This investment was grist for the rumour mill that periodically provided the locality with such weird speculations as that it was all a cosmetic ploy to prepare Rolls-Royce for sale. Even Graham Morris suggested that this period was a cynic's paradise. Denials by Vickers did nothing to permanently quash the rumours; only the morbid interest created by Princess Diana's death provided a diversion for a few weeks in the late summer of 1997. October saw it established that the gossip was founded on fact, with the announcement that R-RMC was again for sale. One obvious, serious contender was BMW, owing to the close working relationship it had forged with RR. By November, VW had declared its interest and the battle for the jewel in the crown of the UK's manufacturing firms had begun.

Surrounded by rumour and uncertainty, the last true Crewe-born Rolls-Royce, named Silver Seraph, and its stable mate the Bentley Arnage, were shown to the associates and dealers before being revealed to about 400 interested onlookers on the town's square early in March 1998. The public were also given a rare glimpse of the company's Silver Ghost. To help the townspeople grasp the importance of the occasion, a live band was hired, along with BBC Radio Stoke's Road Show. Two months earlier, the Silver Seraph had been shown to selected members of the world's press at Wick, in Scotland. Among the publicity pictures from this event are some that show Tony Gott and Graham Morris in Highland dress, which must surely be a statement of some kind. It remains doubtful whether LS, Stafford, Dorey, Grylls and Blatchley would have worn kilts when the Shadow was unveiled. Regarding the launch of the new car, Graham Morris, not knowing what the Vickers' board was planning, claimed that it was the dawn of a new era. It certainly was for him.

The world was afforded the same privilege of viewing the new cars at the Geneva International Motor Show, a far more acceptable venue than the limited space in Crewe town centre. The Silver Seraph, claimed by the company to be the ninth new model in ninety-two years, was the first to be assembled on the newly constructed moving line in the build hall. Priced at £155,000 it was the first car for forty years not to be powered by Jack Phillips's V8. Having died just over two years earlier, he was not around to mourn its passing, nor to wonder at the strange fancy of a BMW engine powering, or, according to most technical experts, under-powering, a Rolls-Royce motor car. For many enthusiasts the aura of the marque was evaporating rapidly.

RHINEGOLD FOR SILVER MARQUES

Despite this new car, uncertainty abounded regarding the purchasers of the plant. A further factor that muddied the water was that RR plc would have the final say in who bought its namesake in Crewe. Frank Culley was informing all and sundry of this fact long before it was aired in the *Sunday Times* in the first week of 1998. By the end of March the deal was done, or so it seemed. BMW's offer of £340 million was accepted, allowing the new owners to examine the books. Pischetsrieder, the BMW chairman, stated that the supply of engines would cease if any other buyer was successful. Whether privy to this or not, VW upped its bid to £430 million, and despite Sir Ralph Robins threatening, yet again, that VW was not fit to use the RR logo, the deal went ahead. Peter Pugh, Richard Feast and Malcolm Tucker have traced, from their various viewpoints, more than the outline of the deliberations and deals that led to the carve-up when BMW removed R-RMC from its home in Crewe, leaving Bentley Motors as the sole occupier of the partially renovated Pym's Lane factory under the ownership of VW.

What concerns us here is the effect upon south Cheshire. Graham Morris resigned, feeling he had no other option after promising the workforce that the Flying Lady and the winged 'B' would remain together. Morris was even unaware that the Crewe car maker was to be offered for sale and to his embarrassment the news broke while he was cruising the Caribbean. This startling fact says more about Sir Colin Chandler and the Vickers board than it does about Morris. Whereas resignation removed his source of income, it restored his honour and improved his reputation locally, unlike that of certain other UK nationals involved in the sale.

A well-known local union official condemned Chandler's attitude as 'horrendous'. Others used words like 'stabbed in the back', 'betrayed and stunned', 'disgrace' and 'bizarre'. The *Guardian* concluded that 'either Vickers has screwed him [Piech of VW], or BMW has, or he could have been stitched by both'. Gloom spread across the town like a blanket of drizzle when it was realised that the marques would divide. Thousands of men and women from the south Cheshire region had earned their living at Royces. Now it was going, and Bentley Motors did not, at that time, seem an adequate substitute.

Chandler's boast about the good price being the end result, as if money were the sole criterion, appeared, to many in Crewe, as another aspect of the unacceptable

View of the car assembly line, *c.* 1978, with a Shadow body in situ ready for mounting the subframes. *(Rolls-Royce Enthusiasts' Club)*

face of capitalism. According to Peter Pugh, in his work on Rolls-Royce, similar sentiments were expressed by Eric Barrass, the President of the RR Enthusiasts' Club. To powerless onlookers within the purview of Pym's Lane, Vickers began to take on the spectre of asset-strippers. The sports field in Minshull New Road was unloaded to a firm of house builders a few weeks before the sale was announced. A few million pounds is neither here nor there in the grand scheme of car building, so why should the land be sold? Many RR employees felt that if certain powers could have got their hands on the historic vehicles at Pym's Lane, then they too would have left Crewe. An indicator of the concern felt in south Cheshire is that the *Crewe Chronicle* of 16 September 1998 was the first issue for a whole year that did not contain any reference to this imbroglio of a sale.

The workers had known nothing of the various moves that resulted in the split of Rolls-Royce from Bentley. That they considered matters in a different light from the directors of Vickers, or Sir Ralph Robins, was natural. The directors were in the business of getting the best deal for shareholders, yet it has to be said that they seemed to have little concern for the economy of south Cheshire. It was difficult, if not impossible, for local people to perceive the qualities Robins possessed that gave him the peculiar ability to differentiate between two competing car giants. Such trafficking suggested that Crewe, even after twenty years of separation, was still a division under the control of Derby and that the executives there knew what was best for the car side of Rolls-Royce.

Passage of time caused the attitude of the workforce to undergo a metamorphosis. From anxiety and anger there arose a settled feeling that VW was the answer to the problems that had afflicted the manufacture of cars at Crewe. Feast maintains that major factors in this shift were the positive briefing, in the autumn of 2000, given to all employees by Tony Gott and two of his colleagues, and the inclusion of every worker in a generous car-leasing scheme. Certainly there were many gleaming VWs, Audis and Skodas on the public car parks of the town, as the scheme unofficially overflowed to near relatives of the employees. A more potent factor must have been the immense amount of VW investment that was changing the state of the factory, something that Vickers had never countenanced.

The change in morale is best summed up by a comment from Steve Taylor, the former convenor, now re-titled senior site representative, who said that the difference between VW and Vickers was that VW had a long-term view. It remains to be seen how long is long-term. Bentley, as part of RR, had been in Crewe for sixty years when VW bought the name. No one can tell the future, and so it would be foolish to suggest with any degree of certainty that Bentleys will still be made in the town in 2050. All that can be hoped is that VW remains at the cutting edge of technology and quality in order for Bentley cars to continue to be attractive to the car-buying public. Just as important, for the people of south Cheshire, is that Bentley production remains at the Crewe motor works, in Pym's Lane, for as long as cars remain a favourite mode of personal travel.

Chapter Eight

The Welfare Amenities Society

The outside social activities of the welfare are designed so that friendship will develop.

Lord Hives, 1953

When Crewe RR was established it was, as we have seen, created in the image of Rolls-Royce at Derby. Rudimentary welfare facilities had been commenced at Derby in 1919, so it was only to be expected that they would appear at Crewe in due course. The idea of welfare should be interpreted mainly as the agency that provided sporting and recreational facilities for the employees, rather than that promised by the Atlee administration when it established the Welfare State. An exception to this, the Rolls-Royce Hospital Sunday Fund, which catered for any severely sick employees, withered away when the National Health Service commenced. It must be made plain that although joining the Welfare Amenities Society was voluntary, over 60 per cent of employees did so, for a nominal sum. In 1980, when there were nineteen sections, each employee who had contracted-in paid 10p a week.

Nothing regarding welfare was attempted in the middle months of 1938 when the Derby seven, and others that joined them, were devoting all their energies to organising a division of Rolls-Royce Ltd at Crewe. The first reference to any sports or competitive movement at Pym's Lane was in November 1938, when it was reported in *The Spanner*, the short-lived Welfare Society magazine, that a rifle club had been formed under the captaincy of Dick Garner. Among the membership of approximately thirty-five was Frank Culley, who acted as first reserve to the competition team of six. Early practices took place in rented accommodation paid for by the Welfare Society. The rifle club was later amalgamated into the Rolls-Royce Home Guard.

In the spring of 1939 the local RR management requested the Air Ministry to buy 15 acres of the Totty's Hall estate, at a cost of £1,700, for a sports ground. This was in Dodd's Lane, or Minshull New Road as it later became, and before it could be used a couple of ponds had to be filled in. Its first car park, with accommodation for eight vehicles, had to be greatly extended as the years rolled by. In 1943 the stewards at Pym's Lane requested that a pavilion and changing facilities, similar to those at Derby and Glasgow, be provided. A memo from Grylls to Hives about this provides an interesting glimpse into wartime industrial relations: 'What we particularly want to avoid is that the scheme should be turned down when we ask for it and then be approved because the Crewe Shop Stewards write to the Minister.' Permission was granted, and a basic wooden structure was erected.

Until the new ground was ready Crewe Gates Farm was used by the nascent cricket section. Ernie Buchan, recently arrived from Derby, was the prime mover in the formation of both the cricket and football sections, remaining as cricket captain for many years. The first cricket match on the new ground was against a RAF team in the spring of 1940. May 1939 saw the recently formed tennis club renting two courts on the municipal playing fields for the exclusive use of RR employees, much to the annoyance of the local non-RR tennis players. Also in May, the swimming club hired the public baths for an hour every Thursday evening, a practice that continued after the war ended.

One of the high days for the children of RR employees, especially in the 1940s and '50s, was an afternoon of sports, entertainment and amusements, or, as it became known, the field day. The first one, arranged for Saturday 8 July 1939 at the new sports ground in Dodd's Lane, was partially called off on account of inclement weather. Instead, it was held in St Michael's church hall, mainly through

A charming picture of the children's field day, *c*. 1955. The vehicle is one of the 'Silver' series that never went through the design office. The driver of the converted Lister truck is Harry Hockenhull of transport sevices. Bert Fowles, a respected crown green bowler, who worked in the main machine shop, has his hand to his eye. Part of Sid Torr's face can be seen in the centre of the picture. In the '40s and '50s it never seemed to rain for these occasions, although Harry seems rather 'fed up'. *(B. Fishburne)*

the ad hoc organising ability of the indefatigable Jack Valentine. Other early organisers were John Morris, R. Woodvine, J. Shaw, W.H. Ward, L. Harper and Jack Moss, a setter from Derby who emigrated to Australia in 1947.

The welfare committee, by persuading the employees to volunteer their services, provided the amusements and the games at the field days. Roundabouts, chair-o-planes, breaking crockery, guessing games, throwing sponges, hoopla and Punch and Judy shows mingled the entertainment with running races, displays and a tug-of-war competition between the more manual departments. Some words by Ted Penaluna give a flavour of the occasion:

> I remember in the late forties going to the children's field day, held on the sports ground in Minshull New Road, with my brother and sister. Our dad, who worked for RR, was allocated tickets. These tickets had tear off strips for various amusements and refreshments. We were full of excitement for weeks before! On the big day, which always seemed to be warm and sunny, the younger children gathered outside the canteen to be taken to the field by truck. The older ones made their own way. I remember running onto the field to get into the first carriage on the Joy Ride. This was a train of two or three wooden carriages pulled by a Lister truck. There were chair-o-planes to ride. Prizes could be won by fishing for metal fish lying on the bottom of a big tub of water with a piece of string with a magnet on the end. The Flying Bubbles was best for winning a prize. This consisted of ping-pong balls, which were blown into the air to be caught in a net. The secret was to wait until the man operating the blower switched it off. The balls came down straight into the net. All these amusements were made by the men in the factory. There was a ticket to be used in the refreshment tent. If you wished you could enter for the races, egg and spoon, sack, three legged etc. the last event of the day was the prize giving, after which we left for home, tired but happy.

At the 1953 field day an office boy named P. Ollerhead entered the balloon race and won 30s when his label was returned from Wahnerheide in Germany.

In addition to this summer open-air entertainment a Christmas party was held every year in the canteen, when each child received a gift from Father Christmas (usually Syd Harvey of inspection, or later Ralph Lloyd), often in the presence of Ernest Hives and his wife. The one held in 1950 catered for over 1,000 children under 6 years old on a Friday evening two weeks before Christmas. Next day, 900 children aged between 7 and 14 were entertained to tea before watching a pantomime written by Sid Torr and produced by Jack Valentine. The large number of younger children is indicative of the baby boom of the postwar years.

During the early years of the war, as a device to prevent the enemy from knowing that Rolls-Royce was in Crewe, the football and cricket teams played under the name of Pym's Lane or Ash Bank. They need not have bothered, for there is in existence an aerial reconnaissance photograph, taken by the Luftwaffe in September 1940, where Crewe RR is plainly indicated by the words 'flugmotorenwerke Rolls Royce Ltd'. There was a frenzy of these 'security' ideas, both nationally and locally,

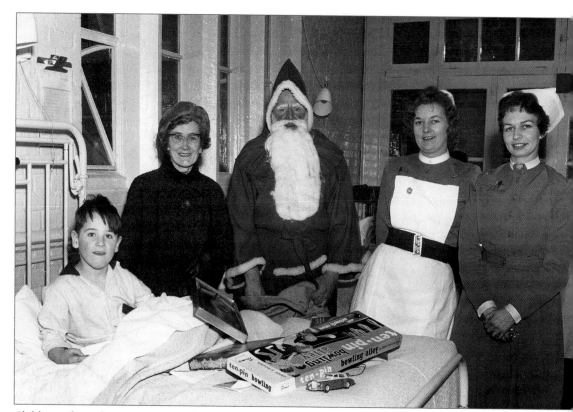

Children of employees were not forgotten if they were in hospital. Here, Father 'Syd Harvey' Christmas delivering presents in 1957 to the now demolished Crewe Memorial Hospital, in company with M Stafford. *(B. Fishburne)*

to stop would-be spies and saboteurs from identifying strategic buildings. One of the silliest to be considered was the removal of the words 'Railway Station' from the destination signs on Crewe's public buses.

Obviously the long hours worked during the wartime years curtailed many sports, yet activities were always available that enlivened the dreary hours. Concerts, arranged by the RR social committee, were regularly held in the Welfare Hall. Even before it was ready, the committee organised a ball at the Mechanic's Institution in Prince Albert Street. A group of instrumentalists, under the name of RR Rythmics, gave a concert at the Plaza in High Street in December 1939. Mentioned in an earlier chapter was the celebration when Jack Payne's broadcasting band played at the opening ceremony of the Pym's Lane works. Over 1,500 were present in the room above the canteen, which was claimed to be three times larger than any local hall. An autographed photograph of the band was auctioned to raise money for the Red Cross. Phillips, the architect, outbid Hives and Haldenby to become its owner at a price of £30.

The sports day was cancelled in 1940, owing to the emergency and the urgent need for increased production, but it resumed in 1941, when sprints, jumps, cycling and even a tug-of-war were arranged. Perhaps the high spot of the day was a march past by the Rolls-Royce Home Guard platoon, with Llewelyn-Smith taking the salute. The same year water was laid on to the ground in Dodd's Lane, enabling the bowling section to start using the recently sown bowling green. Competitive football was resumed on a more regular basis in 1942, and from then until the end of the war the team representing the factory usually fielded former professional players, such as Arthur Turner, Fred Chandler and Ernie Tagg, who had all sought employment in the factory in 1939. In later years Ernie Tagg managed Crewe Alexandra in the fourth division of the Football League. When the war ended they resumed their former calling, leaving RR to return to more prosaic players and more realistic, even appalling, scores, such as the one in November 1945 when RR lost, fourteen goals to nil, to Basford Hall.

On the resumption of peace the Welfare Amenities Society began to organise in a serious way. A branch for virtually every known sport and pastime was started, although from time to time the life of any particular branch depended upon the staying power of its members, some of the more esoteric activities having a very limited life. The first boxing tournament, which was held early in the postwar period, raised £50 for the local hospital. Cricket was played more keenly after the section

ricket section awards presentation, c. 1955. Standing, left to right: A.C. Tagg (clerk), Bill Elliott (millwright reman), Fred Stafford (works manager), Ernie Jones (polishing shop), Jack Amos (tool-maker), unidentified. eated: Mrs Valentine, Jack Valentine (equipment engineer), Mrs Wiggett?, Norman Wiggett (rate-fixer), Mrs uchan?, Ernie Buchan (accounts). (B. Fishburne)

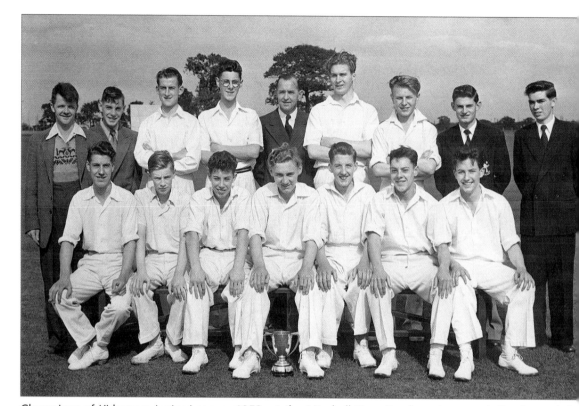

Champions of Kidsgrove Junior League, 1953, at the Minshull New Road sports ground. Front row, left right: Brian Hewitt, Keith Wrighton, Alf Weston, Peter Micklewright, ? Mason, Bill Bailey, Brian Tansey. Ba row: Jock Edmundson, the author, ?, Brian Mycock, Tim Byrne, Derek Gamage, John Taylor, Gordon Harr Maurice Bagnall. Employment at the firm was essential for membership of the team. At least half of t above found employment at the RR factory for the whole of their working life. (Author's collection)

became a member of the North Staffordshire league, and players who graced this section for the next two decades included Jack Prince, a progress chaser in the tool-room and Port Vale's former goalkeeper, Joe Dixon, Jack Amos and Gordon Walker. Under the rules of the Welfare Society, professional players were not permitted until about 1982, when Jeff Maynard became the section's first paid player.

Clan Foundry staff made an appearance on the sports ground when an invitation cricket match was held in 1947. The Houghton Weavers, a nationally known folk group, also played an invitation game at Minshull New Road. In the 1950s Frank Tyson, the soon-to-be England fast bowler, displayed his skills while playing as a professional for Knypersley. Others who went on to play for England, yet appeared against Rolls-Royce, were Ken Higgs, David Steele and Bob Taylor. Inter-departmental competitions were organised for the AID Cup, a trophy presented by the government inspection authority.

Of course the other major sport, which attracted many members and much interest, was football. The final of the Morris Cup, in 1947, when Machine Shop 'B' beat the Tool-room 2:1, attracted a crowd of over 1,000. Eleven years later, when Experimental won the final, Grylls filled the trophy with champagne. It was always understood that an apprentice gained employment in the experimental department as much on the basis of his skill with a ball as owing to his industry at the bench or lathe. Teams always played in the various local leagues under the name Rolls-Royce, Bentley never seeming to be considered by any of the sections as an appellation for competitive teams.

Angling was a popular section that generally attracted manual workers. It was mainly coarse fishing, consequently very few notables ever served on the committee. Llewellyn-Smith and Tom Haldenby provided trophies for individual and departmental winners. In 1946, long before it was fashionable, a few of the women at RR organised a cricket team, and developed sufficient skill and expertise to win the Elworth Cup in 1952. One player, Yvonne Hamer of the inspection department, was good enough to represent Cheshire. Among the other regular players were Nellie Lofkin, a supervisor responsible for interviewing and appointing all female staff in the 1940s and '50s, and Bertha Lowe, from the receiving stores office. The Cantrill Cup was the trophy on offer to the devotees of the short-lived sword fencing section, opened in the spring of 1952. Every activity had its trophy, usually presented by a manager or director. To have one's memory perpetuated by presenting a vase or cup seemed to be an occupational hazard for the great and the good at Pym's Lane.

A few words should be written about the sports ground in Minshull New Road which, despite catching any breeze that was blowing, was the envy of every visiting

Some members and officials of the tennis section, *c.* 1953. Basil Wilman, the paint technologist, is on the right. Others present are Brian Steele, a maintenance electrician, Gordon Banks of the cost office and Fred Stafford, works manager. Stafford showed more interest in welfare activities than did any other senior executive. The dwellings in the background are the wartime Totty's Hall flats. They have since been demolished. *(B. Fishburne)*

team. From 1953, when Len Ord was appointed as head groundsman, it was freely acknowledged that the cricket square was the best in the North Staffs League. That same year saw a programme of improvement undertaken at the 28-acre ground by Barrons of Derby. Hundreds of roses were planted, making the area around the pavilion a riot of colour in the summer, when it was claimed that the display was second only to that in the town's park. A second bowling green was added, along with two more soccer pitches, an extra cricket pitch with another superb square, four more hard tennis courts and a children's play area. Wooden pavilions were constructed for tennis, bowls and cricket. Planning permission was sought for a permanent pavilion, selling Joules Ales and other alcoholic liquors, for the car division's social activities.

A rather unfortunate incident occurred when Lord and Lady Hives officially opened the club on the Saturday of Coronation week in 1953. Directors and representatives from Derby, Hythe Road, British Rail, Kelvinator and the town's council formed the platform party. This was the occasion when Hives made the speech that included the words quoted at the head of this chapter. The festival day

One of the ever-popular dances organised in the Welfare Hall, usually on a Saturday night. This one was in th late 1940s, when ballroom dancing was the fashion. *(Author's collection)*

coincided with a cricket match against a rival team representing the local railway works and a large, rather vociferous crowd watched the LMR team begin to dominate the bowling. One of its batsmen lofted a drive towards a RR fielder, whose attempt to catch the ball was greeted with wild shouts and loud guffaws from a partisan section of supporters. When he dropped the catch the jeers grew louder still, so he turned and hurled the ball at the mocking spectators just as Hives and the official party appeared on the balcony. He never played for RR again.

It is a travesty for local history that when the sports ground was sold at the end of the RR era no reference to its former use was retained. When asked by the house builders for suggestions to link the new roads to names associated with the district, someone in the municipal buildings came up with names of two members of the town's first council, from 1877. Instead of commemorating a doctor and a farmer, the thoroughfares of the new estate should have been named after Jack Valentine and one of the other diligent workers for the welfare section.

In addition to the sports ground, the Welfare Society used the room above the canteen, known as the Welfare Hall, until it was renovated in the late 1960s. From then on it was the Silver Starlight room because of the large number of small lights in the ceiling. All shows were held there, whether flowers, birds or plays. If a section booked early enough the hall could be used for dances, film shows or even indoor sports, as its floor was marked out for badminton and other games. Rolls-Royce Christian Fellowship used it for projection purposes in 1961, when a Billy Graham film was shown on a Friday evening in February. Probably the most consistently well-attended events were the regular dances, with music by Ralph Cowdall and his orchestra and Cyril Shaw as master of ceremonies. Both of these men, and many of the band, worked in the factory.

More sedentary activities were provided for, if enough members of the welfare section requested them. For many years a library of 6,000 volumes, administered by a committee headed by Neville Sadler, a rate-fixer, distributed books from a wooden hut near to the western corner of the main office block. Beginning in 1941, it soon gathered sufficient members to warrant opening five times a week. A photographic society, presided over by George Eardley, a maintenance electrician, and the only worker at Pym's Lane to hold a Victoria Cross, was formed in 1957, developing into a cine club eleven years later.

Following a town-wide evangelistic crusade in Crewe, a Christian Fellowship was formed in 1958, chaired by Lawrence Yarwood and meeting in the Welfare Hall every Monday lunch-time. This was also the venue for regular visits from Elliot Booth, Crewe's first full-time industrial chaplain. Starting two years before this, Charlie Venables and other gardening enthusiasts were moved to organise a flower and produce show in the Welfare Hall each September, as well as the occasional lecture by recognised local and national horticultural experts. A few years later the caged bird section joined them for a combined show.

A motor club, commenced when the design and development personnel removed from Clan to Crewe, soon attracted interest. Treasure hunts and hill climbs were regular events, as were lectures and film shows. Mike Hawthorn, the

First anniversary, in 1959, of the Christian Fellowship, which met every Monday lunch-time in th
Welfare Hall. Left to right: Harry Ellis (labourer), author (centre lathe turner), Enid Pierce (clerk), the Rev
John Holder, George Brammer (estimator), Shirley Bostock (shorthand typist), Larry Yarwood (fitter
(Author's collection)

racing driver, and Sammy Davis, one of the Bentley boys, were just two of the
personalities who addressed a crowded Welfare Hall on a winter's evening in the
early 1950s. A technical quiz was held, with Martindale, Grylls, Dorey, Garner and
Evernden as the experts. As usual, some of the upper echelons of management
(Grylls and Dorey) were persuaded to provide trophies for open competition. The
section even designed its own tie, making it unique at Crewe RR.

In order to comply with the law, Jack Valentine had to apply annually for an
entertainment licence for the Welfare Hall so that the various sections could use it
as a public venue. This also allowed the RR Players to stage two or three plays a
year, and before the era of television these proved very popular, with plays such as
The Chiltern Hundreds or *Where Fools Rush In* being produced. Among the cast
would be the Callaghan sisters, Arthur George, Norman Bentley, Elsie Brown and
Peter Cantrill, an accountant.

Another venture, not strictly a welfare section, was the Rolls-Royce Retired
Employees Association, which commenced in the spring of 1953 at the instigation
of Jack Valentine and Harry Moore, together with a committee that included

E. Beevers, V. Hadfield, J. Taylor and Peter Abraham. Every year three or four coach trips were organised during the spring and summer. For those so inclined, afternoon tea dances were held regularly in the Starlight Room, while for others the Valentine Pavilion in Minshull New Road was opened every afternoon for any member to drop in, meaning a usual attendance of thirty or forty. Every year the RRREA held an annual general meeting, when attendance could reach 200 or 300, to vote in officers and suggest destinations for the summer outings. Norman Evanson, a fitter, who must have assembled more steering columns for RR and Bentley cars than any man alive, was the moving spirit of the Association for most of the 1990s. By the end of the twentieth century there were so many retirees that membership was limited to employees retiring at or within two years of sixty-five or who had served thirty years before being made redundant.

Another almost forgotten facility provided by the firm during its first twenty years in Crewe was the welfare thrift society. Most of the employees used this as a type of piggy-bank where, at the worker's request, a set amount of money could be stopped from wages or salary and placed into the balances of the thrift fund.

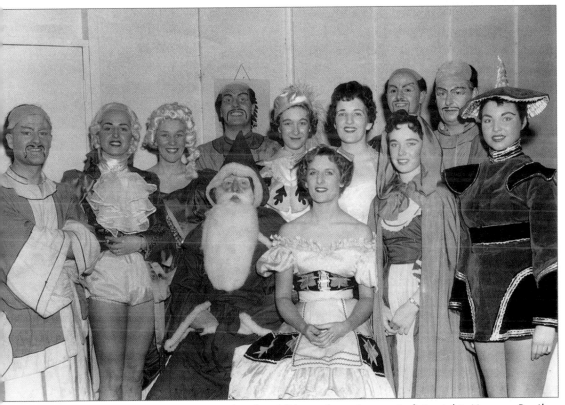

ıe cast of the 1957 Christmas pantomime for the children of employees. Left to right: Norman Bentley, an Alcock, Brenda Tomlinson, Ralph Alcock, Pat Carless, Ellen Pennington, Arthur George, John Leedham ıd Mavis Lewis (later Moore). The three in the centre are Syd Harvey, Enid Hammersley (later Holland) ıd Pat Dodd. *(John Pennington)*

Interest was added, usually at around 2 per cent, and withdrawals could be made on request. In 1952 well over £300,000 was held by the trustees, who also paid the tax on behalf of the depositors. Such a facility might seem archaic to the modern mind, yet to many of the manual workers at Crewe, banks, other than the post office, were alien, even frightening places. Such a resource said much about the firm's paternal concern for its labour force in the early days. When responsibility for the thrift fund was eventually handed to the Midland Bank in Market Street, Crewe, this gave many of the account holders the impetus to use the facilities of the British banking system.

In summary, it can be claimed that the welfare society gave every employee the opportunity to develop leisure time activities. The deliberate policy of the founding managers was to provide activities that would foster fraternal feelings between workers. No group could ever complain that its interests were ignored, as Jack Valentine, or the various welfare managers, always considered favourably every request for new activities. Consequently, the social and sporting life of Crewe was considerably enriched by the presence of Rolls-Royce.

EPILOGUE

As has been made clear in the concluding chapters of this book, Crewe's motor factory continues to manufacture cars in greater numbers than it ever did before, even if none bear the logo of Rolls-Royce. Now proudly displaying the words 'Bentley Motors', the Pym's Lane factory has experienced a much belated makeover, fashioning a twenty-first century automobile production unit far in advance of anything it would have gained if its last owners were still in charge. As this book is concerned with Bentley in conjunction with Rolls-Royce, no useful purpose would be served by describing the factory in its present guise, except to state that at the time of writing the number of employees is rising and production forecasts are optimistic.

Before examining how RR changed Crewe during its sixty years' tenure of Pym's Lane factory, it is instructive to note again the change in the management ethos. In 1961, just before he retired, Ivan Evernden delivered a paper to a distinguished audience at the factory, in which he said: 'Claude Johnson in his day realised the importance of good engineering, and so constituted his Board of Directors that the engineers had a balance of power over the financiers, essential as he realised their function to be. That policy has been maintained until this day, when even the chief executive is one of our own engineers.' By the middle of the 1980s this balance had gone from Crewe, where, for good or ill, marketeers and salesmen had pre-eminence.

The fact that Rolls-Royce came to the town was the second most important event in Crewe's short history, the first being the decision of the Grand Junction Railway directors to commence a repair works in the district. What did Crewe gain from Rolls-Royce's coming? Clearly, first and foremost there was the economic benefit, as thousands of local persons and their families prospered from the wages paid by the firm. Manufacturing aero-engines, and later motor cars, broke the hegemony of the Railway Company in Crewe, enabling the town to expand and modernise as the suburbs were extended and the population increased, along with the rateable value of the property. No doubt the rows of Victorian terraced houses that lined the centre of the town would have been demolished eventually, but the presence of a second major employer in the locality must have increased the attractiveness of redevelopment for the large retail chain stores.

Training in a variety of high skills gave many youngsters a start in life that they would have been hard pressed to gain had Royces not been close at hand. Most, in the 1940s and '50s, came from secondary modern schools and had no educational qualifications, yet through night school, day release and a RR apprenticeship they were able to move onwards and upwards, with the self-esteem that working for such a prestigious firm inculcated. The skill of some of the tradesmen at Rolls-Royce had to be admired, even if it was not always appreciated at the time. Much of this skill was passed on to the young lads who cycled nervously along West Street or Badger Avenue to begin an apprenticeship as tool-maker, fitter or some other of the trades then being utilised at RR. It has to be acknowledged that, as the world has moved on, some of these skills are no longer necessary.

The presence of a prestigious car manufacturer in the town meant that Crewe became a destination for some of the famous and notable persons who graced the second half of the twentieth century. Before the advent of RR, the town was a junction on a rail journey; a journey parodied in the music hall song where Birmingham was desired yet the hapless traveller was put off at Crewe. Once Rolls-Royce began to manufacture cars the factory, and ipso facto the town, welcomed royalty (British and foreign), politicians, renowned sportsmen, film stars, entertainers and that phenomenon of the modern age, the 'personality'. Rolls-Royce caused more celebrities to journey to Crewe than to any other provincial town; needless to say, the visits rarely included anything beyond the perimeter fence of Pym's Lane factory.

Charities, or special causes, were supported on occasion by workshops or departments acting independently of the firm and fund-raising in their own time. Rolls-Royce directors voted sums of money to be distributed to local charities and good causes, always non-political and non-religious. In 1967 Crewe Alexandra football club received a loan of £1,000 at 3 per cent interest, repayable over ten years, to help the club's directors to purchase the ground in Gresty Road. Other typical examples of assistance provided are the grant given to the Air Cadets when they were formed in November 1939 and a RR-sponsored commemorative booklet for Crewe in 1987. Sometimes RR had an official presence at town functions, such as the hospital fête in 1939 when a sectioned Merlin engine was on show in the exhibition tent and a team from the factory failed to beat the LMS brass-finishing shop in a game of push-ball.

Present day theatre-goers can sit in the Rolls-Royce hospitality lounge at the Lyceum in Heath Street, just another link with the town. Rolls Avenue is now an acceptable address, as is Bentley Drive. Drinks and hospitality are available in The Flying Lady and The Merlin public houses.

Almost every home connected with Rolls-Royce had some memento from the factory, albeit obtained unofficially. In the days of coal fires, pokers and poker stands graced almost every hearth in Crewe. Spare parts for cars were made as 'foreigners' with or without the connivance of the supervision. The higher up the ladder, the more open was the manufacture and repair of vehicles. It was not unknown for cars belonging to supervisory personnel to be repaired in the factory under cover of a work number raised by the supervisor in question. One middle manger was successfully prosecuted for covering the floor of his home with carpet intended for Rolls-Royce cars. It is to Fawn's credit that such practices were severely curtailed during his sojourn at Pym's Lane.

Whereas the relocation of RR to Goodwood has broken the bond with Crewe, the memory of the firm will long remain in the civic consciousness. Even though, at the time of writing, Bentley has been solo in the town for two years, it requires an effort of will to prevent the factory being referred to as Royces. What also remain are the many RR and Bentley cars that were made in Crewe. When Alex Henshaw saw a Spitfire fly overhead, filling the sky with the crisp, steady note of a Merlin engine, he heard a wistful sigh from an ex-pilot standing next to him. One can imagine a similar response being evoked from Crewe engineers and artisans whenever they see a Dawn, Shadow, Cloud, Corniche or one of the other models made in Pym's Lane gliding along one of the roads of our land.

All is not over, however, for car manufacturing is continuing in Crewe and the wish of this writer is that Bentley will prove to be even more successful on its own than when linked to Rolls-Royce. May managers and workers match, and exceed, the efficiency of other VW manufacturing plants – with which they will be compared – so that Bentley Motors will still be in the town in 2050. Hopefully, another historian will then be able to trace further chapters in the history of making cars in Crewe, as it is certain that it will not be this one!

Bibliography

PRIMARY SOURCES

Crewe Public Library, Minutes of Council and Committee Meetings, 1938–1970 (including meteorological readings), Crewe Town Council
Pym's Lane Factory, Crewe, Minutes of Crewe Rolls-Royce Works Committee, 1939–90
Rolls-Royce Heritage Trust, Derby, Haldenby's Correspondence File, 1938–50, Rolls-Royce Ltd
—— Minutes of Rolls-Royce Board, 1938–71, Rolls-Royce Ltd
TNA: PRO, Enquiry into Bombing at Crewe Rolls-Royce, 1941
—— Crewe Magistrates Petty Sessions Proceedings, 1942
—— Report of Trials, Chester Assizes, 1942

The following are in private hands.
Culley, F. Diary, 1940
—— Notebook, 1940–3
Details of Proposed Engine Factory at Crewe, 1938, Rolls-Royce Ltd
Elliot, W. Notes of Career at Pym's Lane
Evernden, I. 'An Engineering Heritage, 1961'
Finch, T. 'Industrial Relations at Rolls-Royce Motors, 1988–1998'
Memos Appertaining to VPC Foundry Closure, Rolls-Royce Ltd
Minutes and Memos Appertaining to Redundancy, 1981–2, Rolls-Royce Ltd
Minutes and Memos Appertaining to Redundancy, 1991–2, Rolls-Royce Ltd
Minutes of Redundancy Committee, 1945–6, Rolls-Royce Ltd
Minutes of Joint Production Committee, 1942–5, Rolls-Royce Ltd
Morris, J. 'Notes of Career at Crewe Rolls-Royce'
Spencer, R. 'Rolls-Royce Chassis Division, 1940–1960'

Newspapers, Magazines and Other Sources
Archive Magazine, various dates, Rolls-Royce Heritage Trust
Bulletin, various dates, Rolls-Royce Enthusiasts' Club
Crewe Chronicle, 1938–2000
Journal, Rolls-Royce Motor Cars
Queste, Rolls-Royce Motor Cars
Sale Brochure, 1973, Rolls-Royce Motor Cars
The Aeroplane, 19 July 1939, 26 July 1939
Voice, various dates, Rolls-Royce Motor Cars

SECONDARY SOURCES

Books Relating to Rolls-Royce

Adcock, I. *Rolls-Royce V8s*, London, Osprey, 1994

Bennett, M. *RR & Bentley – the Crewe Years*, Sparkford, Foulis, 1995

Bird, A. and Hallows, I. *The Rolls-Royce Motor Car and the Bentley since 1931*, London, Batsford, 2002

Bobbitt, M. *Rolls-Royce and Bentley*, Stroud, Sutton Publishing, 1998

Bolster, J. *Rolls-Royce Silver Shadow*, London, Osprey, 1979

Buckley, J.R. *A Living Tradition*, Ipswich, Cowell, nd

Feast, R. *Kidnap of the Flying Lady*, St Paul, MN, Motorbooks International, 2003

Frostick, M. *Bentley Cricklewood to Crewe*, London, Osprey, 1980

Gray, R. *Rolls on the Rocks*, Salisbury, Compton Press, 1971

Harvey-Bailey, A. *Hives, the Quiet Tiger*, Derby, Rolls-Royce Heritage Trust, 1985

—— *Hives' Turbulent Barons*, Derby, Rolls-Royce Heritage Trust, 1993

—— *The Merlin in Perspective*, Derby, Rolls-Royce Heritage Trust, 1995

Heilig, J. and Abbas, R. *Rolls-Royce: The Best Car in the World*, London, Apple, 1999

Kirk, P., Felix, P. and Bartrick, G. *The Bombing of Rolls-Royce at Derby*, Derby, Rolls-Royce Heritage Trust, 2002

Lea, K. *The First Cars From Crewe*, Derby, Rolls-Royce Heritage Trust, 1996

Lloyd, I. *Rolls-Royce*, London, Macmillan, 1978

Nockolds, H. *The Magic of a Name*, London, Foulis, nd

Nutland, M. *Rolls-Royce and Bentley*, Dorchester, Beloce, 1997

Price, A. *Rolls-Royce, the Cars and their Competitors*, London, Batsford, 1965

Pugh, P. *The Magic of a Name*, Duxford, Icon Books, 2002

Rimmer, I. *Rolls-Royce & Bentley Experimental Cars*, Paulerspury, Rolls-Royce Enthusiasts' Club, 1986

Robotham, W. *Silver Ghosts and Silver Dawn*, London, Constable, 1970

Robson, G. *Rolls-Royce Silver Cloud*, Marlborough, Crowood Press, 2000

—— *Rolls-Royce Silver Shadow*, Marlborough, Crowood Press, 1998

—— *Rolls-Royce Silver Spirit*, London, Osprey, 1985

Ware, P. *Rolls-Royce B Series Engines in National Service*, Warehouse, Croydon, 1995

Wood, J. *Rolls-Royce & Bentley*, Yeovil, Haynes Publishing, 2001

Books Relating to the Motor Industry and the Economy

Adeney, M. *The Motor Makers*, London, Collins, 1988

Catherwood, F. *At the Cutting Edge*, London, Hodder & Stoughton, 1995

Edwardes, M. *Back From The Brink*, London, Collins, 1983

Georgano, B. *Britain's Motor Industry*, Sparkford, Foulis, 1995

Harrison, M. (ed.) *The Economics of World War II*, Cambridge, Cambridge University Press, 1997

Henshaw, A. *Sigh for a Merlin*, London, John Murray, 1979

Lamont, N. *In Office*, London, Little Brown, 1999

Morgan, E. and Shacklady, E. *The History of the Spitfire*, Stamford, Key Publishing, 1987

Nader, R. *Unsafe at Any Speed*, Toronto, Bantam Books, 1973 (rpt)

Taylor, A.J.P. *English History 1914–1945*, Oxford, Clarendon Press, 1965
Whitaker's Almanack 2005, London, A & C Black, 2004
Who's Who, London, A & C Black, 1970
Wild, R. (ed.) *How to Manage*, London, Heinemann, 1982

Newspapers, Magazines and Other Sources

Commemorative Celebrations: Battle of Britain Memorial Window, 1949, Rolls-Royce Ltd
Directors Reports & Balance Sheets, various dates, Rolls-Royce Ltd
Directors Reports & Balance Sheets, various dates, Rolls-Royce Motor Cars
First Annual Children's Field Day Programme, 1939, Rolls-Royce Ltd
Hives' Commemorative Booklet, 1950, Rolls-Royce Ltd
RR Bulletin, various dates, Rolls-Royce Ltd
RR Crewe Works Souvenir Booklet, 1939, Rolls-Royce Ltd
RR News, various dates, Rolls-Royce Ltd
Specialist Engines Sales Brochures, Rolls-Royce Motor Cars

Index